孙中山与翠亨历史文化丛书

我所认识的孙逸仙

——童年朋友陆灿的回忆

著/陆灿、Betty Tebbetts Taylor
译/黄健敏　校/欧冬红

文物出版社

总　　序

　　孙中山在翠亨村诞生，并由此走向世界。翠亨村及其附近，中西文化的碰撞与交融产生了这里的特色文化，在中国近现代历史上涌现出以孙中山为杰出代表的一批风云人物，这绝非历史的偶然，这个区域的历史人文值得深入探寻与研究。

　　孙中山故居纪念馆把"孙中山与翠亨"作为业务工作的主要聚焦点，亦是必然。孙中山故居纪念馆从 1956 年成立至今已 50 周年。近年来，本馆围绕"孙中山与翠亨"这一业务工作的主要聚焦点，坚持"保护文物及其环境求发展"的宗旨，坚持"有特色才有生命力"的理念，在文物及其环境保护方面坚持"守旧"——守护价值，在管理理念和手段方面大胆创新。我们建立了以"孙中山及其成长的社会环境"为主题，兼具历史纪念性和民俗性、立体和多元化的陈列展览体系，并以现代管理理念及网络化、数字化、智能化的科技手段，运用现代系统理论、ISO9001 国际质量管理标准体系和 ISO14001 国际环境管理标准体系实行科学管理。

　　在孙中山故居纪念馆的业务基础上，我们组建了"中山市民俗博物馆"、"中山市孙中山研究所"、"逸仙图书馆"以拓展业务，相关的研究不断取得成果。本馆与相关部门合作建立"广东省社会科学院孙中山研究基地"、"中山大学中国近现代史教学实践基地"，对本馆业务研究工作是一个很大的促进。我们在努力实现本馆科学研究职能的同时，发挥自身的社会教育职能，积极开展普及性的社会教育工作，建设好"全国爱国主义教育示范基地"。我们注意处理好博物馆学术研究与普及教育的关系，注意处理好博物馆业务职能与旅游服务的关系，取得了良好的社会效益、经济效益和环境效益。

　　在本馆把业务工作的主要聚焦点放在"孙中山与翠亨"，以孙中山及其成长的社会环境开展业务与研究的同时，"孙中山与翠亨"的课题也越来越多地受到了孙中山与中国近现代史研究及民俗文化研究学者的关注，一些学者也积极参与其中，开展了相关的调查和研究工作，我们为这些学者们的工作提供了必要的支持和帮助，他们的研究成果也许是"孙中山与翠亨"主题的重要构成或补充。

孙中山故居纪念馆、中山市孙中山研究所以"孙中山与翠亨"为主题，推出系列丛书，推介本馆业务人员和有志参与这方面课题研究的学者的成果，向读者和游客介绍孙中山及其成长的社会环境，向相关的研究者提供参考资料，以此进一步推进孙中山及其成长的社会环境以及孙中山领导的革命运动和相关人物的深入研究，同时也为实现本馆社会教育职能、开展普及性的工作奠定基础。2006年我们迎来了孙中山故居纪念馆建馆50周年、伟大的孙中山先生诞辰140周年，我们从今年开始推出"孙中山与翠亨历史文化丛书"，有着特殊的纪念意义。今后我们将陆续推出该系列丛书的其他相关资料、文献、图集和著作。

我们不否认我们的进步。但是，我们深知，目前本馆的业务能力和研究水平依然有限。我们希望通过"孙中山与翠亨历史文化丛书"的推出，得到专家、学者以及广大读者的批评和指导，以促进和提高我们的研究水平，进而推动和促进我们其他工作的同步发展。

我们将向着更高的目标不断向前迈进。

孙中山故居纪念馆
中山市孙中山研究所
2006 年 9 月 15 日

陆灿（1874～1949）

陆灿年轻时照

1920年，孙中山题赠给陆灿之父陆兰谷的"博爱"题词。

1921年2月18日，孙中山、孙科参加翠亨同人恳亲会与乡亲摄于广州。前排右四孙中山、右一孙科、右三陆兰谷。

　　旅檀的翠亨乡人1925年4月12日在檀香山首府火奴鲁鲁的夏威夷戏院参加孙中山先生逝世追悼会后摄影。右起第十九人是陆灿。

1940年代，陆灿（二排中）与亲友合影于檀香山。

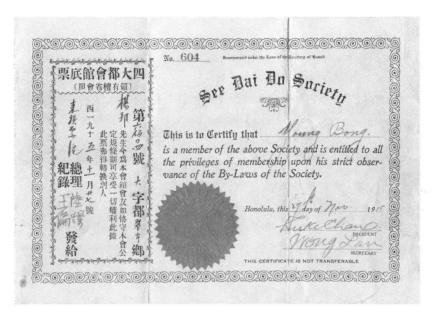

1915年11月27日，陆灿、王伦签发给翠亨村华侨杨邦的檀香山四大都会馆会员证。

20世纪30年代，陆灿撰写的《孙公中山事略》手稿。

翠亨村陆灿故居，原建于1848年，1948年陆灿回乡改建成今貌。

编 译 说 明

本书是孙中山先生童年朋友、翠亨村籍夏威夷华侨陆灿所著的《Sun Yat Sen——As I knew him》的中文译本。

一

陆灿（1874～1949），又名文灿，字立本，号炳谦，别字逸生，广东香山县（今中山市）翠亨村人。其父陆兰谷据说曾在檀香山茂宜岛孙中山长兄孙眉家中担任中文教员，1898年前后因涉嫌参加反清起义被捕，无辜系狱六年。孙中山曾题词"博爱"相赠①。

陆灿于1887年7月离开翠亨村往檀香山求学，就读于泮拿荷学校（Punahou School），是该校毕业的第一个中国学生。1929年前后任亚美利坚花陀士公司苏杭经理、中华绸庄经理②。陆灿也曾在后来发展成为华人资本的金融投资保险公司哈克菲公司（H. Hackfield & Co.）任职，1942年是该公司经理之一③。陆灿热心华侨事业，曾担任檀香山政府外交部华务局长及美国移民局通事，协助赴檀华人登岸。先后参与创办环球中国学生会、四大都会馆、夏威夷华人公所等社团，并连续多年担任中西扩论会主席、四大都会馆主席、夏威夷华人公所主席、万那联义会馆书记等，对于夏威夷华侨公共事业贡献良多。自述"历年厕身社会，皆欲提高侨胞人格，奋起爱国精神，勉励

---

① 孙中山题赠陆兰谷"博爱"手迹现存翠亨孙中山故居纪念馆，陆皓东烈士之孙陆玉昆于2006年11月10日捐赠。
② 《檀山华侨》（第一集），檀山华侨编印社1929年9月印行，"闻人录"第126页。
③ 马充生：《孙中山在夏威夷：活动与追随者》，台北近代中国出版社2000年8月版，第135页。

青年学习中西文字，令入大学专科，以期报效于祖国也。"① 抗日战争期间，担任檀香山的援华会（The China Relief Association）主席，为国内同胞提供援助②。

陆灿是陆皓东烈士堂侄。1883 年孙中山与陆皓东邀集同村少年损毁翠亨村北极殿神像时，陆灿也是在场者之一。1893 年，以檀香山隆记报馆为基地，陆灿与何宽、郑金、叶桂芳等创设中西扩论会。"孙（中山）前为革命失败复来檀时，均在扩论会内报告各事，创兴中会亦在其时。故檀埠助孙革命事业，亦以中西扩论会人为最古，捐书以助革命军饷者甚伙。"③ 1894'年 11 月，孙中山在檀香山组建兴中会，陆灿于年底加入，并参加兴中会组织的华侨兵操队，为日后归国起义做准备。1895 年春，陆灿回故乡翠亨村结婚。正筹划起义的陆皓东每从省城广州回到翠亨，常到陆灿家中倾谈。是年底广州起义失败后，陆灿受孙中山委托，护送孙中山母亲杨太夫人、妻子卢慕贞及两个孩子孙科、孙娫等到檀香山茂宜岛孙眉牧场，他亦因此而被檀香山华侨比作三国时勇救甘夫人与阿斗的"赵子龙"④。在孙中山的建议和鼓励下，陆灿积极参加檀香山的社团组织工作，鼓动当地华侨，筹募革命经费；又任兴中会舆论宣传的主要报刊《檀山新报（隆记）》的翻译，凡关于中国的消息，常与香港《中国日报》总编辑陈少白互相通讯。1912 年中华民国成立，孙中山在南京就任临时大总统，陆灿偕孙科等返国，在总统府秘书处工作。陆灿多次劝说孙中山不要把总统的职位让给袁世凯。稍后，孙中山解职回粤，陆灿任行辕秘书随行。1913 年陆灿回到夏威夷，之后再也没有见过孙中山。20 世纪 30 年代，陆灿在中国国民党党史史料编纂委员会任"名誉采访"之职⑤，撰有《陆皓东公事略》、《孙公中山事略》、《Sun Yat Sen——As I

---

① 陆灿：《孙公中山事略》（稿本），翠亨孙中山故居纪念馆藏，第 66 页。
② Luke Chan and Betty Tebbetts Taylor："*Sun Yat Sen——As I knew him*"，打印稿，第 1 页。
③ 《檀山华侨》第一集，"檀山华侨"部分第 88 页。
④ 郑照：《孙中山先生逸事》，载尚明轩、王学庄、陈崧编：《孙中山生平事业追忆录》，人民出版社 1986 年 6 月版，第 518 页。
⑤ 陆灿：《陆皓东公事略》（稿本），第 6 页，1959 年 3 月 11 日，陆皓东烈士孙媳林文湘女士捐赠翠亨孙中山故居纪念馆收藏。

knew him》、《孙公中山在檀事略》等。

二

《Sun Yat Sen——As I knew him》是 20 世纪 40 年代末，陆灿在
Betty Tebbetts Taylor 的协助下撰写的一部英文孙中山的传记，该书似
乎最后并未正式出版①。中文译本则曾有《我所了解的孙逸仙》出
版②，但与译者所见的英文打字稿相较，此译本时有删节及内容改动，
第十四章全章都没有翻译③；对较少见的地名和人名有些没有翻译，
译出的也有部分欠准确；同时陆灿原文史实错漏混淆之处不少，但此
译本只在极个别地方加以说明。《Sun Yat Sen——As I knew him》作
为目前所见唯一一本由翠亨村同乡撰写的孙中山生平传记，重新翻
译、整理一个更为完整、准确的译本，作为"孙中山与翠亨历史文化
丛书"一种也不无意义。

本书是根据孙中山故居纪念馆所藏该书的英文打字稿复印件④重
新全文翻译，译者尽量查对资料准确译出人名和地名，并加以简单的
注释；对书中明显的史实错误也就译者所知加以说明，以便阅读和利
用。书中各种人名、地名注释和译注说明，是译者参考比较多种不同
资料整理而成，为节省篇幅，一般不再一一注出来源。

本书附录收录《Sun Yat Sen——As I knew him》的英文原稿全
文，通晓外文者大可直接阅读英文原文，当更能体会作者的原意。而
英文稿偶有单词拼写错误及语句、语法不通之处，载入本书时为存其
原貌，原则上不再加以校正与说明。

本书还收录了陆灿的另一份手稿《孙公中山事略》。《孙公中山事
略》为墨笔稿本，原件长 21.6 厘米，宽 28 厘米，每页 21 行，共 66

---

① 就译者所知，台北中国国民党党史会、美国夏威夷大学图书馆及陆灿后
人等均藏有该书的英文打字本。
② 傅伍仪译、季风校：《我所了解的孙逸仙》，中国和平出版社 1986 年版。
③ 笔者曾向该书译者傅伍仪女士请教，是因为所据底本不同还是其他原
因，傅老师表示因距今时间太久，已记不清楚当时翻译的情况，而据以
翻译的英文本是他人提供，译完后便即归还。
④ 该打字稿复印件，16 开，每页 22 行，共 129 页。

页。1959 年 3 月 11 日，陆皓东烈士孙媳林文湘女士捐赠翠亨孙中山故居纪念馆收藏。原稿并无书名，现名为译者根据该稿内容所拟。原稿也未标明写作时间。此稿从篇章结构、内容到表述与《Sun Yat Sen——As I knew him》类同之处颇多，而且较英文稿更能体现作者原意，应该是陆灿提供给 Betty Tebbetts Taylor 撰写参考的主要资料之一，但全稿似未完成，孙中山晚年的事便没有叙及。《孙公中山事略》部分内容曾由黄彦、李伯新两先生整理公布①，但整理时删去部分史料价值不高的章节段落，对部分内容顺序作了调整，改正错字、增补漏字及原文史料失实之处没有加以说明，"让读者们自行研究鉴别"②。本书整理刊入时则依据馆藏原稿全文照录。原稿旧有红色铅笔标点，应是后人所加，较为混乱，整理者现酌加新式标点，并予分段。原稿无法辨认的文字用"□"表示，错字用［］更正，缺字用〈〉补回。该稿某些地方文字欠通顺，史料价值不高，甚至有些表述混乱，但为了尽量保持原貌，亦全部录入，一概不予更改。而对人名及较少见的地名加以注释，史实误记和混淆错漏之处就整理者所知，加以说明，但如在《Sun Yat Sen——As I knew him》译稿中已有注释、说明的，为避免重复则一般只作简注或不再注出。

　　《Sun Yat Sen——As I knew him》及《孙公中山事略》两稿字里行间充分反映了陆灿对孙中山先生的敬仰之情，尤其是陆灿回忆自己亲身经历的那些史事，对孙中山研究尤其是早期生活与革命活动的研究有一定的参考价值。尽管陆灿在序言中指出"在本书中所采用的事实，是建基于我的亲身经历和往事回忆，而不仅仅是道听途说"，但在孙中山革命生涯中，陆灿所亲历的事情毕竟有限，从书稿的实际内容看来，所述仍然不少来源于间接的资料与传闻。陆灿长期担任《檀山新报（隆记）》的翻译，西方报刊关于孙中山的各种报导无疑也是陆灿撰写此书的重要资料来源。尽管作者希望以认真、求实的态度去撰写，但在孙中山去世多年后，在大洋彼岸怀着

---

①　陆灿遗著：《孙公中山事略》，载广东省孙中山研究会主编：《孙中山研究》（第一辑），广东人民出版社 1986 年 6 月版，第 332～372 页。

②　见《孙中山研究》（第一辑）第 332 页《孙公中山事略》"整理者说明"。

景仰和歌颂的心情凭记忆去重塑孙中山的伟人形象，正如其他的回忆性史料一样，对传主的虚饰、溢美难以避免，而史实的误记、漏记、曲解和混淆不清也时有出现，其中部分错误也可能是协助撰写英文稿的 Betty Tebbetts Taylor 所造成的。

此外，译者所见陆灿还撰有《孙公中山在檀事略》① 以及《陆皓东公事略》，因两文内容基本上都已包含在《孙公中山事略》中，所以本书不再重复收入。

三

《Sun Yat Sen——As I knew him》由孙中山故居纪念馆黄健敏初译，中山大学历史人类学研究中心欧冬红校译；译稿的注释、附录文献的整理及全书的统稿由黄健敏负责。

中山大学历史系程美宝教授拨冗审阅译稿，提出不少具体的、有针对性的修改意见，并不厌其烦解答译者提出的"难题"，对提高本书质量大有裨益。译者从修改讨论的过程中受益匪浅，也深为大学时代修读程美宝教授开设的"专业英语"课程时的无心向学而懊悔。

孙中山故居纪念馆萧润君馆长多年来关心鼓励译者从事业务研究工作，本书也是在他的支持和信任下得以完成和出版。孙中山故居纪念馆中各位同仁也给予各种帮助和支持。

在此谨向所有对本书的翻译、整理和出版给予帮助和支持的各位师友、领导和同事致以诚挚的谢意。

译者主观上虽尽力完善译稿，但由于水平所限，误译或理解不够准确之处所在必有，注释中漏注甚至误注的情况恐亦在所难免，这当然应全部由本人负责，也望识者不吝赐教。

译者

2008 年 5 月 12 日

---

① 陆灿：《孙公中山在檀事略》，载郑东梦主编：《檀山华侨》（第一集）"华侨史"部分，檀山华侨编印社 1929 年 9 月印行，第 11～15 页。

目　录

华侨为革命之母

——孙逸仙

献给为革命牺牲之第一人——我敬爱的叔叔陆皓东，献给曾因革命事业而遭受六年牢狱之苦的亲爱的父亲陆兰谷，以及为国捐躯者的一切牺牲。

前　言

抗日战争期间，我被夏威夷火奴鲁鲁①的社团一致推举为援华会（the China Relief Association）的主席，一直无偿服务到 1946 年 8 月。时有美洲大陆的作家来信，请我写一写我所认识的孙逸仙，但是，那段时间我正忙于筹募捐款，所以为这位伟人撰写传记这一大事情，反而一直未能着手进行。

战胜日本后，援华会解散，我便开始收集资料和照片，着手撰写传记。在洛杉矶有一位贝蒂·泰勒夫人，曾经通过三藩市②和火奴鲁鲁的中国领事致信于我，请我提供有关荷马李③将军的资料。我到美洲大陆时，便过去拜访她，并把我在南京见闻告诉了她。因此之故，她自愿协助我撰写这本传记。

因为中国目前正经受内战、干旱、洪水及通货膨胀等等的苦难，笔者将把本书的所有收入用于中国，去援助那些受难者。

我一直以为，孙逸仙的真实经历应由中国人来讲述，以使西方世

---

① 夏威夷（Hawaii），由太平洋一系列岛屿组成，华侨常以"檀香山"称呼这个地方。1898 年后成为美国领地。首府火奴鲁鲁（Honolulu），华侨一般简称"正埠"或"大埠"。

② 三藩市（San Francisco），美国加利福利亚州（California State）西部的城市，华侨一般称之为"旧金山"或"金山大埠"。

③ 荷马李（Homer Lea，1876～1912），亦译作咸马里、郝门李、堪马里、李哈麦等，美国人。1904 年结识孙中山。1910 年 3 月，孙中山、荷马李、布斯等在洛杉矶长堤（Long Beach）荷马李的寓所举行军事会议。武昌起义后，荷马李协助孙中山在欧洲活动。1911 年底随孙中山回国。1912 年元旦参加孙中山在南京就任临时大总统的庆典。同年 4 月因病回美休养，至 11 月 1 日去世。孙中山在 11 月 6 日上海《大陆报》（China Press）刊出的赞辞中，称赞荷马里"是一位伟大的军事哲学家"，"他对中国革命贡献了绝大的心力"。

界更好地了解和获益。关于孙博士①的书已有不少，但往往是从欧美的角度出发；而且中国人也知道许多书对孙逸仙的叙述与描写是错的，但尚未有人去更正。

伟人的真实情况往往朦胧不清，充满了传奇和神秘色彩。在西方世界，孙逸仙被塑造成中国的乔治·华盛顿②和神秘造反者这样的人物。我撰写此书，就是为了澄清这些真假掺杂的叙述。可能我并不比其他很多人更合适撰写孙博士的传记，但至少我在本书中所采用的事实，是建基于我的亲身经历和往事回忆，而不仅仅是道听途说。本书为中国，也为世界上其他国家，提供了对中国第一位总统更清晰、真实的写照，为达到东西方世界更完好地互相理解，可以填补一定的空白。

陆灿

---

① 孙中山从未获授予博士学位或荣誉博士学位，故"Dr. Sun"译作"孙医生"似更符合史实。但自孙中山在世时直到今天，"Dr. Sun"都约定俗成译作"孙博士"，以表示对孙中山的尊敬。在本书附录陆灿撰写的中文《孙公中山事略》中，同是转译1903年檀香山西文报纸报道时，"孙医生"和"孙博士"均有使用。为免混乱，本书中的"Dr. Sun"也按一般习惯译作"孙博士"。

② 乔治·华盛顿（George Washington，1732～1799），美国独立战争时期大陆军总司令，领导美国人民取得了独立战争的胜利。1789年，当选为美国第一任总统。后被称为美国的"国父"。

一 出生和在翠亨村的童年

我和孙逸仙出生在同一个村子里——翠亨村①。"翠亨"表示碧绿透明的翡翠。这是一个中国南部的粤人聚居的小村庄，位于石岐②到澳门的陆路与通往金星港③的水路中间，离广州和珠江40英里。村子离圩市有5英里，平日靠行商小贩流通货物。在10英里外有一个不大不小的村子——唐家④，意思是"唐氏家族"聚居的地方，那里约有2,000所房子。我们或多或少都有点沾亲带故，我的祖母就是唐家人，她的哥哥，即我的舅公，是唐家的长老。

我们村有一百来座砖瓦房子，有中国常见的矮围墙环绕，一些泥草房零星分布在村边。因为偏远，在清朝统治的时候我们也享受着一定程度的自治。

清官员和征收赋税的官吏时不时会出现，并给我们带来烦恼：他们用苛刻、横暴的手段对待我们，有时仅仅为了娱乐就放火烧掉茅草屋的屋顶；但更多的时候，地方官员只要我们缴纳每年一次的田地赋税，就放任不理了。村子太小，所以他们都懒得管——那时在广东，像我们这样规模的村子数以百计。

这种情况下，我们便要利用自己的资源以达到自治，因此翠亨村民发展出来一种独立的精神，特别是在年轻人中间。这种独立精神在

---

① 翠亨村，今属广东省中山市南朗镇，北距广州市约100公里，南距澳门约30公里。

② 石岐，今广东省中山市人民政府所在地，昔为香山县城，因当地有石岐山而得名。

③ 金星港，在珠江口西岸珠海市唐家半岛和淇澳岛两岸夹峙，中有金星岛，附近一片水域水位较深，适宜停泊船只，清中叶起，尤其是西南季候风期间，是珠江口外洋船主要的停泊地点之一，称为"金星港"，距离翠亨村约15公里。

④ 唐家，今广东省珠海市唐家镇，位于珠江口西岸，南距澳门约25公里。

孙逸仙的个性中得到最强烈的体现，当然这也是他反抗压迫和停滞守旧的开始。

翠亨村是香山县一个普通农村，后来为了表示对孙博士的敬意，香山县改名为中山①。翠亨村为群山环绕，发源于犁头尖山、牛头山和五桂山的溪流流过金槟榔山和山门坳②，灌溉着那些肥沃的稻田。稻田每块约 3～5 英亩大小，大部分属于翠亨村或其他较大城镇的地主所有，但耕种的是世世代代在这片土地生活的佃农。

这其中，就有孙逸仙的父亲孙达成③。他们家住在泥墙屋里，耕种村边的十亩地（约等于三又三分之一英亩）。他靠这点土地勉强维持生活和养活他的妻子、两个嫂子、两个儿子和一个女儿④。其中一个儿子很小的时候就夭折了，剩下另外一个儿子，叫阿眉⑤，约 15

---

① 香山县位于珠江口西岸，于南宋绍兴二十二年（1152）建县。1925 年 4 月为纪念孙中山先生而改名中山县，所辖范围大概包括今日广东省中山市、珠海市、斗门县的大部分以及番禺、顺德、新会的一些地区。1953 年从原中山县划出部分地区与原属东莞、宝安的若干海岛合并成立珠海县。1965 年又从原中山县、新会县划出部分地区成立斗门县。1983 年中山县撤县建市（县级市），1988 年升格为地级市。

② 犁头尖山、牛头山、金槟榔山等翠亨村一带山峰均属于五桂山脉，五桂山脉为香山（今中山市）境内主要山脉，面积约 300 多平方公里，主峰海拔 531 米。

③ 孙达成（1813～1888），名观林，字达成，号道川。早岁业农，后在澳门当鞋匠谋生。30 岁左右回乡依靠耕作养家糊口。夫人杨氏（1828～1910），香山四大都隔田乡启运里（今中山市南朗镇崖口管理区杨家村）人。孙达成与夫人杨氏共生下 6 个孩子：孙眉（1854～1915）、孙金星（1857～1860）、孙典（1860～1866）、孙妙茜（1863～1955）、孙中山（1866～1912）、孙秋绮（1871～1912）。

④ 分别指孙达成妻子杨氏，孙学成（1826～1864）夫人程氏（1836～1912），孙观成（1831～1867）夫人谭氏，以及孙达成的儿子孙眉、孙典和女儿孙妙茜。

⑤ 孙眉（1854～1915），字德彰，号寿屏，孙中山长兄。1871 年赴檀香山谋生，后在茂宜岛开辟牧场，拥有不少商店及物业。1894 年底，加入兴中会并担任茂宜分会主席。1906 年 8 月，孙眉宣布破产，带着家人回香港九龙定居。1910 年 9 月，孙眉因"运动劳工入党事，被港政府驱逐出境。"1915 年 2 月 11 日在澳门病逝。

岁，还有一个小女儿。这是一个勤恳劳作但也睿智和厚道的家庭。这一点在当时的中国也是不寻常的，因为在满清政府的统治下，当时的社会因循守旧又落后。

我比孙博士要小七岁，不可能说明他出生时候的情形，但我大概可以准确地向你描绘，那是在 1866 年的 11 月。当时美国正在努力从内战中恢复过来，欧洲正在盲目地走向四年后爆发的普法战争，而中国陶醉于旧传统中，依然是满洲征服者铁蹄下的睡龙。

当时的翠亨村，山岭显得荒凉而贫瘠。天气已经转凉但还不觉得寒冷，北风吹起落叶，散落在一座庙宇的门口。在庙里，有三位神色肃穆的村神，中间一位男神，两边各有一位女神①。男神就是北帝，这个村子的主神，他手握宝剑朝天，拇指向上，令人望而生畏。村民在这里烧香和求签，祈求好运降临。

那时，北帝常常在孙达成家人的脑海中萦绕。一天傍晚，孙达成和他的妻子、两个嫂子谈起了北帝，他们的两个孩子也在一旁安静地听着，神色敬畏。孙达成的妻子，一个皮肤黝黑的小脚本地女人，正怀着另一个孩子。她最近做了一个令人困扰的梦。

她对丈夫说："在梦里，北帝悲痛地走向我，他披头散发地哭着，好像我怀的孩子将会伤害他。我们得想个法子躲避这场灾祸，不如把孩子献给神，让他安心。我们该叫孩子'帝象'——北帝的形象。"

在这点上，她和丈夫有一些争论，但她强烈坚持。因此，当孙达成的儿子在 11 月 12 日（不是很多书中所写的 2 日）出生的时候，他就有了第一个名字（即乳名）：帝象。他们希望把孩子献给神，他就不会去伤害神了。然而，命中注定，帝象不仅会反对村神，而且还会反抗国家与朝廷。

帝象，就是后来的孙逸仙，生长在偏远的广东农村里，过着农民孩子的普通乡村生活。他个子不高，相貌堂堂，遗传了母亲的圆脸和黑肤色。他温和好学、对人真诚，但孩提时就开始反抗陈规。当时我们多数孩子都不用帮家里做家务，但帝象要帮他父亲做些杂务。当他用长竹竿挑着两个陶罐去打水时，他却故意把罐子打破，为了增加信服力，还擦了一些泥水在衣袖上。他对家人说："我摔倒并把罐子也打破

_____
① 指北帝、天后及金花夫人。

了，没办法去打水。"这个法子很奏效。直到有一天，他的哥哥孙眉在他没有觉察的情况下，躲在树后看到了他的"表演"。孙眉从后面抓住帝象的衣领，大力挥着竹棒，喝道："在你做这些小把戏之前，最好确保没有人会看见！"

村子的祠堂里有两所男女合校的中国旧式学塾。学生从早到晚在这里学习，只是在早、晚饭时可以休息。一个中年男教师严格地管教着我们，他规定全班每天朗读的课程，然后我们要逐个背对着他背诵给他听。家境较为富裕的学生自带书桌和椅子，其余学生就使用村塾的旧桌椅。中国传统的教育方法缓慢而单调，可批评之处很多，但这种方法虽然在有限的时间里教得不多，所教的那部分还是很扎实的。一个孩子以这样的方式学习《三字经》，大抵会终身难忘。多年以后，孙博士告诉我，他仍然记得早年在村塾的功课。

虽然当时自由玩乐的时间不多，但玩耍的时候我们还是自己发明了很多娱乐。除了农历新年正月的假期，我们只能在某些节日才能放假①。这时我们会兴高采烈地玩两种游戏。

第一种叫跳青蛙，有点类似美国的"跳房子"游戏。帝象喜欢所有需要急才和调皮的事情，因此总是带领我们玩。四个男孩各拿一只鞋，摆成一条直线，每只间隔两英尺。玩的时候先要右足单脚绕着所有的鞋子跳一圈，再在每只鞋子之间跳进跳出，直至跳完所有鞋子为止。不碰到鞋子又按正确顺序跳完全程的就是胜者。帝象异常敏捷和灵活，所以这个游戏玩得很好。

另一个是最喜欢玩的，叫"砍甘蔗"。我们把一根事先买好的长甘蔗竖直放在地上，顶部放一把小刀。每个男孩轮流拿着小刀从顶端砍一下，尽可能一刀砍下一条长长的甘蔗皮。砍得最长的人，以吃甘蔗作为奖赏，其他的孩子则要分摊甘蔗钱。帝象常常能够吃到甘蔗，而我得遗憾地承认，我很少能吃到。其他的游戏还有放风筝、踢毽子和耍棍棒等。

那时我有一个亲戚在上海去世了，依照中国的习俗，遗体由他的

---

① 　此句原文为"On the Festival days of New Year, Decoration and Full Moon"，"New Year"、"Decoration"等西方节日是当时的中国所无，也许作者认为中国当时有类似的节日，为免混乱，此处只笼统译作某些节日。

儿子运送回故乡翠亨村安葬。他的儿子就是我的叔父陆皓东①，只比我大几年，那时大概12岁。他留下来进了村塾读书，并且很快和帝象成为了朋友。

对我们其他小朋友来说，陆皓东有些特别。他出生在大城市上海，比起我们，可谓见多识广。他是一个优秀的学生，聪明的艺术家，还具有某些音乐家的气质。他的观点非常进步，和帝象一样，不满村民对清政府的畏惧和麻木。他敏捷、活跃，有一双明亮的眼睛和无穷的好奇心，一旦被激发，就有狂热的忠诚。这一点在稍后就被毫无疑问地证明——他后来是为革命牺牲的第一个烈士。帝象与陆皓东志趣相投，成为终生的好友。

这个时候，村里常常谈论夏威夷，许多人家的子弟去那儿成为了商人或地主。翠亨村民收到他们寄回的信中，生动地描述了那里更容易谋生。孙逸仙的大哥孙眉，就是当时在夏威夷发达的村民之一。后来孙眉来信，恳求父亲允许年轻的帝象到火奴鲁鲁和他一起生活并在那里读书，帝象得知后非常高兴。因为自从陆皓东回来之后，听到他讲述外面世界的故事，帝象便非常渴望出外游历。孙达成帮儿子打点好了行装，父母、叔母和同窗好友伤感地一一与他道别——尤其是陆皓东。但对于帝象来说，这将是一次惊险刺激的旅程。我以为他一直是喜欢游历的，甚至在他后来的坎坷生涯中都是如此。

1879年，一个个子不高、皮肤黝黑，文静而充满好奇的13岁男孩，从澳门乘坐英国"格兰诺曲"号蒸汽轮船开始了他的旅途。他毕生的旅程由此开始，他说不想漏掉任何东西，而他也言出必行了。在船上，他大部分的时间向那些跟他讲一样方言的人提问题，并参观了轮机舱，观察那个机器怪物是怎么运转的。

经过三个星期的愉快旅程，孙逸仙到达了火奴鲁鲁。他穿着中式长衫，辫子很整齐地盘在红钮绸帽的下面。哥哥孙眉到码头接他。建筑物、棕榈树和海浪拍岸声，白皮肤、蓝眼睛的白人，怪声怪气的说话，还有那些衣着鲜艳的海岛居民——对一个来自中国农村的男孩子

---

① 陆皓东（1867~1895），名中桂，字献香，翠亨村人。1895年第一次广州起义中，因返回销毁革命党员名册而被捕牺牲，孙中山称他为"中国有史以来，为共和革命而牺牲者之第一人"。

来说，这里处处都是新奇景象。

帝象目不暇给地观察眼前的景象，几乎没有听到孙眉在和他说什么。孙眉说准备把他送到一个由英国圣公会主办的、名为意奥兰尼的教会学校①去上学，学校由韦礼士主教②主持。但遗憾的是孙眉住在偏远的茂宜岛，他在那里经营牧场③，所以帝象得在学校寄宿，只能偶尔去看望他的哥哥。然而，或许帝象正喜欢这样，可以远离家庭的约束而自行其事。

韦礼士主教是一个与众不同的无私的人，后来我去夏威夷时，他也是我的老师。他把这群中国年轻人聚集在身边，花很多精力在他们身上，并给他们充分和健全的教育。为了让这群年轻人可以很容易地成为寄宿生，他每年总共才收 150 美元。

韦礼士主教十分关心帝象。帝象不会讲英语，但他勤奋认真地学习。他在意奥兰尼学校所受的教育，当然与我们在村塾里单调地背诵中国的传统经典是完全不一样的。对于帝象来说，一切都新奇而富有吸引力，他第一次开始完整地认识这个世界和世界上的事情。不过，这也使得他对中国的生活更加不满。

他进步很快，1882 年，他进意奥兰尼学校三年后，便获得了英语语法的二等奖。奖品是一本关于中国的书，由海岛的国王卡拉卡瓦亲自当众颁发给他。④

这时，他已经能讲流利的英语，但仍然对周围的一切保持着强烈

---

① 意奥兰尼学校（Iolani College），是檀香山英国圣公会主教 Staley 于 1862 年 10 月创办。在檀香山各外人所办之学校中，该校可说是与华侨关系最密切之学校。

② 韦礼士（Alfred Willis），或译作"威利士"，1872 年接任檀香山英国圣公会主教。孙中山就读意奥兰尼学校时，他是学校的主持者。

③ 茂宜（Maui）岛，夏威夷群岛第二大岛，位于夏威夷（Hawaii）岛和奥鸦湖（Oahu）岛之间。位碌古埠（Wailuku）为岛上最大市镇。1881 年，孙眉离开火奴鲁鲁，搬到茂宜岛的茄贺蕾（Kahului）开设商店，1889 年向夏威夷政府承租菇剌（Kula）牧场。

④ 据当时在孙眉牧场打工的陆华造回忆，奖品是由主教牧师韦礼士亲自送到畜牧场孙眉手里。（1935 年杨连合采访陆华造记录，见杨连合：《孙中山先生的幼年生活》，广东省政协文史委员会藏稿。）

的兴趣。这种好奇可能太强烈了，以至有一次他去看望哥哥孙眉时说：他希望和意奥兰尼的其他学生一起受洗成为基督教徒。

孙眉自然感到震惊，他做梦都没有想到事情会发生这样的转变。他送弟弟到学校去只有一个目的，就是让他获得教育。帝象想要放弃中国的神而信仰基督教的想法，令孙眉大怒，他要帝象完全打消这个念头。孙眉也立即写信给父亲详细报告了这件事情。孙达成回信命令孙眉马上把帝象送回故乡，在信中，孙达成还说："我要把这种耶稣的谬论从他的脑袋里抹得一干二净。"

帝象很不愿意地乘坐一艘驶往香港的蒸汽轮船回国。在回翠亨的途中，他乘坐一条当地的小船，驶经汲水门①的小岛前，船长告诉船上的乘客，要顺从海关官吏的检查，如果有人与他们发生争拗，将会给全船人带来麻烦。

这些海关人员是些贪婪的官员，他们有时还索取贿赂。在第一次检查之后，帝象重新收拾好了行李。然而不久，第二批海关人员来了，要求打开行李再次检查。帝象一声不吭，再次顺从配合。第三批查缉鸦片的海关人员佩带刀剑来了，当他们要求开包再检查一次时，帝象感觉受到了侮辱。然而，这次检查后还没有把行李重新收拾好，身穿制服、全副武装，声称是煤油检查员的第四批官员又过来了，他们说必须再一次检查行李。帝象认为这太过分了，他粗声告诉他们，他的行李已经被检查过三次了，他们只要看看他行李的大小和形状，就可以清楚知道里面并没有空间可以藏有像煤油这样大的东西。

那些官员很快就转身走了。

这让船长和旅客们惊慌不安，他们哀叹道："任何抵抗的行为只会给我们所有人带来麻烦。船会被扣留，直到他们高兴的时候才会批准放行！上午我们走不成了。"

帝象平静地说："当船进港之后，我将为你们向更高级的官员上诉。"

船长和乘客们都讥笑起来。他们对他说："这里没有上诉这回事的，如果你去找更高级的官员，只会给我们带来更多的麻烦。"

船长告诉他一个故事，有一次有个乘客从香港带了一些香肠回

①　汲水门，原称急水门，位于香港大屿山东北及马湾之间，维多利亚港西面的出口，是由南中国海往珠江流域的重要水道之一。

家，两次过关都被贪婪的官吏没收了。第三次他放了一些毒药在香肠里，还是这个官吏，他吃了香肠后很快被毒死了。

这给了帝象一个很好的机会去鼓吹改革的必要性。他告诉大家，这样的检查不是必然的，我们应该反对，健全自由的政府给予每一个人平等的自由与权利。不论他是否对这一小群惊恐的乘客有所影响，但他抓住每一个机会去反抗不公平的权威，并把自己想法和大家分享。令人费解的是，检查的官吏并没有再来找麻烦，船很快就被放行了①。

在村子里，我们知道帝象被送回来了，不过17岁的他很不情愿回到偏僻的翠亨村，他已经是一个和四年前离开的男孩完全不同的年轻人了。西方文化在他身上留下了不可磨灭的烙印。他满脑子新想法，对村子里人们的因循守旧有更多的不满。过去在他身上表现的独立和果断的性格，现在已变为公开的反抗与挑战。

乡村生活的落后让他感到不快。他深切意识到，和世界上的其他地方相比，同乡们多么缺乏自由和发展机会。他看到，传统观念和狭隘的教育，加上清政府的粗暴统治，成为村民身上牢不可破的枷锁。他不是第一个或唯一一个意识到这些问题的中国年轻人。当时中国的秘密社团星罗棋布，他们用各种方式希望进行改革，或者推翻政府。有一些零星但影响不大的起义发生，最近和最接近成功的是19世纪40年代的太平天国起义，持续了14年。但所有的起义最后都失败了，不是因为清政府保持了高度警觉性，封锁所有的通讯和消息，就是有外国势力的干涉。对中国大部分有识之士来说，成功反抗和推翻清政府看起来几乎不可能了。

也许我们该先有一个简明的中国政治史的图像，才能明白革命及其结果给中国带来了什么。

在真正由汉人统治的明朝的200多年里②，中国总的来说算是享

---

① 据林百克《孙逸仙传记》记载，孙中山反抗之后，"果然不出船主所料，乘客真的受着麻烦了，因为这些吏员把这沙船扣留，不准开行，直到第二天早上，船主纳贿给他们，沙船才得开行。"

② 原文"Under the Mings, who were truly Chinese, China enjoyed for the most part a benevolent rule of some two thousand years."但明朝实际只存在276年，故译文根据史实改为"200多年"。

有仁政。当然，任何地方都有好的和坏的统治者，但他们往往都是能干而精力充沛，尽自己的能力帮助国家和人民的，在他们的统治下，国家安定而繁荣。对于那个时代来说，这是一个很好的管理体系。问题是当清朝也用这个制度治国时，这个体系已是逐渐过时，但清朝统治者却拒绝改革。

古老的统治制度下，住在北京的皇帝（或者称天子），是人民精神上和道德上的领袖——但是更多地被认为像是父亲与孩子的关系。对于父亲，孩子有一定的自由和责任，但相应地，父亲要引导和保护孩子免受伤害。天子是绝对的君主，但附属于其权力之下也有一系列机制去维护其统治。

每个省的总督或者巡抚是政府官员，在所管辖的地区是最高统治者，除了规定的上缴赋税和向皇帝报告，其他方面他都可以自己做主。公职必须通过竞争甚大的科举考试选拔，也就是说高官不可能根据个人意愿而随意卖官或安插官员。官员晋升是基于没有偏袒的实际政绩。这些手段，减轻了皇帝所能恩赐的权力，被认为起到了约束皇权的作用。同时，还设立了都察院，主要监察执权者和日常行政官员，由是进一步限制皇权。

在真龙天子有名无实的统治下，这事实上就是一个依靠个人关系的各省自治的联邦。省的管理权实际掌握在各省官员手中。城市依靠商人或手工业者行会及商会来运作。乡村则依靠长老来管理。各省设有巡抚，或是数省归一个总督管理。巡抚或总督是政府官员，直接向皇帝负责，但如无必要，他不会被请求插手地方的事务，也不会有人期待他这样做。在他头上的，当然就是皇帝了。

因此，对于大多数的人民，政府不是太重要。就像流淌的河水，这边波涛汹涌，那边波澜不兴。但在明朝的统治下，人民完全有权去反对或者推翻软弱无能的管理者，对于地方上的统治者是如此，对于皇帝自己亦然。这种权利是一种"反抗"的权利而不是"革命"。这意味着在危急时刻，他们可以推翻那些无能的长官或统治者，但不代表他们可以根本改变帝国这种形式或者政府本身。

在这种制度下，来自北方的满洲人征服中国并在北京推行统治之初，广大人民对此表示漠不关心的态度，就变得不难理解了。

满洲人虽然粗鲁但聪明。他们认同明朝实行的那种已经运作了

2000 多年的统治体系的主要价值，并决定保留下来，其中又加入了一些他们自己的东西。

正是这些新加的举措，令中国人终得直面失败的痛苦，并由此产生对满洲人不灭的憎恨。从一开始，满洲人就依靠武力治国而非像明朝一样实行德治，这令汉人感到被冒犯。由于担心失去刚得到的权力，清政府完整地保持了军队并驻扎到每一个省份，并尽可能让满洲人统领汉人官吏和官员。所幸并非在所有地方都可能这样，因为满洲人并没有足够的人才到处安插。臣服于清朝的读书人和官员，终身都背负着羞辱感。

清政府对出版物和所有的舆论信息执行严格的审查。他们知道，维护胜利果实的代价，就必须时刻保持警惕。他们还建立了复杂而深入的间谍系统。这无疑是他们可以维持 268 年统治的部分原因。

虽然清朝为适应统治需要而改变明朝的制度，不过满清政府头150 年的统治还不是太糟糕。初期出现了几个强硬而又能干的皇帝，例如康熙①和乾隆②这对祖孙，他们精明、善于经营，又勤政励治。妇女被严格排除在政治之外，皇帝亲自处理国家大事。第一代清朝统治者带来活力，对于中国来说，好多于坏。

清统治真正的问题，始于家庭——也就是说在他们的宫殿里面。为了确保皇子接受满洲传统教育，防止腐化堕落，皇子只能在紫禁城内过着狭隘而孤独的生活。让这群年轻的统治者了解外面的世界和事物的任务被寄托在老师身上，但人生的意义是没有办法教的。生命的意义必需通过生活才能完全明白，但晚清的皇子只是朝廷的傀儡，根本没有机会去体验生活。嘉庆③、道光④两个皇帝都是孱弱、奢靡和

---

① 康熙（爱新觉罗·玄烨，1654～1722），1661～1722 年在位。从康熙中叶起，清朝出现了相对繁荣的局面，到雍正、乾隆年间，国力达于鼎盛，这段时期被称为"康乾盛世"。

② 乾隆（爱新觉罗·弘历，1711～1799），1735 年继位，在位 60 年。嘉庆元年（1796），传位第十五子颙琰（嘉庆），自为太上皇帝，是中国历史上掌权时间最长的皇帝。

③ 嘉庆（爱新觉罗·颙琰，1760～1820），1796～1820 年在位。

④ 道光（爱新觉罗·旻宁，1782～1850），1820～1850 年在位。道光即位之初，中国正面临严重的内外危机，史称"嘉道中衰"。

放纵的男人。后期的统治者让朝廷变得一年比一年奢靡和堕落。女人开始干涉政治，由于她们狭隘的眼光和有限的教育，加深了争执。而一直等待权力旁落的老谋深算的太监，一俟时机出现，便迅速地抓住了机会。

接下来的是更年轻的统治者。咸丰①在1850年登基时年仅19岁，同治②当皇帝的时候只5岁，光绪③做皇帝的时候还只是一个4岁的小童。实际上这是在摄政，权力掌握在慈禧太后④的手上，这个权力她渴望已久。

一系列政治上的惨败逐渐证明满清政府没有能力去统治和保护中国。持续了14年的太平天国起义是第一个打击，也几乎致清政府于死地。之后，两次鸦片战争的结果是向"蛮夷"让步。最后，1860年俄国要求割让北方领土得逞。所有的这些事情使清政府不仅在中国而且在全世界都丢尽了脸面。统治家族的堕落，加上慈禧太后与日俱增的专政——这时她已是残酷无情而又贪恋权力的老女人了，使汉人对清政府极度反感。

因此，帝象和许多积极思考的中国年轻人，看清了这套荒唐的制度并希望改革，这一点都不奇怪。不过我觉得他当时还没想过自己去改变它，他希望帮忙把其他人鼓动起来，直至进行改革。

他常常和我的叔叔陆皓东讨论这些问题，因为他们俩都感兴趣。事实上，在广州衙门招募新兵时，陆皓东甚至自愿报名参加了清政府

---

① 咸丰（爱新觉罗·奕詝，1831～1861），1850年继位，在位期间，经历太平天国起义、第二次鸦片战争和义和团运动。

② 同治（爱新觉罗·载淳，1856～1875），1861～1875年在位。一直在慈禧太后控制之下，十八岁亲政，次年即病死。这一时期，国内外局势稍趋平和，清室亦兴办洋务，颇有发愤图强之心，此段时期被称为"同治中兴"。

③ 光绪（爱新觉罗·载湉，1871～1908），1875年继位时年仅4岁，由慈禧太后"垂帘听政"。1889年亲政，但朝中大权仍掌握在慈禧太后手中。1898年6月，光绪帝力排众议，宣布变法。9月，慈禧太后发动政变，光绪帝被囚于瀛台。1908年11月14日，先慈禧太后一日卒于宫中。

④ 慈禧太后（1835～1908），清咸丰帝奕詝之妃。满洲镶蓝旗人。同治、光绪两朝实际最高统治者。

军队的操练。参加操演回来后，他把帝象叫到一旁，厌恶地说：

"50个训练有素的士兵就可以击溃这样的军队和摧毁保卫广州的虎门港。"

"那为什么没有这样的军队呢？"帝象若有所思地问，"如果有的话，我们就可以夺取政权，中国就能够在世界强国中取得应有的地位了。为什么没有人开始做这件事呢？"

陆皓东笑道："也许你就是做这件事的人。"

对陆皓东来说，这不过是随口讲讲的笑话，但对追求改革理想的年轻的帝象来说，却像悄然埋下了一粒种子，他知道国家需要有人干一番大事业，而这值得他去做。

任何形式的起义都是帝象和陆皓东现在最留心的事情。他们讨论失败了的太平天国起义，这场起义1846年由洪秀全发动，最初是基督教运动，但后来演变成为有组织的反清斗争。他们注意到，起义是从破坏旧偶像开始的。

帝象从中受到启发，他决定扫除自己与神明、家庭以及传统的一切联系。他把一些孩子叫来，包括陆皓东和我，告诉我们他从夏威夷回来之后，曾被迫去庙里烧香，但他只是做做样子而已，他根本不信神。他接下来的计划更让我们感到震撼，因为那实在太令人兴奋了。他说他将带着我们到庙里面去扫除迷信，捣毁那个他一生下来就被奉献给它的北帝。这对于华南广东的一个小山村的年轻人来说真是一件惊人之举，他没有任何后盾，只有为人民、为中国而奋斗的伟大理想和坚定决心。

我们大白天去到庙里，那里没有人，只有一个守庙人在外面睡觉，我们留下两个人盯着这个守庙人。帝象和陆皓东走进庙里，帝象砸断了北帝那只朝天的手指，而陆皓东则带着小刀，刮掉了一个女神脸上的油彩。

我和我的同伴当然对庙里面所发生的事情非常好奇，因而没有留意到守庙人已经醒了，他马上发出警告，我们所有人都逃回家里。然而，帝象被看见了，而且还被认出是带头的。从我前面所介绍的背景，你们可以想象，恐慌象野火一样在翠亨村里迅速散播，他们认为这种卑劣的行径是前所未有的。

乡中的长辈们冲到孙达成家告诉他，他那胆大妄为的儿子在庙里面的所作所为。孙达成费尽唇舌、卑躬屈膝地为帝象和全家向他们道歉。他不知道为什么他的儿子做出这样的事情来，他向乡人解释他也感到不安和丢脸，他很生气，但不知如何是好。长辈们于是说，如果不把帝象驱逐出村子，就不能安抚神灵，这样会给全村带来灾祸。孙达成一家的辩解并不能抵御全村的压力。这次恶作剧的最终结果出乎我们任何一个人的意料：帝象被迫忍辱离开了翠亨村。我们谁都没有意料到帝象污损神像会有这样的结果，不过其实帝象自己在计划和采取行动时，已经很清楚这种危险性了。我后来才认识到，他从不在尚未权衡得失就去做任何事。也许这就是他为什么在忍辱离开翠亨村时能这么冷静和镇定，并终于开始他自己的独立生活。我从未听闻过有什么事情可以令他惊惶失措，无论是多么重大的事情。他一个人身无分文地去了广州，镇定自如，就像他后来就任中华民国第一任大总统时一样。

二　学医、结婚、第一次起义

我不再称呼他帝象了，因为这个乳名只用于他在村里的青少年时代。当他怀着新的理想与信念离开翠亨村——几乎成为一个全新的人物时，我相信他将会大有作为，并称呼他为孙逸仙。

他到了广州，没有钱，没有朋友，甚至没有活干。不过他意识到自己拥有一种很有价值的才能——在意奥兰尼学校的训练使他说得一口流利的英语。年轻的孙逸仙找到广州英美医院①的一个领班，凭着他的语言能力，找到一份学徒的工作，任普通杂役和翻译。虽然工作繁重而琐碎，但他再一次认识到与现代技术相比，自己国家的医生迷信和不完善的医术是多么落后。

一位名叫嘉约翰②的主治医生很欣赏这个严肃认真又勤奋刻苦的年轻人，他们成为了朋友。一天，嘉约翰医生告诉孙，香港的教会不久将为华人开办一所医科学校。资助开办这所学校的是何启③医生，他在苏格兰毕业，是一位律师和医生。他的苏格兰夫人随他回国，死后留下了一笔基金。在香港一个教会的帮助下，何启利用这笔基金开办了一家医院，并将之命名为雅丽氏纪念医院，以纪念其亡妻。听到这个消息，孙逸仙燃起了通过先进医学去帮助同胞的想法。"我想进那所学校。"他对嘉约翰医生说。嘉约翰医生也为这所新学校得到这

---

① 原文 the Anglo - American Hospital in Canton，所指应是博济医院。孙中山约于 1886 年夏秋间入院学医。

② 嘉约翰（John Glasgow Kerr，1824～1901），美国基督教北长老会（North Presbyterian Churches）传教医生。1855 年起在广州的 Canton Hospital（中文初称广济眼科医院，1866 年改名博济医院）内开办授业。

③ 何启（1859～1914），字迪之，生于香港。早年习医于英国鸭巴甸大学（Aberdeen University）。1887 年捐款创建雅丽氏纪念医院。同年 10 月，香港西医书院创校，并以雅丽氏纪念医院为教学和实习场地。何启出任香港西医书院荣誉秘书，并任教法医学及生理学。

样一个干劲十足的学生而欣喜。

回头看看我们的村子，这里发生的一些事情也影响着年轻的孙逸仙的生活。他的父亲在一年前去世了①。母亲觉得儿子已20岁了，因此她就写信告诉他，依照习俗，他该结婚了。母亲帮他选了邻村一位卢姓姑娘②，她跟孙逸仙的母亲一样，也是本地人。即使是孙逸仙这样反叛的人，在当时如果要违抗母亲的意愿，也会是闻所未闻的。他履行义务似地回到翠亨村去结婚。他不认识这个女孩，也从来没有见过她，按习俗，他们要直到婚礼之后才能见面。婚礼按照中国传统举行，饶有趣味。不过，孙逸仙在婚礼举行后旋即回到香港，为进医科学校做准备。在等待学校开学的时候，他决定请美国公理会的传教士为他举行洗礼③。他这个时期的生活似乎是新旧混杂的。

1887年6月，康德黎④医生从英国到来，开办这间中国的医学院⑤。医学院秋天开学，孙逸仙从一开始就是个能干并且真心实意勤奋学习的学生。无论是从个人成长、医学院学生还是未来医生的角度，康德黎医生对孙逸仙都关心入微。像孙逸仙拥有的大多数友谊一样，康德黎跟他的朋友关系始终如一，至死不渝。

孙在同学中却是很少有知己。他平静的外表下对祖国的一腔热情，也吸引了一些同学，他告诉他们，他的希望是有一个新政府，也

---

① 此处叙述有误。孙中山与卢慕贞于1884年5月7日结婚。近4年之后，1888年3月23日，孙中山父亲孙达成才去世。

② 指孙中山元配夫人卢慕贞（1867～1952），广东香山县外壆村（今珠海市外沙村）人。1884年5月7日与孙中山结婚，婚后，生子孙科，女孙娫、孙婉。1915年9月，在日本与孙中山协议离婚。

③ 此处说法有误，孙中山于1883年底在香港受洗入基督教，当时就读于香港拔萃书室，亦尚未结婚。1884年，孙中山转学香港中央书院，1886年秋入广州博济医院学医，1887年9月，方转入香港西医书院求学。

④ 康德黎（James Cantlie，1851～1926），英国人，外科医生。1887年夏天到香港，参加香港西医书院的创办工作。1889年至1896年担任西医书院教务长。1896年，孙中山被伦敦清使馆诱捕，康德黎倾力营救脱险，并帮助孙撰写《伦敦被难记》。

⑤ 所指应是香港西医书院，1887年10月成立，原名 The College of Medicine for Chinese, Hong Kong；1907年改为 The College of Medicine, Hong Kong，1913年并入香港大学。

迫切希望发展正规的教育和促进农业。通过孙的眼光，那些年轻人开始领会，国民应该有权对其统治者提出诉求。这种想法是非常激进的，虽然就像孙逸仙所解释的一样，其基本原则很简单，人民必须要有饭吃和受教育。通过集约耕作可以实现前者，通过先进的教育方法和现代的平权理念可以实现后者。这样，人民就完全没有理由不可以管理自己的社会。对于这群青年学生来说，这是激动人心的思想——年轻人永远是革命的温床，但没有人知道该怎么去做，在这个时候，也没有一个切实可行的行动计划，连孙逸仙自己也心中无数。他和同学们都充满热情，觉得有些事情必须要做，但都尚未清楚这要如何进行。因此，孙以他一贯寄热情于冷静的能力，继续潜心学医。他仍然相信，专业的医术是他服务同胞的最佳途径。

这时的中国，各色秘密社团星罗棋布，这样的情况，早就"蔚然成风"。但这些社团大部分是说的比做的多。其中一个比较活跃的新兴社团是三合会，其头目是孙逸仙的一位郑姓同学①。我年轻的叔叔陆皓东也是这个社团的活跃分子，因为和陆皓东的亲密友谊，孙逸仙也对这个社团产生了兴趣。各种各样的历史事件不断激发这个社团更积极地传播革命学说。首先，日本成功地把台湾变成附属地。对于这群有关怀的年轻人来说，这证明了军事力量和"现代化"对于国家安全至关重要。为了表现他们新的爱国主义和尚武精神，陆皓东设计了一面旗帜，蓝色天空上一个白色的太阳②，这后来成为中国国民党的党旗。后来蒋介石领导军队从广东北伐到北平并统一国家，青天白日旗被采用于红色旗子的左上角③，作为中华民国国旗。

1892 年，夜以继日勤奋学习的孙逸仙成功地成为医学院的首位毕业生④。同一年，他和陆皓东一起在香港受洗成为基督徒⑤。他继续坚定地逐步帮助同胞们摒弃旧的生活方式，无论是心理上的、身体上

① 当指郑士良。郑士良（1863～1901），号弼臣，广东归善（今惠阳市淡水镇）人，三合会员。1886 年入广州博济医院学医，与孙中山结为好友。参与发动和领导广州起义和三洲田起义。
② 今一般称为"青天白日旗"。
③ 今一般称为"青天白日满地红旗"。
④ 香港西医书院首届毕业生有孙中山、江英华两人。
⑤ 孙中山与陆皓东 1883 年底已在香港受洗。

的还是精神上的。他正式丢弃了"帝象"这个名字，称自己为孙逸仙。当然，孙是他的姓，就像史密斯或者琼斯一样。逸仙，粗略地翻译成英语大概是"自由神"的意思，或者广义地理解，有敢于特立独行的意思。

不过在这个时候，"自由"要实践起来也并非容易。首先，当孙选择在澳门开业执医的时候，那里的葡萄牙医生嫉妒这个懂得现代医学技术的中国人，恐怕他威胁了他们的生意。另一方面，作为一个放弃了传统医术而改行西医的中国医生，他还需赢得当地中国人的信任。

刚开始的时候，生意非常惨淡，不过孙通过几个病例就证明了自己是一个极出色的大夫和外科医生。在澳门行医之余，孙和各种秘密社团的成员一起议论政治和政府，他惊喜地发现许多年轻人对中国怀着和他一样的想法和希望。这当中有许多和他一样是教会学校的学生，透过游历和接受西方教育开阔了视野。他们回来之后，很自然地看出国内的缺点与落后，并希望为此做点什么。即便今天的年轻学生，从接受教育的大城市回到故乡，不也是把两者进行比较并发现家乡的落后吗？但在那个时候，差别是如此之巨大，他们发现这根本没有办法比较。诉诸政府不仅毫无用处，而且作茧自缚，徒惹来牢狱之灾甚至杀头。他们也不用指望从长辈处得到支持，长辈若非太囿于传统而无意改变，就是打从心里惧怕清政府。

尽管清政府在甲午战争和俄国、英国的百般需索中丢尽了颜面，但慈禧太后在中国仍然牢牢掌握着大权。孙逸仙博士发现他对设法让老谋深算的慈禧太后为人民做些事情比行医更有兴趣。他告诉一个朋友："如果我只是一个医生，一次只能希望治好一个病人；如果我帮助中国获得解放，我一下子就救活四万万人！"因此，他准备孤注一掷。孙逸仙毫不犹豫地离开了澳门和他的行医事业，就像他当年离开他出生的村子一样。这都是为了同一个原因——尽自己所能力帮助同胞。

他和他的朋友陆皓东一起回到广州。孙是一个天生的演说家，他们很快就让他去公开演讲，他的声音打动了不少听众。他是一个平静、从容的演说者，对于听众来说，他的声音清晰而具有说服力。但是，对于孙来说，开始的时候也并不容易。他花了很长时间去练习，以达到完美。不过就像他希望掌握的每件事一样，他的演说很快就达到了一个很高的水平。除了是个杰出的演说者之外，孙生来就是个领袖，他的朋友们很快就认识到了这一点。除了演说宣传他们的梦想，他们期望做更多的事情，把梦想变为现实。

孙博士回到广州后，在一个药店里设立了他的总部，作为他活动的掩护所。1893 年，他和陆皓东一起从汉口到北京做了一次短途旅行，亲身考察清政府的政治制度。他发现这是一个腐败而沉滞的政府。这位年轻的革命者当时决定通过李鸿章①上书政府，呼吁进一步改革教育和农业，不过很快就被李鸿章拒绝了②。

政府的拒绝，使孙博士和他的追随者证实了走和平道路永远不能达到他们的目标。他们终于认识到武装革命才是唯一的道路。少年中国会在那时已经秘密集会，他们筹款购买武器，一切都在极其秘密地进行着。

第二年，即 1894 年，清政府忙于和日本开战，孙看到这是一个革命的机会。然而，经费对他们的事业至关重要，他决定到夏威夷寻求孙眉的帮助。他的哥哥最终被说服，也相信革命别具大义，并和另一位夏威夷华侨邓荫南③成为第一批支持革命事业的富商。他们倾尽全力帮助年轻的孙逸仙，并帮着动员其他本地人加入新成立的兴中会。1895 年孙离开火奴鲁鲁时，这个新社团已有近百名会员。

邓荫南和孙博士一起回到中国，帮助他在香港成立兴中会总部。他们计划以广州作为起义的发端。

在香港，兴中会开办了乾亨行（一家进口贸易公司）作为掩护，在广州则用“农学会”作为掩护所。

---

① 李鸿章（1823～1901），字子黻，号少荃。安徽合肥人。淮军创始人和统帅。1870 年，继曾国藩任直隶总督兼北洋通商大臣，并参与掌管清政府外交、军事、经济大权，成为清末权势最为显赫的重臣。

② 此段叙述有误，孙中山与陆皓东到北方短期游历，是在 1894 年 7 月。孙中山曾回忆，上书李鸿章被拒之后，“予乃与陆皓东北游京津，以窥清廷之虚实；深入武汉，以观长江之形势。”（《孙中山全集》第 6 卷，中华书局 1985 年 3 月版，第 229 页）

③ 邓荫南（1846～1923），原名松盛，又称邓三，广东开平人。檀香山华侨富商，与孙眉交往甚密。1894 年加入兴中会。次年变卖家财充革命经费，回国参与筹划广州起义。

九月九日①，因为武器装船时的疏忽，广州海关的官员发现了他们的 600 支手枪。政府的密探通知官兵包围广州总部，陆皓东、丘四和朱贵全不幸被捕。孙博士在前往总部的途中收到风声而得以及时逃脱。

那时，我从夏威夷回乡结婚，虽然我知道发生了什么事，但传到长辈处的谣言让人惶恐不安。陆皓东狂热地为革命事业而付出，甚至变卖年轻妻子的首饰去资助革命运动。我有一个姑妈住在广州，她在来信中谈到陆皓东的情况，让村子里人心惶惶。当然，他们中没有一个人知道，这些不顾后果、他们难以理解的年轻人，正在进行一场革命。

对于这个勇敢的小政党来说，这是一个悲惨的开端。在翠亨村，却很快引起了令人恐惧的反响。我的姑妈很快来信告知陆皓东被捕入狱，而孙逸仙被迫逃亡。

我后来从孙博士那里知道，他从广州逃往内地找唐雄②——一个他在意奥兰尼学校时的同学。他半夜到唐雄家把他叫醒，请他找一个轿子，让他到澳门并坐船去香港，在香港这块英国的割让地上他应该会安全。他说他曾想去美国领事馆看看他们能否帮助陆皓东。

陆皓东坚决拒绝向清政府提供任何情报。

我刚在翠亨村举行过婚礼，在这里，我们也有一场小小的革命。当我的叔公（他是村里的乡正③）收到我姑妈的来信后，这位老人很是沮丧。

他激动得在椅子上跳起来又坐下去，念着信中的内容，说这些年轻人都疯了，他们会使全村人丢脑袋的！他悲叹道，现在对孙逸仙及其同党的缉捕令已经发出，由于他是长老，他们可能要他为此事负责的！他十分害怕，不知所措。我当时可能是太年轻了，还不懂事，只

---

① 公历为 1895 年 10 月 26 日。

② 唐雄（1865～1958），字谦光，广东香山县恭常都唐家村（今珠海市唐家镇）人。1883 年和孙中山一起在香港受洗加入基督教。唐雄当时住在香山县唐家村，唐家在广州的南面，珠江口西岸，离澳门约 25 公里，所以原文用"inland"（内地）似不合适。

③ 据陆灿《孙公中山事略》所记，这个陆灿的叔公、陆皓东的叔父名陆星甫，当时是翠亨村乡正。据陆仁协主修的《香山隔田河南郡陆氏族谱》（清同治元年抄本）载，陆星甫，生于清道光十一年（1831），名如铎，字廷深，号惺甫，其父陆仁车是陆皓东祖父陆厚车的长兄。

觉得看着他穿着长衫像木偶一样跳上跳下的样子非常有趣，思量着灾祸何时会降临。

最后他问我："难道你不害怕吗？"我说我不怕。我还说，我敢打赌，我舅公——他是另一个大村唐家村的长老，也不害怕。我建议，如果他因为这件事情而觉得陷入困境，可以去找找舅公这个亲戚，征求他的意见。这正合他意，恐惧也稍稍平复下来。不过他又说自己年老体弱，要我代他去。他很着急，当场就找了一顶轿子要送我去。我说明天上午去的话也还来得及。

于是，第二天一早我就坐着轿子到了唐家。我穿上了我最好的长衫，因为舅公是个官员，我必须按传统的习俗去拜会他。不过，由于我已经离开家乡，到夏威夷上学，过惯了自由的生活，这次只是最近为了结婚才回来，所以对于这样的繁文缛节已经不太习惯了。

舅公家位于一座小山上，非常宏伟。他的两个兄弟的房子也在同一座山上。唐家村有大约 2000 幢房子，是我们这个地区的集镇，由他们三兄弟管理。

登上 21 级台阶，才到了舅公家，他家有漂亮的花园环绕。舅公在门口迎接我，我合手作揖，并三鞠躬。这位老人一身清朝官服，留着稀疏的长胡子，会视情形摆弄他的胡子以表达他的情绪。终于我们在客厅坐下来了，我们开始寒暄，谈论天气、花园、季节等等，直到舅公开门见山地问我："你这么早来找我有什么事？"我明白可以说出此行的真正目的了。

我客气地回答说："舅公，只是来向您请安。我们很少来看您，祖母很想知道您的近况。"

舅公摸摸他的胡子说："你不会一大早老远过来就为了这个。来，告诉我你真正的来意吧。"

他这样吩咐，我就可以告诉他实情了。于是我把村子里的困难一概相告，并告诉他村里的长老——我的叔公，不知如何处理是好。

起先，他觉得这几个学生只是志大才疏，并无大害，对他们这样哗众取宠的行为感到好笑。但当我详细说到姑妈的来信，并谈到她的外甥陆皓东已被捕入狱，可能很快就要被斩首时，我这个当官的舅公扯着他的胡子并从椅子上跳起来说："没有钱、士兵和军舰，你们这些小村民怎么有那么大的胆子搞推翻政府这样的大事？这是造反！这是大逆不道!"他继续训斥,而我只是顺从地沉默着,直到他平息了怒气重新坐回椅子上。

"您的阅历丰富,"我说,"请您一定要告诉我们下一步该怎么办。清兵若到村里搜捕孙逸仙和搜查陆皓东家,我们该怎样应付。"我们当然都知道,如果可以的话,官兵一定会查封这两个莽撞的年轻人的房子,扣押他们的家人。不过他们都已经离开了。孙博士把家里人都送到香港藏起来了。

舅公坐着猛捋他的胡须,先捋一边,再捋另一边,一面在思考。最后,他问我翠亨村的长老是否有谈及缉捕程序的书。我说我不知道。舅公拿出他的那本,说长老应该读读关于如何应付奉命搜查缉捕的官员的那几段。他说村里的长老们要客气地接待那些官兵,对他们毕恭毕敬,陪同他们四处搜查。我们在书上找到一段说这些官兵可能根据他们搜查时所走的路程收取"报酬",所以要尽可能带他们走偏僻的道路。舅公只能想出这个对策了。如果那些官兵收取了报酬,又没有发现什么可以"查封"的,他们或许会马上离开。

我带着这个建议回村,希望可以安慰叔公。他收到那本关于官兵缉捕程序的书,全神贯注地阅读。他打算完全按照舅公的建议来进行。但我还是另外做了预防措施,布置了一些带枪的人在周围的山上,以防大规模的扣押或屠杀,最后果然没有出现麻烦。到来的官兵心不在焉,他们收了"报酬",让我们带他们到孙逸仙空无一人的家中,然后就平安无事地走了。孙家在知道起义的消息时早就已经跑到香港去了。

期间,孙博士在香港为援救他的朋友陆皓东而作出不懈的努力。他联系了美国领事为他出面求情。他还找了陆皓东工作的电报公司,保证陆皓东只是他们所雇用的一个学生,不会真的参与造反活动。但所有朋友都没有充分估计到这个年轻人的革命热诚。美国领事去到衙门,发现陆皓东已经写了供词。他向他的朋友们解释说,他希望成为革命事业的第一个献身者,他还说清政府可以杀他一个,但杀不尽数以百万计后继的革命者[①]。在起义失败后的第15天,他被

---

① 陆皓东牺牲后,陆灿采访狱卒记录的陆皓东的供词,中有"但一我可杀,而继我而起者,不可尽杀"的句子。

斩首了①。

　　孙博士捎话来叫我去香港见他。陆皓东的死对他来说是一个沉重的打击，但也更加坚定了他继续革命的决心。他告诉我他将会到日本神户去避难，并在那里开展工作，准备另外一次起义。他问我可否带同他的妻子、母亲和三个孩子一起回夏威夷②，委托他们给孙眉照料，因为他们留在中国已经不再安全了，我欣然同意。我们一群人很快就一起出发到夏威夷了。

　　在香港和他分别时，我感觉到这是一个新的孙逸仙——热情果断，又像将军那样冷静和深思熟虑。那个冲动的男孩——帝象，已经转变成一个我们期待的精明的、坚定不移的领袖。

　　即使经过无数次的失败，对这样不屈不挠的精神来说，都不算什么。虽然之前我许多亲密的朋友付出的微薄努力，最后都以失败告终，但和孙逸仙谈话之后，我觉得我第一次对中国有了明确的希望；而我自己也决心竭尽所能，为这个大业贡献力量。

---

①　1895 年 10 月 27 日（农历九月初十日），陆皓东被捕。1895 年 11 月 7 日（农历九月二十一日），陆皓东英勇就义。

②　此处叙述有误，此时孙中山只有孙科和孙娫两个子女随陆灿到檀香山。孙中山的次女孙婉 1896 年 11 月 12 日才在檀香山出生。

三 在日本和夏威夷

我们乘船到达火奴鲁鲁后，把孙博士的家人安顿到了茂宜岛他哥哥孙眉那儿。当然在那里我们也直接或间接听说了孙逸仙在日本的活动。

孙博士的朋友资助他到达横滨。他说他把横滨当作流亡据点，是因为那里离中国近，是领导今后革命运动极好的地点。

1895 年中日签订的和约对孙逸仙去横滨有所帮助，但即使有了和约，他还是要时时防备清政府的追捕。清政府悬赏十万元巨款买他的人头，密探遍布日本。除此以外，引渡法已在两国生效，一旦被捕，他会被中国领事送回中国去审判和处决。

不管如何，在他从事革命事业的早期，他已经习惯了这些生命经常受到威胁的日子，对他来说，其激励意义更大于威吓。

这时候，掩饰自己本来的身份十分重要，于是他改穿西服，蓄起胡子，把辫子也剪掉了。他肤色很黑，所以很容易被当作是日本人而通过检查。事实上，后来人们常常说，他穿着整洁的黑衣服，蓄着修整的小胡子，像一个精悍的法国人多过像中国人。

孙博士在神户呆了一年，在他的中国朋友和同情他的日本友人的帮助下，建立了革命工作的总部①。他发现日本人对此很感兴趣，很留意他的计划并且给予帮助。这在后来对他的事业的确发挥了影响，但他们在当时的帮助已至少让孙可以为将来的革命活动打下基础。孙博士和他的小团队，在神户与世隔绝地为了革命不知疲倦地努力着。

---

① 1895 年 11 月 13 日，孙中山抵横滨后，旋组建兴中会分会，但未见有在神户建立革命工作总部及长期活动的记载。1895 年 11 月中下旬，孙中山离开日本赴檀香山，后在美洲大陆、英国及加拿大活动，至 1897 年 8 月初才再次到日本。

　　夏威夷是特别同情和支持孙博士的地区。首先，我们都是广东人，并和他关系亲密，在广州的第一次起义中也紧密合作。在那段早期的日子里，火奴鲁鲁的人们对孙博士的革命热情高涨，同时也越来越多人估计他的革命成功。我们中的大部分人都在夏威夷受过西方教育，都喜欢新的、自由的生活方式，因此我们都非常清楚地看到旧的中国政体需要变革。我们都看到了进步和现代的方法可以达致什么成果，也热切希望可以把这种变化带到中国去——如果需要的话，甚至会不顾一切。孙博士认识到来自太平洋彼岸的中国进步青年支持的重要性。他必须争取道义上和经济上的帮助，没有其它地方比夏威夷更能得到这两方面的帮助。

　　我们听说他计划于1896年初来火奴鲁鲁。中国领事知道他要来的消息时，准备安排一个盛大的欢迎仪式。不过他后来听说孙博士竟然是被满清政府通缉的革命党首领！他马上改变所有的计划，甚至不敢与孙会面。

　　然而我们一大群人去迎接他。众人对这个敢反抗"真龙天子"的年轻革命家所表达的崇高敬意，马上可以感觉得到。得益于意奥兰尼学校教育的我们，都敏锐地意识到了中国必须变革。但更令孙中山惊讶和感动的，是夏威夷的老华侨给予他的真诚关怀和忠心支持。在旧制度下，这些旧时代的人会如此盲目地追随这个年轻而激进的领袖，是不可思议的。尤其是当时孙中山是一个流亡的革命者。他们的支持坚定不移。实际上，被唤醒的思想所提倡的新的社会秩序已经被接受和产生切实的影响了。

　　看望了家人和密友之后，孙开始为革命事业开展扎扎实实的组织工作。虽然有同胞的坚定支持，但工作进展仍然缓慢，然而孙把救中国的信念和计划放在第一位，不知疲倦地投入热情和努力。他就象一个新的传教士向第一批信徒传教一样，为了让人明白，用简单的语言缓慢地、煞费苦心地解释。他从不采用那种华丽夸张的讲演方法，而代之以简明易懂的比喻和日常口语。然而这种真率简朴比慷慨激昂更能感动他的听众。他保持了一贯的冷静和说服力，并成长为一个令人信服的演说家。

　　宣讲了几个月之后，他已经充分建立起了一个稳固的基础，让人们对革命有了完整的认识。于是在他的朋友何宽①家里，他召开了一次会议，邀请了约 30 位有名望地位的人参加。

这是一个非常有意思的会议。在孙博士的主导下，决定成立一个固定的组织，名为"兴中会"，也就是"振兴中华的会社"的意思②。每一个成员进行简单的宣誓，表示他们会效忠于这个组织和它的主张，愿意服从领袖的指挥，任何时候都为革命事业竭尽所能。

孙博士第一个宣誓，他把手放在圣经上，平静地请上帝为他的誓言作证。其他人也很快跟着这样做了。他们大多是年轻人，能干、精力充沛且热情澎湃，他们多少受过一些西方教育，是热诚上进的年轻领袖孙逸仙的理想同伴。

在兴中会刚成立后的几次会议上，加入者稳步增多，但这些年轻人除了捐钱和听演讲之外，想做更多的事情，他们想亲自参加为中国争取自由的运动。

有人认为，真正的战斗是不可避免的，军事训练对他们的事业来说就必不可少。很快，他们就从兴中会的队伍里选出了一位年轻的中国指挥官和一位副官——叶桂芳③和钟工宇④，并聘请了一个丹麦人维克托·贝克作教官。贝克曾是军人，虽然他只能在芙兰·蒂文⑤牧师的院子里训练这些中国年轻人，却不乏真正的军事训练⑥。在大洋彼岸，中国革命的车轮终于开始转动起来。

---

① 何宽（1861～1931），广东香山县黄竹蓢乡（今中山市三乡镇竹溪村）人，15 岁到檀香山。在檀香山卑涉银行任职三十二年。何宽在兴中会成立会议上被选为副主席，后又担任主席。
② 檀香山兴中会成立于 1894 年 11 月，而不是广州起义失败之后的 1896 年。
③ 叶桂芳（Yap. William Kwai Fong，1873～1935），广东惠阳县人，生于檀香山，1894 年 12 月加入兴中会。1899 年后长期任职于夏威夷银行，曾任中西扩论会总理及书记。
④ 钟工宇（Chung Kun Ai，1865～1961），广东香山县西山乡（今中山市三乡镇西山村）人。1879 年随父至檀香山，就读于意奥兰尼学校，与孙中山为同学。钟公宇参加第一次兴中会会议，并曾资助出版《自由新报》。
⑤ 芙兰·蒂文（Frank Damon），华侨多喜欢译作"化冷爹文"，亦有译作"佛兰爹文"，是基督教教会人员，曾在广州服务多年。
⑥ 这次军事训练是在 1894 年冬，兴中会成立后不久，而不是在 1896 年。

　　孙博士继续在夏威夷获得支持，革命事业所需的资金不断注入。那年 6 月已经募集到了大约 6000 美元①，这在当时来说是一笔巨大的款项，其中有不少是某些捐赠人全部的积蓄。孙非常高兴，决定在三藩市也尝试用同一种组织方法，那里有很多在淘金热时期来到美国的广东人定居。他希望在加利福尼亚的富商中找到像火奴鲁鲁的商人那样热情又忠诚的支持者。虽然清政府的侦探仍然等待捕获他的机会，但他却能冒着危险，愉快而乐观地独自一人出行。他看来只有一个信念——尽快实现中国革命的彻底胜利。就像罗伯特·布鲁斯②，他的失败只会促使他再接再励，重新投入更大的精力和决心去继续奋斗。

---

　①　此处筹得捐款 6000 余元，是指兴中会成立后，1894 年底归国筹备起义前所筹得的款项。（冯自由：《中国革命运动二十六年组织史》，商务印书馆 1948 年版，第 16 页）1895 年底，广州起义失败后，孙中山在檀香山筹款，"然当时新败，和者寥寥。居檀数月，遍游夏威夷群岛，力劝侨胞赞助革命，效果绝少。"（冯自由：《华侨革命开国史》，良友印刷公司 1928 年版，第 36 页。）

　②　罗伯特·布鲁斯（Raibeart Bruis，1274～1329），苏格兰国王，曾领导苏格兰人取得民族独立，而被尊称为民族英雄。

四　加利福尼亚与英国

在火奴鲁鲁逗留的前期，孙中山很偶然地遇见他以前的老师康德黎医生。康德黎医生和夫人当时正在回英国的途中，刚好在火奴鲁鲁要停留一天。康德黎医生带着妻子和日本女仆坐着马车在岛上四处游览，路上遇到一个男子和他们打招呼。这个男子蓄短发，穿着西服，留着短而修整的胡子，他们以为他是日本人。康德黎医生叫女仆过去和他谈谈，看他有什么事。

孙笑了，并用英语跟他们说话，但这时他们仍然认不出他来，孙只好告诉他们自己是谁。对于他的新动向——从事革命事业，康德黎夫妇非常感兴趣，并建议他去英国进一步宣传他的主张，到时他们可以接待他。孙答应说如果他去伦敦的话一定去找他们，但他解释说，目前他最大兴趣是加利福尼亚以及在那里居住的大量中国人。

1896 年 6 月，孙逸仙从夏威夷乘船到三藩市。在他身后，留下的是一个由他的同胞组成的，活跃而且组织优良的夏威夷社团，成员几乎包括了岛上十之八九的中国人①。

三藩市的唐人街简直就是一个移植的"小中国"，当地华人早已准备好热情地迎接孙逸仙的到来。他们都注意到他的工作，并且从中国和夏威夷的亲友那里听说了在广州夭折的第一个革命尝试。在那里，孙逸仙平静而热诚的演讲并没有白费。富人和穷人都来听他的演说，并留下来向他许诺，将竭尽所能给予支持。他们加入迅速壮大的

---

① 1896 年 6 月，孙中山离开夏威夷时，檀香山兴中会"成员几乎包括了岛上十之八九的中国人"的说法或有夸张。孙中山之所以转赴美洲大陆，主要原因之一是"总理留檀半载，多方活动，均难收效。乃兄德彰及何宽等均谓当此新败之余，人心咸怀疑惧，在檀进行，徒费心力。美洲华侨较众，当有可为，宜改从新方面入手等语。总理从之，遂于丙申夏六月首途渡美。"（冯自由：《中国革命运动二十六年组织史》，第 26 页）

兴中会，宣誓效忠革命，大笔的钱源源不绝资助革命事业。

从三藩市开始，孙博士还到加利福尼亚的一些边远的小城镇作简短的巡回演讲，在那里耕田和种菜的中国人都来聆听他的演讲（而且他再次立刻得到了热烈且忠诚的支持）。有些人能提供的捐助不多，但他们能奉献的是对革命的信念，恰恰是这个信念使他们意识到支持和统一行动的必要。另外，在那里，兴中会又吸纳了不少新成员。

他穿越美洲大陆，到他的下一个目标——纽约。途中他在主要的城市短暂停留，继续演说和组织兴中会的新分会。所到之处，他感受到年轻人的狂热。而从一些长辈那里，至少看得出他们真的感兴趣——要那些长者相信这场初生的革命可以取得实际上的成功，当然是比较困难的。

在中国，革命并不是什么新鲜的东西，即使在古代也十分普遍——但都遵循着某种模式：讲的比做的多，少数是流血革命，更多是持久的反抗，但最终的结果都是成就其少。孙逸仙建立自由民主中国、废除旧传统的理想，几乎令人难以相信。这个理想很可怕又很美妙。如果能够实现，将是一件不世奇功；如果失败了，人们将会在清政府的混乱之中趁火打劫。

对于一个普通人来说，孙逸仙的追随者都意识到他们的形势极度危险，不仅是他们自己，还包括他们在国内外的亲属，也是如此。只要一发现蛛丝马迹，清政府就会毫不留情地满门抄斩和查封财产。尽管如此，人们还是毫不畏缩地忠诚于革命事业和这位新领袖。许多人为了革命贡献了所有的财产和毕生的积蓄，甚至生命。兴中会发展之迅速，令人吃惊①。

---

① 作者关于孙中山在美洲大陆演说、活动以及兴中会迅速发展的描述，不无夸张之处。孙中山曾自述 1896 年游美，"美洲华侨之风气蔽塞，较檀岛尤甚。故予由太平洋东岸之三藩市登陆，横过美洲大陆，至大西洋西岸之纽约市，沿途所过多处，或留数日，或十数日。所至皆说以祖国危亡，清政腐败，非从民族根本改革无以救亡，而改革之任人人有责。然而劝者谆谆，听者终归藐藐，其欢迎革命主义者，每埠不过数人或十馀人而已。"（《孙中山全集》第 6 卷，第 231 页）冯自由所著的《中国革命运动二十六年组织史》也记载"是时旅美华侨风气异常闭塞，十九缺乏国家思想，与谈革命排满，莫不掩耳惊走，在耶教徒中因同情总理而加入兴中会者，仅邝华汰数人耳。"（见该书第 27～28 页）

在纽约，孙博士住在朋友唐雄那里，他是孙在意奥兰尼学校的同学，现在经营着一家古玩店。孙打算不久后就乘船去伦敦。他不知道，他到了纽约的消息已被当地清政府的人员获悉，知道他要去伦敦后，他们便打电报让伦敦清使馆逮捕他。当然，孙博士启程赴英时对此一无所知。

孙逸仙一般出行都非常谨慎，他清楚无时不在的清廷特务所带来的危险。他用假名订了船票，但因为某种原因，他觉得英国颇为安全。当然，现在他已经收到消息，知道驻华盛顿的中国公使曾尽力要把他俘虏并送回中国，但计划失败了。孙博士还不知道伦敦清使馆已经收到电报，他还以为自己很安全。

到了伦敦，他去拜访康德黎家并受到热情的款待，并作为康德黎家的贵客住在那里①。

孙博士此次访英有两个目的，一是组织当地的中国人参加革命运动；另一个是如果可能的话，吸引一些英国同情者的关注和财政援助，但这两方面他都没有取得显著的成绩。在英国的中国人很少，至于他希望从英国人那里贷款购买军火，也是徒劳无功——英国人都非常友好和同情，但并不想卷入这一前所未有的、前途未卜的革命事业中去。不过，他们并没有直接拒绝他，而是说他们将观察和等待一阵子，并表示孙日后还可以再去找他们。

风暴在十月一个平静的星期天爆发②。孙博士去教堂的途中，一个中国人和他打招呼，问他是日本人还是中国人。因为孙博士剪掉辫子、改穿西服，他常常被当作是日本人。他解释说他是广东人，那个人说他也是广东人，他们一边走一边用广东话聊天。不久，又有一个

---

① 在被伦敦清使馆诱捕前，孙中山并没有住在康德黎家。孙中山甫至伦敦，住在泰晤士河北岸河滨路中的赫胥旅馆（Haxell's Hotel）。1896 年 10 月 1 日，往访康德黎，康氏为之在寓所附近的葛兰法学院坊（Gray's Inn Place）八号宝勒特小姐（Miss Pollard）开设的私人公寓找到寓所。1896 年 10 月 11 日，在被伦敦清使馆诱入囚禁之前，孙中山一直居于此。1896 年 10 月 23 日获释后，孙中山才多居于康寓。1896 年 11 月 2 日，迁回葛兰法学院坊八号。

② 下文所述关于孙中山伦敦被难过程显然主要基于传闻与想象，过程细节与其他相关记载多有出入，译者不再一一指出。

中国人加入进来，这两个人力邀孙博士到他们家里聊天。孙博士说他还要到教堂和康德黎医生见面。这时第三个中国人加入进来，而第一个则离开了。他们经过一间开着门的房子，余下的两人突然强行把他拉进去。他仍然没起什么疑心，直到他们使劲关门上锁，他才吃惊地发现，他被关在中国公使馆里面！

自从华盛顿公使发电报给伦敦，他们就一直在寻找他。这时他们立刻清楚地告诉他，他已成为因犯。他被捕时身上一张纸片都没有，这让搜查他的人非常失望。但他们知道他住在康德黎医生家，应该有留下文件在那里。他们迅速派人去找。幸运的是，康德黎医生以孙不在为由拒绝了他们。

据孙博士说，当时马格里爵士①是他的主审官。马格里爵士告诉这位革命家：他将会被用船送回中国，并且要一直被关押到船启航为止。公使馆为未能得到孙博士的文件而感到十分懊恼，如果他们拿到手的话，就可以知道所有革命积极分子的姓名和地址，而这将会在中国引起巨大而悲惨的后果。

孙博士被关在公使馆楼上的一个房间里已经 12 天了。他听说他将被当成疯子用船运回中国。他知道除非他在被送上船之前设法逃跑，否则在到达中国之后肯定会被处死。他决心尝试给康德黎医生传信，收买公使馆的人是不可能的，但他口袋里的财物并没有被搜走。

他的房间在临街的楼上，看出去就是两栋楼之间的通道。孙博士决定写一个便条给康德黎。他把写好的纸条包在一个硬币的外面，尝试把它扔到人行道或大街上，那里有很多人经过，可能会发现它。不过，他第一次的努力完全失败。

不是纸条和硬币分开了，就是根本没有扔出屋檐。终于有一次成功地扔到了大街上，却被公使馆的人捡到了，因此对他的看管比以前更严了。孙博士几乎绝望了，他向神祈祷，准备接受命运的安排。他后来说，这是他仅有的一次绝望时刻。

---

① 马格里（Halliday Macartney，1833～1906），英国人。1859 年底，随英军往中国参加第二次鸦片战争。1862 年助李鸿章训练淮军。1875 年底被任命为中国驻英公使馆的参赞和翻译。1885 年 8 月被封为爵士。

　　所有的希望都破灭了，因为公使馆采取了措施，令他再不可能从窗子往外扔便条。一天，孙博士独自坐着，一个仆人进来为炉火加煤。他灵机一触，他向仆人说明了自己的处境并请求他传个消息到康德黎医生家。那个仆人小心谨慎，但他至少听完了这个故事，并且接受了孙写的纸条和剩下的钱。此后焦虑不安地等待的几个小时，是孙一生中最难熬的时刻。

　　那仆人完成该干的活后离开使馆，孙博士从房间的窗口目送他离去，心里十分清楚，那是他脱险的最后机会。他把便条递给仆人时，夹了 150 英镑，并说：“我在这里非常危险。他们将用船把我运回中国并杀死我。这是一张便条，请送给唯一可能帮助我的那位朋友，他住在这条街上。如果你把这张便条带给他，这 150 英镑就是你的了。”

　　然而，这个仆人并没有直接去康德黎医生家，他带着便条和钱回家和妻子商量。幸运的是，他妻子是一个精明机敏的女人，她说，当然他们必须帮助这个可怜的人。她急忙写了一张给康德黎医生的便条，拿着孙所写的纸片，披上围巾，亲自送到康德黎家，尽管这时已经晚上 11 点半了。她担心丈夫的名字和这件事关联会令公使馆找他的麻烦，所以在便条上的落款只是“一个朋友”。她把纸片塞进前门，按了门铃就离开了①。

　　康德黎医生穿着睡衣走到楼下，发现了两张纸条。他没有丝毫犹豫，立刻换好衣服到苏格兰场②。在位于堤区的警察厅，警长坦白告诉他，这与苏格兰场无关，他们不会采取行动。康德黎医生很清楚，孙的形势危急，必须争取时间。无可奈何之下，他跑到外交部，那里有他的一个有私交的朋友，在这里他终于得到了帮助。他的朋友马上把情况向索尔兹伯里勋爵③禀报，勋爵毫不迟疑立刻打电话到苏格兰场，要求他们包围清使馆，营救孙博士。

---

①　据 1896 年 11 月 2 日仆人柯尔的陈述词，代递信函的不是柯尔的妻子，而是清使馆的女管家霍维夫人（Mrs. Howe）。

②　苏格兰场（Scotland Yard），指英国首都伦敦警务处总部，负责包括整个大伦敦地区的治安及维持交通等职务。1890 年后总部位于维多利亚堤区（Victoria Embankment）。

③　索尔兹伯里（Salisbury，1830~1903），旧译“沙士勃雷”，英国保守党领袖，时任英国首相兼外交大臣。

　　这时，离孙被送回国处死只有 20 小时了。苏格兰场魁伟的便衣包围了囚禁孙的大使馆，一个带着帽子表情严肃的警察巡官用拇指大力急按清使馆的门铃。

　　看到眼前的武力包围，清朝大使吓得要命，不知所措。于是他装病，叫他的秘书到门口应付那些野蛮人。如果我们可以猜想的话，他们的对话大抵如下：

　　"我是苏格兰场的巡官某某某。请问大使在吗?"

　　"大使阁下病了。我是他的私人秘书。有什么可以帮您的?"

　　"是这样的。我们了解到有一个孙博士被囚禁在你们这儿。我们想见见他。"

　　"噢，大概有些误会吧，巡官。我们这儿没这个人。"

　　"没有? 那么，你不会反对我们搜查一下这个房子吧，我们必须就这些传闻追查究竟。"

　　"可是……，你们没有这个权力。"

　　"我们有正式的搜查令。要么你就立刻交出孙博士，否则我们就要从上到下彻底搜查这个房子。"

　　"这是对中华帝国的侮辱!"

　　"可能吧。但是你要明白，现在你不是在中国——你现在在英国!趁早交出我们想要的人，这对你和你的帝国都有好处!"

　　几分钟之后，脸色苍白但面带笑容的孙逸仙和他的朋友康德黎医生重逢了。

　　这是最紧张的一次死里逃生，却也是最广为人知的一次，因为英国报纸把它当成重要新闻报道，他们还要求孙博士为伦敦《泰晤士报》写一篇关于此次惊险过程的文章。一时间，中国的孙逸仙博士名扬天下，成为全世界谈论的话题。

　　这次的宣传让孙博士非常高兴，不是为了他自己，而是因为他的革命事业终于为世界和中国人民所知，他希望这将帮助他更容易争取到援助。

　　他在康德黎家住了一段时间，为更好地继续开展他所热爱的事业，不停地学习和工作。康德黎医生后来谈及此事时说，孙从来不会浪费一分钟。

　　他坚持不懈地阅读军事著作、宪法史、政治学，为使中国跃升为一个共和国这一伟大事业做好准备。他知道，必须有人去为群众讲解他所提倡的新型政府的基本原理。面对一切困难和看上去似乎不可逾越的障碍，他从未对他建立自由中国的梦想丧失信心。

五 欧洲，海峡殖民地和
重返中国

孙博士离开伦敦的途中，到欧洲其他几个大城市布鲁塞尔、巴黎和柏林作了一次短暂的游历①。但那些地方很少有中国人，真正能有所作为的地方是英属海峡殖民地②，尤其是新加坡，那里有很多东方人和富商。

欧洲的银行只给了他含糊的答复和空洞的承诺。他们反问，怎么能借钱给一个尚未成立的政府呢？他们的同情只是为了维系一个他日或者有用的关系。

在英属海峡殖民地，情况大不一样。在这儿，孙博士再次在华人中找到对革命忠诚和坚定的支持。他努力而耐心地对富人和穷人进行游说工作，最后筹募到大约60000美元的资金③。新加坡人明白，还需要很长的时间才能看到为自由而进行的奋斗出现些许成功的希望，建立革命基础需要时间，不过他们愿意耐心地等待。新加坡成为革命党最坚定的据点之一，随时准备保护或援助孙博士；而孙在逃避满清政府的追捕时，也多次利用这个有利条件。

---

① 此处紧接第四章伦敦被难后，所述容易引起误解。伦敦被难获释后，孙中山继续呆在英国，至1897年7月1日离英赴加拿大。1897年8月2日离开加拿大坐船赴日本横滨。1904年12月再访伦敦。1905年上半年在布鲁塞尔、巴黎和柏林活动。1905年7月初在回日本横滨的途中，在新加坡短暂停留，与尤列、陈楚楠、张永福等会晤。因此，此处所述应是孙中山在1905年后的活动。

② 英属海峡殖民地，指18世纪后期至20世纪中期英国在马六甲海峡的殖民地，包括槟榔屿（Penang）、新加坡（Singapore）、马六甲（Malacca）和拉布安（Labuan）等。

③ 据当时的记载，新加坡同盟会成立初期，孙中山在富商阶层筹款多受挫折，新加坡广帮七大商翁都对革命派没有好感。

认识孙博士的人都会觉得奇怪，孙博士怎样设法与散处各地的分支机构保持密切的联系，尤其他老是在东奔西躲。然而，他不仅明了各地组织的活动情况，而且还让他们也了解自己的工作进展。大量的信息由夏威夷的组织负责传达；同时，这里也发送信息给身处海外的孙博士，并从组织的基金中给他提供个人活动经费。

孙博士从不为自己谋算，在后来的日子里，我常常责怪他身无分文地到处走，并说像他这样的领袖走到哪儿就得向哪里要钱，是不体面的。他总是笑着说："我不需要钱，无论我去哪里，我都能得到我想要的。"这倒也没错。

革命组织一旦建立起来，他凭着个人的威信就能够走遍天涯海角。人们总是为他准备好交通工具、房子、食物，还有他提出的需要的费用——除了工作所需之外，他很少提其他需求——甚至汽车和船都能提供，如果他需要的话。

第一次起义失败后，孙博士来到夏威夷，那时我的叔叔陆皓东已被清政府处死，我告诉孙博士，我想做一个医生，打算去学医。孙说："为什么你要那样做？我已经是一个医生了，但我放弃了。在我们前面还有很多伟大的工作。如果你真的想学点什么，就跟着康有为①学习，学政治与政府管理吧。"

康有为是中国的一位大学者和开明人士，他曾经被清廷起用，就建立一个较现代化的政府向年轻的光绪皇帝提建议。

不过我对孙博士说，我年纪太大了，不能上学了。"那么，如果你想帮助我的话，"孙说："就在这里参加政治活动，在夏威夷做社团组织工作。"我告诉他我愿意干这个。此后我多年担任社团的负责人，并常常应孙博士的要求，从社团基金里给他提供经费。

我父亲②被谣传和革命有关系，满清政府逮捕了他，我的工作因此变得更加困难。为了父亲，我只能悄悄地进行地下工作。也因为这

---

① 康有为（1858~1927），字广厦，号长素，广东南海人。晚清著名的学者和思想家。

② 陆灿的父亲陆兰谷，广东香山县（今中山）翠亨村人。据说曾在檀香山茂宜岛孙眉家中担任中文教员。1921年2月18日，曾与杨灿文、杨德初等率翠亨同乡到广州拜会孙中山，并摄影留念。

个缘故，虽然我生活在夏威夷，我不得不留起辫子10年，因为剪掉辫子会被视为革命行动，而这可能会置他于死地。

可怜的父亲早已退休，在我们村里生活，当然和革命运动毫无关系。民国成立后，他成为当地的耆老。有一天，他到村外田间散步的时候，突然被逮捕并关押在广州。

幸运的是，他是个读书人，会写东西，他们让他干些书记的活，但他被关在监狱里达6年之久，其间为了让他获释，我试尽了一切我能想到的办法。最后，我通过中国驻华盛顿大使伍廷芳①把他救了出来，但那时我已经在中国法庭白白花了一万块钱。

孙博士希望在日本建立一个常设总部，因为这里靠近中国，而且横滨和东京有大量的中国人。那时东京有很多中国留学生，孙想如果能引起他们的同情和兴趣，他们非常合适在国内帮他传播学说。他进出中国日益困难，清政府布下了抓捕他的天罗地网。很多日本人对他的革命活动表示友好，他们提供金钱资助和一切可能的援助。

尽管当时重金悬赏买他的人头，孙博士仍然设法回国多次。旅途中他通常乔装改姓，但能够躲过侦察，仍然算是奇迹。他打扮成乞丐、苦力、渔民，有时甚至扮成女人，好在每一次都很幸运。他知道由他亲自宣讲革命原理的重要性，因为整个运动几乎是建基于他极富吸引力的人格魅力之上。虽然他总能让不同的听众明白他的学说，但他也很清楚他不可能到所有地方去。于是他计划把他的学说写出来，在地下的革命小印刷所印刷，然后在各地的茶楼中散布。在那里，他们可以大声读出来。

也许你们会惊讶他用这种又笨又慢的方法传播新学说，但考虑到中国的语言复杂多样，这实际上是唯一可行的办法。

四万万中国人中，大部分都只懂他们自己省份和阶层的方言。即使到今天，中国也没有"通用"的语言，这要等将来慢慢实现。因此对群众发表演说，往往要再"翻译"成几种方言。当然官员们一直用

---

① 伍廷芳（1842～1922），字文爵，号秩庸，后改名廷芳，近代著名的外交家、法学家。伍廷芳1897～1902年和1908～1909年两度出任驻美公使。据本书附录陆灿所撰《孙公中山事略》载其父被捕时在戊戌年（1898），6年之后就是1904年，伍廷芳恰恰不在驻美公使任上。

官话沟通，但当时只有少数人是读书人，有闲暇学它的人也不多。

虽然很少人识字，但每个村子里至少都有几个能读会写的人。因此，他可以把书面的东西"翻译"成方言告诉他同村的人。书面文字好就好在，各地的方言虽然不同，但文字却总是一样的。因此，同一份文字经过本地的读书人"翻译"成各地的方言就容易普及开来。这样，向所有人传播革命思想的难题就解决了。于是，中国人民终于被革命事业唤醒，开始集结在新领袖的旗帜下。在满清政府枷锁下沉睡多年的巨龙慢慢地苏醒过来，开始有生命力地抖动各处的束缚，合紧的口慢慢张开。260 年的死气沉沉之后，神州大地再一次重现生气。

中国在 1894～1895 年的中日战争中惨败，这让世界，尤其是中国本身，意识到进行变革极为重要；否则，中国将会亡国或被瓜分。甚至皇帝也觉醒了，年轻的光绪皇帝在学者康有为的指导下，开始了一系列的"改革"。1898 年 9 月，他颁布条例，废除在科举中只考八股的制度，鼓励出国留学接受西方教育，设立学堂和实现军队现代化①。

所有的这些改革广泛而彻底，事实上，可以说是太过广泛而彻底了。很多人觉得应该更缓和些，而不是一蹴而就，但宫廷里势单力薄的维新分子这样匆忙是有原因的。他们知道老谋深算的慈禧太后随时可能阻止他们，他们要避免这个威胁。在推行改革的时候，年轻的光绪皇帝命令袁世凯将军包围慈禧太后的宫殿并囚禁她，这是一个大胆的行动，也将很有用——如果这个计策成功实行的话。不过，袁世凯是个不讲信义的两面派，他通过金钱买来的权力，可不想在这个时候失去。他看到这是个他利用一方反对另一方以谋取个人私利的好机会，于是他偷偷跑去慈禧太后那里，佯称光绪皇帝命令他置她于死地。当然这是最大逆不道的，慈禧太后现在掌握了夺权的充分"理据"。在袁世凯的帮助下，她迅速采取行动，年轻的皇帝被囚禁起来。慈禧悬巨赏收买康有为的人头，而康的弟弟和其他五个参与变革的改革者则被斩首②。康有为逃到一艘英国船上，流亡到日本避难，就像

---

①　这一系列的变法措施是在戊戌变法期间陆续颁布，非仅限于 1898 年 9 月。

②　指 1898 年 9 月 28 日，惨遭清政府处死的康广仁、谭嗣同、林旭、刘光第、杨深秀、杨锐六位维新志士，后被合称为"戊戌六君子"。

孙博士当年那样。慈禧太后很快就宣布所有的新法令都无效。

　　孙博士继续写作他的革命讲义，在国内，有越来越多的读者期望读到。他的著作中，尽可能运用中国的经典著作和简单的中国历史举例说明其中的含义。他解释说，人民需要更好的食物、教育和更多的自由以求进步，中国必须在进步中求存。他煞费苦心地指出，历史上腐朽无能的政府都被推翻了，因此人民必须要有信心，现在要大无畏地行动起来了。

　　同时，孙博士继续领导着零星的起义。大家都说，在最终胜利之前，他尝试过九次①。早期的大部分起义因为计划的仓促不周、行动缺乏配合或者被敌人提前发现而夭折了。

　　有一次，一桶武器在码头被打开了，计划只好放弃。第二次，两支队伍的兵力在关键时刻没有成功会合。又一次，某个仓库的炸药意外爆炸了。一次接一次的失败，让那些对革命事业最忠诚的信徒都失去了信心。在欧洲，孙的革命运动被当成笑话——一个狂热分子妄想赤手空拳移动一座山。

　　但孙博士并没有动摇，如果有任何改变的话，只是他的热情着随每一次失败而更加高涨。他顽强地前进，不断往他的团队中增加新的力量，用他自己坚定的决心所引发的激情和力量来凝聚他们。

　　然而，中国开始变成一个动荡不安的基地，行动将从这里爆发，新的地平线正在冒升，向着它招手。

---

　　① 据孙中山自述，在武昌起义之前经历 10 次武装起义的失败，包括：1895
　　年，广州起义；1900 年，惠州三洲田起义；1907 年，潮州黄冈起义，惠
　　州七女湖起义，钦州、廉州、防城起义，镇南关起义；1908 年，钦州、
　　廉州、上思起义，河口起义；1910 年，广州新军起义；1911 年，广州三
　　·二九起义。

六　美国和欧洲的组织

尽管慈禧太后自光绪皇帝的变革尝试失败之后，再次用绝对的君主专制统治清廷，但世界列强和中国人自己都认识到，旧式政府不会维持太久了。

中国被迫对其他国家让步，失去了台湾和朝鲜，向世界暴露了其内在的虚弱程度。1897 年，德国强占胶州。1899 年，法国占领了广州湾。

即使是憎恨西洋方法的慈禧太后，也觉悟到中国需要捍卫自己了。

她现在有两个反对朝廷的敌人——孙博士和正在日本避难并宣讲君主立宪制度的康有为。她憎恨蛮夷，蛮夷古怪的政府制度启发了这些人，以致无法无天。因此，她更乐于采纳朝廷里那些投机取巧又精明的谋臣的建议——倘若他们可以帮助她赶跑那些可恨的洋鬼子；这一切都是洋鬼子搞出来的。

紫禁城内的这场骚乱酝酿和破灭的时候，孙博士忠实地继续推行他自己改变中国政体的计划。伴随着皇室的动荡，什么事都有可能发生，他意识到他决不能错失这次良机。

他再次从日本出发到夏威夷、美国和欧洲。第二次的出访各国比第一次更加成功——主要因为世界至少对"孙逸仙"这个名字以及他为中国所做的工作略有所闻了。

当他到达三藩市时，他发现不仅中国人，还有一些美国人对他的革命事业也很感兴趣。某天晚上他演讲之后，一个驼背的美国青年走了过来，他是斯坦福大学的学生。

"我很钦佩你为中国所作的努力"，他告诉孙博士，"我愿意追随你。"

这两个严肃认真的年轻人顿时志趣相投，互相钦佩。

这个美国人是两个年轻的中国学生带来的，他们向孙博士介绍说他叫荷马李，是个了不起的军事天才。未几，孙博士让这个美国青年做了他的军事顾问。他还安排荷马李和两个即将从纽约启程回国的中国青年一起到中国去。

然后孙博士就沿着旧路线再去纽约，在途中的大城市作短暂停留，向他的追随者演讲。所到之处，革命运动蓬勃发展，分支成员显著增加，为革命事业募集到的经费持续增多。孙博士自己也不禁对如此快速的发展感到吃惊。

就像在美国一样，在欧洲，他受到更热烈的欢迎。银行对于财政援助仍然不愿意作出明确的允诺，不过他们同意采取观望态度。

很多时候，这种表面上的成功，对那些与革命有密切关联的人来说，没有用处。面对一次接一次的失败，甚至坚定的追随者都开始沮丧，很多人建议孙博士放弃，但他仍然坚定决心进行下去。我相信，是他无畏的精神和钢铁般坚强的意志最后带来了革命的胜利。

很多人倾向于把这次革命当作仅仅是中国政治史上的一个阶段，但如果你认真考虑在整个革命历程中所遇到的巨大困难，你不会不意识到这是整部中国历史上最伟大、影响最深远的变革。

想一想革命兴起的背景。一个思想活跃的广东乡村青年，他的思想被西方学说深深影响。他的后面总有为数不多但热情高涨的一群中国青年，他们亦深受西方或欧洲的影响。这一小群人以大无畏精神面对两千年的传统。你不妨想象一下，这是一个生活着四万万人口的辽阔国土，国民多数是文盲。这里不存在统一的语言，资源只有极少的开发，运输和通讯也不发达。这片土地深深沉浸在祖祖辈辈自古相传下来的传统中，在自我隔离的长城后面沉睡了数个世纪。这样延续了几千年的文明，竟被一个人的理想所威胁。这个人不但要改变同胞们的政府，而且还要改变生活的各个方面。怪不得中国和海外的人民都怀疑这是否有些许成功的可能。更奇怪的是，不管成败的几率如何，全世界竟有那么多各行各业的人，心甘情愿与这位不屈不挠的年轻领袖孙逸仙同甘苦共命运。

自从在朝鲜一役①失败后，清政府不得不承认需要学习更多先进国家的经验。这让慈禧太后难以忍受，自从光绪和康有为企图变革以

---

① 朝鲜一役，指 1894 年中日甲午战争。

来，她对"蛮夷"的憎恨达到了新的高度。因此当她的奉承者端亲王①提出把所有洋鬼子赶出中国时，她觉得采纳这个建议的时机已成熟。

1900 年义和拳之乱②从北方开始，持续用血腥暴力对付白人和中国的基督徒，直到英、法、美和其他国家的联军镇压，耀武扬威地进驻北京为止。

皇室被迫逃亡到西安③。即使在败逃，慈禧太后仍然是一个顽固且老谋深算的老狐狸，十分狡诈地统治着她的领土。她囚禁光绪皇帝，继续悬巨赏收买孙博士和改良主义者康有为的人头。因为孙博士年轻的军事顾问荷马李参与了义和拳事件，她又另加了一万元悬赏缉拿他。

义和拳起义爆发之初，孙博士还在国外，但他后来又回到了在日本的基地。三个造反者，孙、荷马李和康有为当时都在那儿避难，并计划他们下一步的活动。

孙博士找康有为商议，看看他们的革命活动是否可以联合起来，但康有为拒绝了。他解释说，孙博士提倡与旧传统彻底决裂，建立一个真正的共和国，他不同意，因为他觉得中国还没有准备好接受如此激烈的变革，现在应该首推君主立宪制，把光绪皇帝重新送回皇帝的宝座。荷马李，现在是李将军了，从军事的观点来看整个事情症结所在，他认为在这个时候团结起来比他们个人对中国变革的目标的看法有所分歧更加重要，必须先推翻清朝的统治，才有可能尝试任何形式的新政府制度。

当荷马李明白合作已经不可能时，他告诉孙博士，他准备回美国，在那里更能发挥自己的作用，为革命训练中国军事干部和筹募经费。他建议这些志愿者军队稍后秘密回中国，渗透进清政府的军

---

① 端亲王（爱新觉罗·载漪，1856～1922），满族，隶镶白旗。在戊戌变法期间，成为慈禧势力的骨干。1900 年初慈禧立其子溥儁为大阿哥；同年任总理各国事务衙门大臣，与庄亲王载勋等力主慈禧利用义和团排外。八国联军攻陷北京，随慈禧至大同，任军机大臣。议和开始，被列强指为"首祸"，不久被夺爵罢免。

② 义和拳之乱，一般称义和团运动。

③ 原文"flee to north to Si Ann"，但从地理位置看，西安在北京的西南方。

队中。这样，革命一旦发动，他们将有助于瓦解清军。其时，孙博士继续为创立共和国而工作，康有为和他新成立的保皇会①（意为"保救年轻皇帝会"，目的是使光绪皇帝恢复自由）则鼓吹维新学说。一旦推翻清朝的目标圆满完成，时间足以化解他们个人之间的分歧。

在荷马李离开日本前，孙博士介绍荷马李认识一个人，他是革命总部的二号人物黄兴②将军，他骁勇善战，忠诚于孙博士及革命事业。

黄是一个出色的剑手，他曾经在日本习剑，他用重量级的武士剑来练习，这使他肩膀和手臂的肌肉非常发达。他所有时候都很沉静、能干，是孙博士赋予军事重任的忠诚战士。他们决定，在中国和国外招募的军事队伍都由黄将军直接指挥，荷马李将军则负责制订作战计划和最后执行。

当荷马李将军回到美国，开始秘密为革命事业组织和训练军事干部队伍时，孙博士继续发动零星的起义，这些起义虽然都注定失败了，但让中国和他的革命活动持续引人注目。他计划在1900年秋天发动一次起义，队伍已经做好了进攻的准备，成员一部分来自在外国受训的军官，一部分是日本和西方白人的支持者。虽然只有一支小部队被派出，他们设想第一次胜利之后，将有当地的爱国队伍参加进来。这些起义者隐藏在澳门附近，等待着孙逸仙的到达。

孙博士乘船从横滨出发，但到香港时被拒绝登岸，因为清政府警告英国，一场起义正在策划中。清密探们都很尽力，起到了作用。孙博士当然没有办法溜上岸，但他发现，携带起义经费的司库也被拒绝进入香港，而被迫去了新加坡。孙随后到达，却发现此人在那里已被逮捕，而钱也被当局扣留了。因为时间极为重要，孙博士费尽唇舌想

---

① 保皇会，全称"保救大清皇帝会"，1899 年 7 月康有为与李福基等在加拿大创设。

② 黄兴（1874～1916），号克强，后改名兴。湖南善化（今长沙）人。1905 年 8 月，中国同盟会成立，黄兴被选为庶务，成为同盟会中仅次于孙中山的重要领袖。此后，他以主要精力从事武装起义。1912 年 1 月 1 日，南京临时政府成立，任陆军总长兼参谋总长。

取回这笔钱，他对主管官员说他需要这些钱继续他的生意——但很谨慎地避免提及具体是什么生意。他最终成功地取回了钱，但仍然浪费掉了不少宝贵的时间，他被迫坐下一班船赶回香港。这次他没遇到什么麻烦就顺利上岸，但英国对他的活动进行严密的监视，他不能直接去找他的同伙。他通知把会面地点改到另一个地方去，但意料之外的延误导致他等了很久①。现在突袭已经不太可能了，但是起义军正是指望以突袭作为最主要的武器。清密探通知广州总部，大量武装士兵在附近，广州方面马上派部队截断他们。4000 个官兵很快把 600 名勇敢的革命者组成的小部队打得溃不成军。

孙博士和那些随他逃出来的革命同志，被迫再次到日本和新加坡避难。清廷对入境港口施加越来越多的压力，孙博士几乎不可能登岸或者离岸，甚至中国的条约口岸现在也对他关闭，最后连日本也拒绝他登岸了。但在克服种种困难之后，他回到了横滨总部，在那里他马上又开始为下一次起义做基础准备工作。

1901 年，慈禧太后被迫和八国联军签订和约，赔偿 4500 万两银

---

①　本段叙述非作者亲历，所述与当事人的回忆颇有出入。1900 年 6 月 8 日，孙中山与宫崎寅藏（也就是文中所说携带经费被捕者）等乘船离开日本赴香港。他们于 6 月 17 日抵港，并与杨衢云、陈少白等在船上商议起义计划，之后孙中山赴越南西贡。宫崎寅藏等先赴广州与刘学询密谈，再留在香港数日办妥孙中山委托之事后，坐船往新加坡，并于 6 月 29 日到达。宫崎寅藏等到新加坡后被误会欲刺杀康有为，于 7 月 6 日被捕，在宫崎的寓所搜得银单二万七千元，现银二百五十元。孙中山于同日自西贡赴新加坡，向当局声明款项为自己交给宫崎，并为宫崎等作证担保。7 月 12 日，宫崎等获释，与孙中山等被殖民当局逼令离境，即日乘船赴香港。7 月 14 日，英国首相兼外交大臣索尔兹伯里电示香港总督卜力：对孙中山的五年驱逐令仍然有效。孙中山等所乘坐的"佐渡丸"号在香港停靠后，孙中山被禁止登岸，只能与港革命同志于船上相见。7 月 20 日，孙中山与宫崎等离港赴日。而惠州起义在 10 月 6 日爆发，半个月后失败，从时间上看似乎与孙中山在港是否与部下延误见面没有必然关系。（陈锡祺主编：《孙中山年谱长编》（上），中华书局 1991 年 8 月版，第 208～223 页；宫崎寅藏著，佚名初译、林启彦改译、注释：《三十三年之梦》，花城出版社、三联书店香港分店 1981 年 8 月版，第 180～217 页）

子（大约 6250 万美元）的赔款①。这是对皇室统治的又一个耻辱，中国开始更多地思考变革的必要性。1903、1904、1907 年的起义都不成功，在这几年中，荷马李在美国、康有为在日本、黄兴将军在中国坚持不懈地筹募经费、训练队伍，保持燃烧的革命之火。

1904 年，孙博士去了夏威夷和美国，尝试筹募 250 万美元，这是他继续革命事业所需要的，所到之处，他都受到热情的接待。他很惊喜地看到了李将军训练志愿兵队伍的进展。这支队伍从在旅美华侨中招募，甚至有一支队伍是在马尼拉组成的，当然夏威夷也有一支。他们之前都没有接受过军事训练，然而他们转变成为最好的队伍，尽管他们多数是拿着扫帚柄开始受训的。

1905 年春天，孙博士去了欧洲，在那里，他再次向当地的银行恳求援助，但基本没有取得成功。他们也再次没有强硬拒绝，但也似乎很佩服他的坚韧。在其欧洲之旅中，孙博士从始至终都鼓吹三民主义和五权宪法，他这套思想以美国的立国理念——"民有、民治、民享"②——为楷模。他也在比利时的安特卫普省建立了当地第一个分会③。在柏林，有三十个成员宣誓入会。第三个分会在巴黎成立，有三十个成员。革命运动终于可以说是真正具有国际性了。

经过持续的实践锻炼，孙博士已经成为一个卓越的、强有力的演说家。他的演讲除了有说服力、吸引力，还增加很多有用的技巧去提升听众的激情，通过联想的力量去鼓动他们。他的名字在中国和海外

---

① 所述赔款数字有误。1901 年 9 月 7 日，清政府与列强签订的《辛丑和约》规定：中国向各国赔偿白银四亿五千万两，分 39 年还清，连利息在内，共九亿八千二百多万两，史称"庚子赔款"。

② 1863 年 11 月 19 日，美国总统林肯在葛底斯堡（Gettysburg）发表演说时，提出要建立"民有、民治、民享政府"（government of the people，by the people，for the people）的重要见解。

③ 此处叙说有误，1905 年 1 月中旬，孙中山在比利时首都布鲁塞尔留学生中建立革命组织，但并未见有在安特卫普建立革命组织的记载。7 月下旬，赴德国柏林及法国巴黎成立革命组织，"是时会名尚未确定，但通称革命军三字。直至乙巳年冬，得东京同盟会本部来函，谓已确定会名为中国同盟，于是德、法、比三处始一律通用同盟会名号。"（《中华民国开国前革命史》（上编），良友印刷公司 1928 年版，第 188 页）

华侨中家喻户晓，并深得欧美其他种族人士的同情。

他之所以受欢迎，在某些情况下因为他是一个基督徒，在另一些情况下是因为他受过英语教育，还因为他是一个改革者，为启蒙中国而努力奋斗——所有这些因素都很重要。一些聪明的领导者从私利角度出发，认识到更重要的一点——孙博士现在已成为中国公认的领袖，他的革命应该会成功的；所以任何人都应该准备好去支持这位胜利者。

每一个和中国有贸易条约或通商口岸协定的国家，都在对最后的结果下赌注。他们认识到即使一个衰弱、动荡、治理不济的中国，从经济的观点来看仍然是一个资源丰富和有强大潜力的国家，并且是最终平衡世界强国的力量。他们开始认识到，一旦孙逸仙把计划付诸实现，将毫无疑问领导中国。银行对孙的兴趣终于开始明确起来，看来国内外的忠诚革命者再也不用面对沉重的财务负担了。

七　家　庭

我想至少用一个短章节来介绍一下孙逸仙的家庭。很荣幸，我非常熟悉他们。

一直到今天，中国家庭是一个紧密结合的团体，并且是构成每一个成员的人格的不可分割的一部分。因为每个人在家庭团体里都有其明确的定位，从来不会逾越，所以我就从家长——父亲讲起。

孙博士的父亲孙达成是一个贫穷但正直诚实的农民，是我们村里的长者。我记得，这位老人手里总是拿着一把小扇子，散步时边走边用扇子轻轻地拍打自己的大腿。他佃耕了大约三英亩半土地，按照中国的惯例，他要和地主分享所收获的稻米。

虽然村里面大部分的房子是砖瓦房，没有树木和草坪的那种；不过孙家的房子的边上，是三座有庭院包围的大宅，由三个在香港发财的富商所建①。我记得我们常常去那里，就像去公园一样。

除了他的妻子和孩子们，孙达成还把他两个弟弟的妻子接到家中。这两个"叔母"或多或少是由大哥来照顾，因为她们的丈夫出远门谋生，再也没有回来。一个去了加利福尼亚淘金，无疑已经死在那里了②；另一个去了宁波，也没有回来③。那个时代的通讯极端缓慢

---

① 指杨启文、杨启操、杨启怀三兄弟在翠亨村兴建的住宅及花园"韵园"。杨氏兄弟据说均由"卖猪仔"（即苦力贸易）致富，并各捐得"朝议大夫"等官衔，后在港澳经商。

② 指孙学成（1826～1864），孙达成二弟。早年务农，为谋生，与同乡到美国加州淘金，据说死于当地（亦有回忆说后病死于乡）。娶妻程氏，香山南朗安定村人，生女妙桃。

③ 指孙观成（1831～1867），孙达成三弟。年轻时为谋生，前往上海做工。清咸丰十年（1860）前后回乡。后因家境艰难，再次到上海谋生，后在上海附近船上病死（孙中山胞姐孙妙茜之孙杨连合回忆，则说孙观成死于美洲）。娶妻谭氏，香山南朗崖口乡人，生一女孙殿（又作孙缎）。

和不可靠，因此这两个妇女直到死都仍然不知道她们丈夫的命运。然而，她们失去夫君的经验让人们觉得外面的世界可怕而悲惨，这种印象难以磨灭，因此，孩子们如果想离家，就不得不和家里作斗争。

家里的第二个家长是孙逸仙的母亲，她来自邻村，身材匀称，相貌清秀，是一位皮肤黝黑的小脚本地女人。年老时，有人给她画了幅肖像画。她活到八十多岁，但不幸地她在儿子成为中华民国大总统前就去世了。

阿眉，即孙眉，是他们的大儿子，第二个儿子很小的时候就夭折了，在孙逸仙之前还有一个女儿①。后来，孙逸仙还有一个妹妹②。大哥孙眉第一个出去，他选择了夏威夷，因为当时有很多同乡在那里打工。他是一个年轻的勤劳刻苦的农民，在火奴鲁鲁郊外安顿下来。他一去就发了财，不久就回村招收了更多中国劳工去夏威夷的农场工作。回到火奴鲁鲁后，他先在茂宜岛开了一个商店做生意，这个投资成功之后，他在库拉附近买了一个大牧场养牛。他是茂宜岛上最早经营牧场的人之一，也是非常成功的一个。

我记得大概在这个时候孙眉安排了他的妈妈去看望他，又娶了一个邻村的女孩子，育有一子二女③。他的妈妈到了茂宜，对所有东西都留下深刻的印象。我们不妨稍作猜想，如果不是为了另外一个儿子，她会背井离乡留在那里。

她回到村里后，我们聚到一起听她讲她的见闻。她印象最深的是夏威夷的"活动"房子——这让我们都难以置信。她解释说，那些不是

---

① 指孙妙茜（1863~1955），孙达成女儿。嫁同县隔田乡启运里（今中山市南朗镇崖口杨家村）杨紫辉为妻。孙妙茜向史家叙述过不少关于翠亨孙氏家世及孙中山早年事迹的史实，同时保存了有关孙氏家族历史的一批珍贵文物。

② 指孙秋绮（1871~1912），孙达成女儿。与同县四大都西江里（今中山市南朗镇西江里村）旅美华侨林喜智结婚，生女林耀梅、子林帝镜。

③ 孙眉只有独子孙昌（1881~1917），字建谋，号振兴，生于檀香山。孙眉与妻子并无育有女儿，陆灿所称孙眉的"二女"当指孙顺霞与孙细银。孙顺霞（1886~1957）是孙眉的养女，后适香山南屏容吉兴。孙细银（1881~1954）是孙眉收养作为早夭的弟弟孙德佑（1860~1866）嗣女，后适香山南屏容当。

我们这种坚固结实的房子，而是木屋，所以可以从岛的这头搬到那头！

孙眉让他的弟弟到夏威夷，目的是给他提供教育，他当然预见不到接下来的后果。他期望孙逸仙最后可以和他一起做生意，他甚至很快就慷慨地把自己的一半财产正式分给了他弟弟。然后，糟糕的事情接踵而来，首先是孙逸仙想成为基督徒，接着他又损毁了村神北帝。当这些严重的行为传到孙眉耳中，他命弟弟到夏威夷找他，他责备弟弟的所作所为并要求弟弟正式归还那一半财产给他作为惩罚。孙中山欣然在律师的见证下签署了归还财产的文件。他向孙眉解释说，钱财和产业对他来说毫无意义，他从未改变过他这方面的想法。在孙眉这个辛勤的商人和牧场主看来，孙逸仙此举幼稚愚蠢到极点。但孙逸仙反过来尝试说服他的哥哥，告诉他旧秩序的改变对于中国来说至关重要。当然，孙眉对这个看法置若罔闻，什么都没有听进去。对弟弟的所作所为，孙眉感到震惊和耻辱，并直截了当地告诉他。

孙逸仙回广州继续学医①，但在他上京向清廷上书改革教育和农业未遂后不久，他认识到要改革就离不开武力与行动。因此再次到夏威夷找孙眉。这时，他差不多已经成为一个演说家了，虽然他不懂商业策略，但逆着孙眉的意思，说服他自己是对的。从加入孙逸仙的行动那一刻开始，孙眉给予弟弟一切可能的援助，利用他可观的财富去推动这个事业，忠诚地为革命不倦工作，可说是第一个追随革命事业的殷商。

孙逸仙的父亲在他学医的时候就去世了，活了七十多岁。之后他的妻子成了一家之主，她写信给孙，告诉他，她已经为他选好了新娘②。

这样由家里为儿子挑选媳妇，在西方人看来也许有些奇怪，但实际上很多西方国家一直到现在都是这样做的，如法国、西班牙、葡萄牙、意大利等。这种婚姻方式在许多方面是成功的，因为它往往能够把两个在社会地位、品味和信仰方面都一致的家庭匹配起来。

孙逸仙母亲选中的女孩来自邻村，是个本地的乡下女孩，肤色甚

① 孙中山在归还孙眉所赠予的财产后回国，于1885年8月在香港中央书院复学。一年之后，1886年秋，才入广州博济医院学医。
② 孙中山与卢慕贞于1884年5月7日结婚。将近4年之后，1888年3月23日，孙达成才去世。

至比孙的母亲还要黑一些。

婚礼的程序是相当冗长而认真的。首先，孙的母亲要请媒人去问女方的母亲要女孩的生辰八字。这通常会写在一张红纸上，交给男家一个月。

然后，男方的母亲会请算命先生看看双方的命相是否相配。如果没有不利的迹象，她就请送年庚纸来的人回去问女方母亲，订亲需要多少聘金、礼饼、猪肉和首饰。女方母亲收到聘礼后会送一套衣服给新郎以作回礼。如果双方同意，新郎就带着一顶花轿，连同他自己的年庚纸和彩礼，一起去到新娘的家里。

然后，红盖头遮面的新娘坐上轿子，被接到新郎家。花轿到达时，要烧鞭炮欢迎。新郎打开轿门，一个老年妇女扶着新娘，跨过屋前的小火盆，直接进新房。最后才请新郎进屋与新娘相会。

男宾和兄弟们陪新郎进入新房。他用扇子挑开新娘的红盖头，这是新郎和新娘的第一次见面，但他马上又和其他人一起离开了新房，新郎和新娘的合欢宴稍后再单独举行。为了好运，新郎会先夹一块鸡肉。新娘家里跟来的妇人这时要祝福这对夫妇和睦相处，讲完之后，除了家里人和远道而来的宾客之外，所有客人都散去了。

新郎和新娘返回卧室，但第二天一早，新娘还得完成另外一套仪式。按习俗她要端着热水服侍婆婆洗脸，跟着奉上茶和甜食。稍后，新娘和新郎穿上他们最好的衣服，向父亲、母亲和家中的长辈叩头，以示服从与尊重。

三天后，他们要回新娘的家中表达敬意，最后新婚夫妇宴请至亲。

以家庭纽带和经济稳定为基础的中国式婚姻，与西方社会旋风式的恋爱结婚相距甚远，但也许由于它传统而庄重，这种结合往往知足而持久，并从中产生深厚的感情。我相信孙逸仙欣赏他的新娘的许多贤惠品德，如果不是当初全神贯注于学业、后来又投入革命工作中，我相信他们之间会更加互相了解对方。事实上，孙逸仙几乎一结完婚就离开了新婚的妻子，独自回到香港完成他的医科学业①。卢氏留在

---

①　此时，孙中山尚就读于香港中央书院。至1886年秋，才入广州博济医院学医，开始他的医科学业。

翠亨村孙家，期间她和丈夫总共生了三个孩子，即儿子孙科和两个女儿①。然而，孩子的父亲很少回家，妻子和母亲自然也常常为此而抱怨。我从来没有认识一个比孙逸仙更仁慈和体贴的人，我知道他如果不是为了救中国，无疑会放弃工作回家以取悦家人，但他关注着中国的前途，任何事情都无法让他背离这个目标。

当第一次起义准备就绪的时候，孙博士意识到稍有差池就会给他的家庭带来危险。因此，他让他们离开翠亨村，搬到在香港租住的房子里，希望他们在英国的割让地里安全生活。本书附录的《孙公中山事略》则说，孙中山家人是起义失败后才迁居香港的。"公太夫人、夫人及其子女因公首次义举失败，不能安居于翠亨，遂迁居香港。一八九五年编者回华娶妻于翠亨村，复檀时并代他带家属来檀，与其兄长眉公同住。"两处说法虽同出陆灿之手，却互相矛盾。

孙老夫人苦苦抱怨小儿子的行为令到她这个时候要离开村子。他们在香港租住的房子并不像孙所希望的那么秘密，第一次起义失败以后，清政府的密探就到来要求搜查房子，幸亏那个房子的主人是个英国人，他表示除非能出示搜查令，否则不会让他们搜查，并说如果他们什么都搜查不到的话，他会因为受到骚扰而起诉他们。双方争论一轮之后，他们只好离去。

孙意识到对于家人来说，即使香港也不再安全了，因而他让我把他们送到夏威夷孙眉那里去。

当然，当她们再次被告知这时必须到国外去生活时，这两个女人就更加愁苦和不快了。她们的抱怨并没有随着岁月的流逝而减少，每当我到孙眉在茂宜岛的牧场看望她们时，老母亲常常告诉我对于儿子所作所为的失望与忧虑，可怜的卢氏一提起革命就流下眼泪，这两个妇女既不了解也不关心孙逸仙正在做的事情。在中国，妇女常常是不干涉政治的，她们的生活圈子就是家庭。卢氏感觉到她被欺骗了，当然，以我们的标准来看，她的生活确实不寻常。她不错有孩子，和婆婆以及孙眉的夫人和子女一起，在孙眉的家中过着舒适的生活。但是，她几乎看不到丈夫。她常常听说丈夫的麻烦事和遇到的危险，但什么都帮不上忙。做称职的孙的妻子对任何女人来说都很困难，对于

① 孙中山的次女孙婉1896年11月12日生于檀香山，而并非在翠亨村。

一个对婚后迅速改变的生活感到困惑的简朴农村女孩来说，就更是加倍的困难。

孙逸仙一直很喜爱他的孩子们，特别是他的独子孙科，一个聪明和活泼的男孩。他的父亲送他到火奴鲁鲁一所天主教学校圣路易学校读书，后来他还上了哥伦比亚和加利福尼亚大学①。现在，他是中华民国的副总统②。

孙的两个小女儿，一个很年轻的时候就死了，另外一个是曾任驻墨西哥大使的戴恩赛③的夫人。

孙的家人大部分在革命胜利后回到中国，现在仍然住在那里。孙眉在澳门定居，他的母亲也曾住在附近④，虽然她在儿子就任大总统之前就去世了。卢氏仍然住在澳门，当然孙科和他的家人也住在那里。他们的流亡生活在1911年结束，恰如许多其他的革命追随者一样。

对孙博士1914年在日本和宋庆龄结婚的事⑤，有很多的议论和一

① 孙科1912年8月考入加州大学，1916年5月毕业，获文学士学位。1916年9月入哥伦比亚大学研究院，主修政治、经济、理财、选修新闻学，后获硕士学位。

② 孙科未曾担任过中华民国的副总统。1947年4月，国民政府改组，孙科被选为国民政府副主席兼立法院院长。1948年4月，孙科曾参加副总统选举，但以143票之差败于李宗仁。

③ 戴恩赛并未担任过驻墨西哥公使。戴恩赛（1892~1955），广东长乐（今五华）人，美国哥伦比亚大学法学博士，曾任广东军政府外交部秘书，梧州市政厅长，陆海军大元帅大本营财政部梧州关监督兼外交部特派广西交涉员等。孙中山次女孙婉于1921年3月与戴恩赛在澳门结婚。1929年，戴恩赛任驻巴西公使。

④ 1906年8月17日，夏威夷联邦法庭正式宣布孙眉破产。1907年春夏间，孙眉从夏威夷奉母杨太夫人及弟妇卢慕贞等回香港，在九龙牛池湾开辟农场。孙眉与杨太夫人等家人一直在港居住，至1910年7月19日杨太夫人在港去世。同年9月28日，孙眉因运动劳工入党事，被港政府驱逐出境，往广州湾开设店铺，继续开展革命运动。1912年底，孙眉才定居于澳门。

⑤ 孙中山与宋庆龄于1915年10月25日在日本结婚，并非1914年。宋庆龄（1893~1981），原名庆林，海南文昌人，生于上海。1914年3月，宋庆龄开始担任孙中山的英文秘书。

些批评。我见过庆龄的姐姐蔼龄①，也就是后来的孔夫人，当时她是孙博士的秘书。我没有见过庆龄，但她很适合孙逸仙，不仅可以帮助孙从事救中国的伟大工作，而且可以和他一起展望未来，这是可以理解的。孙中山与她的家庭熟悉多年，因为她的父亲宋查理②是他的心腹之交。当然，在中国人的心目中，抛弃一直对自己忠贞可靠的结发之妻并不恰当；不过就像年轻一代所解释的，中国不再生活在过去，也不再以过去的生活为准则了。它正在摆脱老路子迈步向前。我认为新旧两套主张各有利害，当然，孙逸仙一生都没蓄意做过什么自私或见不得人的事情。无论如何，他把他整个生命奉献给了中国，我知道中国也是感激他的。

---

① 宋蔼龄（1889～1973），海南文昌人，1912年4月始任孙中山秘书。1914年9月与孔祥熙在日本横滨结婚，婚后辞去秘书工作。

② 宋查理（1861～1918），本姓韩，名教准，字嘉树，号耀如，英文名 Charles Soon，昵称 Charlie（查理），海南文昌人。曾在美国范德比尔特大学神学院专修神学，归国后在上海、苏州一带传道，被孙中山誉为隐传革命之道的"隐君子"。除长子早殇外，还有子女蔼龄、庆龄、子文、美龄、子良、子安六人。

八 为 1910 年作准备

革命党人在孙博士领导下终于到达真正胜利在望的阶段了。他们在国内外的组织强大而生气勃勃。他们获得了很多美国人和有势力的欧洲人的同情和资助，这些欧美人士看到了清朝越来越不稳定，而孙博士及其追随者的实力和人数都在不断增长。这个时候所有看到孙逸仙的人，都觉得他情操高尚、品格真诚、全身心投入到革命事业中去。他的正直是无庸置疑的，他的信誉使他和他的朋友结成了深厚的情谊，其他任何东西都难以取代。

1908 年，这位年轻领袖和他的团队又多了一个有利条件——慈禧太后去世了。1908 年，在无耻的御医和太监李莲英的帮助下，她先是毒死了年轻的光绪皇帝。然后便让另一个小孩溥仪①登上了帝座，那时他才 3 岁左右。为了维持清王朝的统治，她召集组成了一个选民有限的资政院——一个虚假的议会，就像孙博士所料，这个假议会最后是无疾而终。

中国不再被动接受清政府虚伪的承诺，这要归功于孙博士的著作和演讲，以及报纸开始在全国各地的广泛传播。孙博士的第一张报纸《中国日报》创办于 1899 年②，他委派陈少白③到香港去担任这份报纸的主编。

他那时到各地活动仍然不容易，甚至日本都不再装作不知情而让革命党人登岸；但他以一贯的沉静，尽可能隐姓埋名地四处行动，亲

---

① 溥仪（爱新觉罗·溥仪，1906～1967），清朝末代皇帝，1908～1912 年在位，年号"宣统"。

② 《中国日报》创办于 1900 年 1 月 25 日（光绪二十五年己亥十二月二十五日）。

③ 陈少白（1869～1934），原名闻韶，号夔石，广东新会人。与孙中山、尤列、杨鹤龄并称"四大寇"。1900 年 1 月《中国日报》创办后，任主编兼发行人。

自检查各项活动的最后细节。

荷马李告诉他，在美国训练的军事学员已经准备就绪，并请他过去视察。黄将军在中国的军事力量也已经集结待命。康有为当时正在美国视察他的保皇会。荷马李认为，既然光绪皇帝已经死了，这时康应该和孙博士合作。孙博士并不需要康有为，他有自己的追随者，人数和力量都强大得多，康有为无论在什么方面都不能提供助益。尽管如此，孙博士还是看到，一旦中国向世界宣告他自由了，有一股联合的力量还是有利的。

康有为并不像谦虚稳重的孙逸仙，他以学者和宫廷顾问的身份全副穿戴去美国，他的名字让沿海城市那些出身卑微的广东人感到敬畏。他住在纽约沃尔多夫·阿斯托维亚酒店①的套房里，举行豪华的接待会和宴会。在美国的华人很快就发现，这个领袖不像孙博士那样毫不张扬、衣着朴素地到来，发表完充满信念和希望的激动人心的演说后，又在晚上静静地离开。

虽然康有为有着显赫的背景，但并没有留下孙逸仙那种持久的、可亲可敬的的印象。看到康有为是一个不懂军事的人，荷马李的中国部队中开始产生不安，队伍中的绝大部分人都意识到一个不懂军事的领袖会带来的危险，他们对此并不乐意。而那些已经加入保皇会的人，现在准备参加孙博士的党了。

荷马李将军尽力迎合康有为这个显赫人物，这是把公众的注意力从埋头苦干的孙博士那里转移出来的高明的政治手段，孙博士正忙于为即将到来的革命作最后的努力。康有为被安排与罗斯福总统会面，这给了李将军一个合理的借口陪同这位维新人士去纽约，而他此行的真正目的是去见孙博士。

孙逸仙现在已经为解放中国做好了起义的准备，他希望这是最后的一次。他在洛杉矶停留了一段时间，向忠于革命事业的华侨演讲。在此之前，他也曾多次向他们演讲，但通常是隐姓埋名的，只是以支持革命的演讲者的身份出现。而这是一次大型的华人集会，其中也有一些荷马李将军邀请来的对革命事业感兴趣的美国人，在这里孙博士

---

① 沃尔多夫·阿斯托维亚酒店（the Waldorf Astoria hotel），或译"沃多芙酒店"，当时纽约最豪华的酒店之一。

向他们表露了自己的真实身份。

那些听了他演讲的人说，这是一个激动人心、一针见血的精彩演讲。听着他深沉、诚挚地发誓要建立一个自由和民主的中国，听众们认识到这个人就是他们合适的领袖，不仅仅是领导革命运动，如果革命成功，他还要领导中国。

在纽约碰面后不久，孙博士、康有为和荷马李之间又开始了在中国建立民主共和还是君主立宪的旧争论。但是，就像李将军对康有为所说的，康已经不再有那么多追随者，因为他的团队中大部分人已经转向孙博士；而且自从光绪皇帝去世以后，"保救年轻皇帝会"（即保皇会）的存在已经缺乏正当理由。一边是李将军率直而有力的论证，另一边是孙博士冷静而又有说服力的逻辑分析，康有为最终向孙博士作出让步，同意竭尽所能帮助建立共和国。

随着领导层不再有分歧，孙博士把发动起义的日期确定为 1912 年 1 月。孙博士和荷马李都确信这次能够成功。他们长期努力，苦心打下了起义的坚实基础，之前的错误又让他们得以避免某些缺陷。中国各地遍布李将军训练的军官和黄兴将军斗志昂扬的部队。北京城里甚至清朝军队内部都遍布卧底和革命支持者，随时响应号召。人民也准备好了，全世界的中国人都已经准备好追随孙博士解放中国的事业。孙中山现在关心的，就只剩下贷款和贸易协定的最后安排，以确保新政府一旦成立就得到承认。

为了这个目的，孙博士完成在美国的活动之时，李将军去欧洲找罗斯柴尔德家族①。李将军可以在国外公开地旅行，当时他应德国威廉皇帝②邀请去检阅皇家军队。他的著作《无知之勇》在 1908 年出版③，书中对现代战争敏锐的科学分析很快使他扬名世界。

但是，人算不如天算，这些计划注定要被打乱。

---

① 罗斯柴尔德家族（Rothschild family）是欧洲著名的金融家族，发迹于 19 世纪初，其影响渗透到欧美及殖民地经济生活的各个角落。
② 威廉二世（Wilhelm II von Deutschland，1859 年～1941），是末代德意志第二帝国皇帝和普鲁士国王，1888 年到 1918 年在位。
③ 荷马李的名著 "The Valor of Ignorance"（《无知之勇》）初版于 1909 年，出版商为 New York，London，Harper & Bros。

　　1911 年 10 月 10 日，孙博士在丹佛收到了黄将军的一封电报，译解电报的密电码本锁在了行李箱中，他想这不过是一封例行公事或请求经费的电报，因此决定等到明天早上再看。当他下楼到饭厅去吃早餐时，那封未破译的电报还放在他的口袋中，他随即瞥见早报上大字标题"革命军控制武昌"，他立刻买了一张报纸，读了那条报道他毕生的梦想已成为现实的新闻——这发生在万里之外。黄将军的电报译解后，证实了这条新闻所言非虚①。

　　1911 年 4 月 27 日，黄将军和他的部队攻打广州的总督衙门。虽然黄将军失去了两根手指，他的敢死队牺牲了 72 个队员②（这些牺牲的烈士稍后被埋葬在黄花岗），他们的战斗壮烈而英勇，向风雨飘摇的清政府展示了新的革命军队的气势与能力。清政府面对的不再是乌合之众，而是受过良好训练、经验丰富的队伍，每个人都坚毅不屈，斗志昂扬。

　　黄将军的队伍被驱散，在强弱悬殊的情况下只能撤退，他们仍然要求再次起义，但遭黄将军阻止。直到 10 月 9 日，一颗储存在（汉口）俄国租界的炸弹意外爆炸，"砰"的一声引发了革命。

　　革命总部马上遭到搜查，30 名革命党员连同党员名册被带走，起义势在必行了。剩下的党员用孙逸仙的名义展开了真正的革命运动，各省都接到通报，指挥自己的士兵响应起义。大约几个星期，15 个省

　①　本段所叙述与孙中山自述颇有出入。孙中山曾自述："武昌起义之次夕，予适行抵美国哥罗拉多（Colorado）省之典华城（Denver，即丹佛）。十余日前，在途中已接到黄克强在香港发来一电，因行李先运送至此地，而密电码则置于其中，故途上无由译之。是夕抵埠，乃由行李检出密码，而译克强之电。其文曰'居正从武昌到港，报告新军必动，请速汇款应急'等语。时予在典华，思无法可得款，随欲拟电覆之，令勿动。惟时已入夜，予终日在车中体倦神疲，思虑纷乱，乃止。欲于明朝睡醒精神清爽时，再详思审度而后覆之。乃一睡至翌日午前十一时，起后觉饥，先至饭堂用膳，道经回廊报馆，便购一报携入饭堂阅看。坐下一展报纸，则见电报一段曰：'武昌为革命党占领。'如是我心中踌躇未决之覆电，已为之冰释矣。乃拟电致克强申说覆电延迟之由，及予以后之行踪。"（《孙中山全集》第 6 卷，第 244 页）

　②　1911 年广州三·二九起义中，战死及被捕牺牲者实际并不止 72 人。

被革命军占领，他们在各地都取得胜利。清军发现它已经被军队内部的革命军卧底和支持革命者背叛了，使他们溃不成军，被迫投降。

孙博士最初想尽快回国，但经过考虑之后，他大公无私地认为，现在更有利于中国的是去欧洲帮助李将军完成财政和商务的工作。

这对中国来说是一个伟大的日子——最终，我们可以向世界列强展示实质性的成果，从而换取了他们对中国是自由、平等国家的承认。

九　革命成功

——孙逸仙被选为第一任总统

孙博士马上乘船去英国，一到伦敦，便立刻赶到他的朋友康德黎家。

几天来，已有一些给孙的电报送到了康德黎家。在他到达以前，有一封给孙文（孙博士的正式名字）的电报错写成清政府大使馆的地址，因为收信的康德黎夫人不能证实孙已经到那里去，那个信差打算把电报退回去。但是，在退回去之前，康德黎夫人吃力地把这份电报上的中文字抄在另一张纸上。后来孙博士到达康家时，她把这份电报抄本给他。直到第二天早上，孙博士谦逊地证实这是一封邀请他担任中国第一任大总统的电报时，她对这封电报的好奇心才得到满足。

康德黎夫妇听到这个消息非常高兴，但孙博士对他们说，他仅同意在找不到更合适人选的情况下，临时担任总统。

李将军与孙博士在伦敦会合，他们集中精力，为新政府筹募迫切需要的贷款而尽最后的努力。银行告诉他们，首先他们必须证明新政府是一个稳定、职能健全的政府，有常设的总统和议会。当然，要做到这一点，孙不得不先回中国。所以，他希望奉献给新共和国的钱便未能到手。但他还是有一点收获，那些银行家们同意立刻停止对清政府的贷款。

孙博士由李将军陪同，从法国乘船经过苏伊士运河回中国，对他来说，这某种意义上是一次胜利的游行。当船停泊在新加坡时，孩子们把鲜花抛掷到他脚下，到处都是人民的笑脸，向这位胜利的英雄致意。在欢呼声中，孙博士心里高兴，但表情平静，仍然保持谦逊谨慎。他没有选择去出风头，不像大部分人那样认为斗争已经结束了，他看到，为了维持胜利果实，中国还面临着更艰巨的斗争。

经历漫长的艰苦岁月，他第一次公开踏上中国国土，12 月 24 日他用正式的名字孙文在上海登岸①。他立刻就被拥护为新共和国的当然领袖。

当被问到是否为新生的政府带回急需的资金时，他伤心地回答说，他只是只身回国。但他指出，一旦新的中国政府在永久性的基础上成立了并得到正式承认，世界各国将会贷款给中国。

回国5天之后，17省的代表在南京集会，选举孙逸仙为中国的第一任总统②，南京被选为国家的新首都。

这是中国历史上最伟大的日子。在精心策划和实施下，这场革命几乎不流血，中国终于成为一个自由的国家！经过多年的艰苦、努力和无私奉献，孙逸仙这个凭着理想和愿望驱策自己的乡村孩子，带领人民从黑暗中走向光明，并希望建立一个安定、自由的共和国。

1912年1月1日就职庆典期间，他在明孝陵前接受祝贺和检阅时③，意识到工作才刚刚开始。对于中国来说仍然还有太多的工作要做，他非常盼望新生的共和国可以生存下去。也许，在某种意义上，他忧心迫在眉睫的问题更多于国家的未来发展。

这时我在檀香山的公司给我一个假期，于1912年1月16日乘船往中国，同行的还有另外20个同盟会的海外会员。我还带着年轻的孙科，当时他20岁。

我们一到中国就去了南京，发现孙总统已陷于众说纷纭之中。

孙博士为人民制订了一些初步的法律，如采用世界通用历法、剪掉辫子和禁止缠足，这些改革是我们都期望看到的。所有人都感到满意，但总统的顾问却分裂成两派。

从海外归来的年轻进步人士忠实地追随和献身于革命事业，他们要求彻底的改革和建立全新的政府；而那些老一辈的读书人，却希望他保留旧制度中的有益部分，并结合到新政府中，给中国一个机会去逐步适应变革。

---

① 1912年12月25日上午9点45分，孙中山乘"地湾夏"号到达上海。

② 1912年12月29日，孙中山被选为中华民国临时大总统。

③ 1912年1月1日孙中山并没有到过明孝陵。1912年2月15日，孙中山才率各部及右都尉以上将校赴明孝陵行祭告礼。也是在这一天，袁世凯被参议院选为临时大总统。

对于孙博士来说，后者似乎亦属忠言。他生平第一次变得小心翼翼起来，害怕犯错误而危及新生的共和国。他说，这群年长者长期宦海浮沉，经验丰富，而且他们中间也有一些年轻人，包括孙中山的秘书和笔杆子、曾获益于旧制度的汪精卫①。

第三种顾问人数较少，包括军队、李将军和黄将军，他们指出目前最迫切的任务是立刻挥师北上，完成把清廷驱除出北京的工作，从而统一全中国。他们向孙恳求说，如果这件事不马上做的话，整个革命事业——如果不是立刻——终将失败，到时所有的一切都要重头来过。

但另一方面，那些文官顾问向总统解释说，这些军事行动将花费不少金钱，而目前没有这么多钱。他们指出这样安于现状就很好，无论如何，他们已经控制了中国。现在更重要的是确保中国马上被世界各国承认，而征服少数惊恐的满人和北方的省份，却什么时候做都可以。

对于新中国来说，这是多么可悲的建议啊！就是这小撮亲北方的人在未来全中国统一的问题上制造了分裂。如果那时候采取了统一中国的步骤，就不会有后来多年不统一的问题，而在政治上，中国也将进步许多。

然而，孙和其他许多人听信这个建议，失败注定要来临。今天已发展为国民党的兴中会②，他们取消了所有进一步的军事行动。之后不久，李将军中风，回到美国后去世了，但是临行前，他再次告诫孙不要放弃进军北方。

我知道黄将军也有同感，因为我无意中听到他和总统办公室汪秘书电话里的交谈。总统秘书生硬地告诉他，总统命令他停止军事行动。黄将军提出疑问，汪回答说："这是总统的命令，你能怎么样？"

---

① 汪精卫（1883～1944），名兆铭。1905年参与组建同盟会，被举为评议会议长。1910年3月，谋炸清摄政王载沣，事泄被捕。1911年10月武昌起义后，汪出狱并结识袁世凯。在袁的指使下，与杨度组织"国事共济会"，呼吁停战议和。12月，充当南方议和参赞，参与南北和谈，主张孙中山让权，推举袁世凯为临时大总统。

② 1905年8月，中国同盟会成立，兴中会并入同盟会。

接着挂了电话。

第二天黄将军患了出血症，很多人说，这是因为他对此事反应强烈而导致的。

作为一个私人朋友和军队领导人，黄兴一直十分忠诚于孙博士，在这件事情上，他也像往常一样跟从指令，但这却有违他自己的意愿。

有一个人很快从军事运动的结束中得到了好处，他就是袁世凯①。他统领着清朝军队，是个有实力又奸诈狡猾的人，总是能够扭转局面而有利于自己。他确信新共和国已经站稳了脚跟后，就赶快投入共和国的大军去。

但是，事情的发展证明了袁世凯不仅是一个投机者，而且是共和国的主要敌人。我想有必要在这里简要地谈谈这个人的背景。没有比袁世凯更像孙中山的反面的人了②。

袁世凯来自北方的河南，他家属于小官僚家庭，祖父辈曾当过大官。他年轻时是一个放肆浪荡的人，花钱如流水，这是他一个从未克服的缺点，他曾经在一晚的赌博之中把妻子的首饰都输光了。不巧的是，第二天他的妻子要去给父亲祝寿，她的父亲也是做官的，非常富有，按照习惯，他的子女和客人照例都会盛装出席。由于首饰都没有了，袁的妻子不得不穿得比其他人朴素，以至父亲的一个女仆问她，为什么穿着这么寒酸的衣服来。这对于袁夫人来说是极大的羞辱，她还没有见父亲就离开了娘家，又气又哭回到家中。她当然知道为什么会发生这样事，不过奇怪的是袁其实怕她。

当袁回到家时，发现妻子哭得很伤心。她大骂袁，以致袁不得不吹嘘说如果有机会，他也可以去北京弄个一官半职。令他感到惊奇的是，妻子居然相信他的话，还从自己的积蓄中取出500元给他，但又嘲笑他不可能成功。

在妻子嘲笑的刺激下，袁世凯立刻动身去北京。当然，在他到达目的地之前，就已经花了300元在赌博和喝酒上。但他的一生总是见

---

①　袁世凯（1859～1916），字慰庭，号容庵。河南项城人。北洋军事政治集团首脑。

②　以下所述袁世凯的事迹，不少出自稗官野史和传闻，译者不再一一注出。

鬼似的走运。在北京，他找到一个当官的河南同乡商量。这个同乡建议袁进军校，因为袁的叔叔是高级军官，可以帮助他。但这个建议对于袁来说既慢又笨，他改向后来成为光绪皇帝的老师的前辈学者徐世昌①请教。徐告诉袁世凯，如果他希望取得功名，他必须学习各种应付科举的经典。在困难面前，袁再一次畏缩了，他要求徐给他其中一本常用的考试书，以便将来可以抄袭以通过考试。

徐世昌告诉他，倘若考试是以此书为基础命题的话，这种办法倒也不坏，但这种机会只有千分之一。然而，袁的好运再一次降临，考试的命题基础和他手上的是同一本书，他抄袭通过了考试，并获得功名。接着他进入军队当了军官，在他叔叔的关照下，他去了朝鲜负责管理那里的中国驻军。

在朝鲜他故态复萌，侮辱了日本大使，并因玩忽职守导致最终失去了朝鲜。他逃到了上海，但很快就壮起胆量向寡廉鲜耻的太监李莲英买得清廷的一个官职。李莲英得到慈禧太后的宠信，他成功地使袁被委派为去编练新军，即后来的北洋军。李知道这样做，还会得到源源不断的回报。

我已经讲过袁如何背叛年轻的光绪皇帝，歪曲事实向慈禧太后告密，以及如何在慈禧太后的新亲信中，成为朝廷派系中更强有力的人物。终于，当慈禧太后去世时，袁世凯看到他当皇帝的机会来了，如果他出对牌的话。

慈禧太后遗命一个男孩溥仪当皇帝，由溥仪的父亲摄政②，直到

---

① 徐世昌（1855～1939），号弢斋。河北天津人。1879年与袁世凯结为盟兄弟，得袁资助北上应试。1897年袁世凯在小站练兵时，徐成为袁的重要谋士。1911年5月，清廷裁军机处改设皇族内阁，徐任协理大臣。辛亥革命爆发，徐力主起用袁世凯镇压革命。1914年5月，袁世凯任命徐世昌为国务卿。次年袁公开推行帝制，徐以局势难卜求去。1916年3月袁被迫取消帝制，恢复民国年号，起用徐为国务卿。袁世凯死，徐为之料理后事。

② 溥仪的父亲，即爱新觉罗·载沣（1883～1951），溥仪继位后，载沣以摄政王监国，在皇族成员支持下将袁世凯开缺回籍。1911年10月，武昌起义爆发，各省纷纷响应。载沣无法控制局势，不得已再度起用袁世凯。

他可以执政为止。但溥仪的父亲察觉袁世凯想谋朝篡位的图谋，他对此十分担心和恐惧，随身带着枪，甚至企图杀死袁。这个不成功，皇室便给袁红罗赐死。袁世凯未能"蒙恩"，而是辞官回到河南的家，在那里一直呆到革命爆发。

革命一爆发，庆亲王①——吓坏了的皇亲国戚中的一员——亲自到袁的家里请求他回来领导清廷的军队②。

袁这时可以漫天要价了。他说，如果要他回去，不仅要完全控制全部军队，而且皇室也要听他的。当清廷无奈地答应了他这些要求时，他回到北京。但他是在观察时机，当他确认胜利的一方时，便赶快去和革命党人做交易。他是一个官场经验老到的人，当他表示自己真心拥护共和，并为过去所犯下的错误感到歉疚时，孙博士相信了他。

唯一可以解释孙信任袁这样一个人的理由，就是孙自己所具有的高尚道德和情操，让他相信所有人。袁世凯毫无感到良心不安，他诡计多端和狡猾奸诈，宫廷的经历又使得他善于玩幕后操纵的把戏。由于袁曾把孙博士的秘书汪精卫从监狱中释放出来，救了他一命，因此汪便欠下袁世凯一笔人情债。这使袁很容易便说服汪，让汪怂恿孙逸仙把中国总统的位置让给袁。

还有一些人也像孙一样真诚地信任袁。但那些年轻的中国人，特别是那些从海外归来的以及在军队里的年轻人，他们的眼睛并没有被蒙蔽。他们知道袁世凯只对大权独揽有兴趣，无意建立一个自由的共和国，由于他的军队控制了国家，他便可以开辟通往皇帝宝座之路，像清王朝一样统治。

在上海举行的南北和议上，他指示他的代表鼓吹君主立宪政体，但南京代表伍廷芳要求在讨论其他政府组成形式之前，首先承认共和

① 庆亲王，指爱新觉罗·奕劻（1838～1917），1903 年，任军机大臣，旋又管理财政处、练兵处事务，集内外大权于一身。奕劻初主军机时，袁世凯就用重金笼络，使之成为袁在朝廷中的内援。武昌起义后，竭力主张起用被罢黜的袁世凯。

② 武昌起义爆发后，1911 年 10 月底，清廷任命袁世凯为钦差大臣，节制湖北水陆各军及长江水师。11 月 1 日，袁所指挥的军队攻入汉口。同一天，清廷任命袁世凯为内阁总理大臣。

政体。袁的代表被迫同意了这一点。袁对此非常恼火,他召回代表,通过电报的形式继续余下的和谈。

孙逸仙和他多年的追随者之间,从这个时候开始有了第一条裂痕。我和其他一些孙的童年时代的朋友以及海外会员,恳求他放弃把辛苦得来的总统之位让给象袁世凯这样的人的想法。

在他工作完毕后,从晚上7点到11点,我们在他的办公室开会,要求总统重新考虑他的决定。

孙说:“你们这些华侨不清楚中国的状况。袁世凯是一个能干和有经验的人,况且只有他能让皇帝退位,而这是很必要的,我们要向世界表明我们有一个真正的共和国而不是临时的。”

在汪精卫和其他人的支持下,要孙中山改变主意是很难的。于是我们要求他即使不改变主意,但至少应该派兵北上完成统一中国的任务。

孙告诉我们,目前财政上并不允许北伐。我们说在这之前我们筹过款,我们可以再去筹款。但总统的秘书汪精卫再一次以诸如浪费时间、金钱和精力等理由反对,孙听信了他。汪后来证明了自己是一个软骨头,在最近的战争期间①他成为日本在上海的伪中国政府的傀儡统治者。不幸的是,在共和国历史的第一个危急关头,在孙逸仙身边的是这类人。

很多回国支持孙的华侨看到留下来也起不到什么作用,又回到海外了。因为我的假期比较长,我仍留在那里。孙逸仙想让人民接受袁世凯,却未能马上奏效。这个人不受欢迎,报纸登载长篇故事揭发他的真正面目,为了制衡这些报道,孙命他的秘书刊载了一些有关袁世凯的正面的事迹,讲述他的政绩,为他建立总统候选人的形象。孙逸仙的名字自然在人民中很具有分量,人们即使不一定心甘情愿,但最后至少在表面上也接受了这位领袖的主张。

皇室提出的议和条款成为年轻的革命党人另一个棘手的问题。这些要求包括:紫禁城仍归皇室使用,保留宫廷卫队,用国家税收满足皇帝的个人需要,皇帝有权接受晋见。我们很多人都觉得,清政府没有权再要求任何东西,我们也反对旧制度有丝毫的延续。但孙逸仙再

---

① 指抗日战争(1937~1945)。

次相信了袁世凯，说最重要的是保证清帝马上退位。于是，条款在少数人抗议和多数人埋怨的情况下签订了。孙始终认为他所做的是对中国最有利的。这当然是他所犯的最严重的也是唯一的错误。选择其他任何人都可能好一些，但袁世凯是完全靠不住的。

悲哀的是，孙的忠实朋友开始黯然离开，而他被老谋深算的袁及其支持者所包围，那些年长的保守派为了这样或那样的理由要他把还在襁褓中的共和国交给袁世凯。

1912年2月12日，清朝皇帝退位。三天之后，孙逸仙辞去总统职务①。从世界各地发来的电报都恳求他至少完成这一任的任期，但他坚持他的决定，因为这样不用进一步的战争就能推翻满清政府。

我随他回到广州。在他的办公室工作时，我遇见过宋蔼龄，她是后来成为孙夫人的宋庆龄的姐姐。

孙博士被任命为全国铁路督办②，他接受了。但经费在短短的三个月就用完了，而工作也随之终止。

孙博士要我继续留在中国，但我告诉他，因为我已经不能再做什么实质性的有益工作了，我将回夏威夷。这是一次悲伤的也是最后的分别，从此以后我就再也没有见过他。

---

① 1912年2月14日，孙中山率各部总次长赴参议院辞职。参议院接受孙中山辞职后通电各省："新总统未莅宁受任之前，孙总统暂不解职。"1912年4月1日，孙中山正式解除临时大总统职务。

② 1912年9月9日，袁世凯颁布临时大总统令，授予孙中山"筹划全国铁路全权。"

十　第一个政府的混乱

——背叛

尽管信任袁世凯，孙博士还是采取了防范措施，把忠诚的黄将军安排在南京，监视新总统。然而，袁世凯老奸巨滑，他背着黄将军扩充和武装了自己的部队。

袁世凯当上总统时，已经五十多岁了。他颇有军人风度，但本性难改。他仍然酗酒、抽烟和沉迷赌博，还抽鸦片烟。当了一年总统，他就花费了四百万元，大部分用于个人挥霍和收买密探、军队和其他随从以保护他的安全。

他觉得在北方更安全，于是坚持拒绝南下选定的首都南京。他改为在北京实行统治。以后的几年，许多革命者企图刺杀或毒死他，但他高薪雇用的密探太机警了，所以他们总是失败。有一次，他乘坐的轿子受到袭击，但只打死了一个轿夫。他又一次走运。

1913 年，南京议会选举袁世凯为总统，黎元洪为副总统。后者是清官员，曾在两个省任都督①。他们是合适的搭档，虽然两个人中黎比袁要更软弱，也不如袁阴险，但他们消灭反对派却是同样的毫不犹豫。

有一件事是孙逸仙没有估计到的，他的辞职影响到由于他担任总统而获得的贷款。因为他辞职，大部分的贷款被取消了，有的只是这个稚嫩的新共和国，而没有资金去正常地发展。这个时候，资金是至关重要的，清王朝统治下的中国已经比其他国家落后很多了，重新筹

---

① 黎元洪（1864～1928），字宋卿。湖北黄陂人。出身北洋海军。1912 年 1 月，南京临时政府成立，黎当选副总统，并兼鄂督。1913 年 10 月，袁世凯、黎元洪分别当上正副大总统，12 月，袁将黎从武昌接到北京，并与之结成儿女亲家。但黎对袁世凯复辟帝制采取抵制态度。1916 年 6 月，袁世凯死，黎继任大总统。

募资金、恢复国家建设、发展工业等艰巨的工作都必须立刻展开。

事实很快便证明，袁总统的声名狼藉是其来有目的。未经国会同意，他就和欧洲签订了二千五百万英镑的贷款协议，并开始推行从满洲老师那里学来的铁腕专制统治。他是一个背信弃义、残酷和无耻的人。

早在 1913 年 5 月初，孙博士就得知袁世凯计划谋杀他。孙博士发现袁世凯使用外国贷款进一步装备他的军队，于是写信给各国要求停止贷款给袁。这深深激怒了袁。当孙中山到他的朋友李医生家拜访时，袁命令军队包围李家，要求他们交出孙，并在北京受审和斩首。孙博士对袁世凯的行动感到吃惊，在他的朋友们在李家的前门和军队交涉的时候，他就从后门逃走了。回到家后，他得悉家里也被人访查和监视了。

孙博士再次隐姓埋名，他试图联系他忠实的追随者黄将军，但三个星期过去了，都没有成功。最后，他去了香港，又从香港去了广州，最终到达黄将军在湖州的总部①。他请求黄将军帮忙把他的家人送到日本。这两个朋友相约暂时分开，稍后在日本重会。他们一路伪装成水上人，这样使他们能够在沿海地区频繁活动。孙博士坐着一艘渔船从澳门出发，十二天后在日本门司②登岸③。他一到达就听说忠诚的黄将军已经到长崎五天了④，并圆满完成孙博士交给他的任务。

孙博士再一次流亡，他写信给袁世凯，言辞激烈地谴责他背叛了自己的国家和人民。他还说，他将发动起义反对袁，就像反对满清政府一样。他终于认清了袁的虚伪面具下的本来面目。

尽管孙博士的朋友和追随者再次劝他，出于对自己的考虑，应采取一条阻力最少和符合当前政府政策的路线，但孙仍然坚定地相信中

① 据记载，黄兴这一时期一直在上海及南京指挥反袁斗争。

② 门司，位于今日本北九州市北部。

③ 1913 年 8 月 2 日，孙中山偕胡汉民乘德轮约克号离开上海，至福建马尾。8 月 4 日，改乘抚顺丸号船赴台湾基隆。8 月 5 日抵基隆，换乘信浓丸号船赴神户。8 月 8 日，抵日本门司港，未登岸，会见记者后，旋驶往神户。8 月 9 日抵神户。

④ 黄兴于 1913 年 7 月 31 日乘日轮静冈丸号离开上海赴香港。8 月 3 日抵香港。8 月 4 日晚乘三井物产公司装煤船第四海运丸离港赴日本门司。8 月 9 日到达门司前六连岛，在下关上岸。

国人民决心要为自己争取公正的待遇。

大部分孙博士的追随者到日本和他会合，其中包括宋家。孙博士让蔼龄的妹妹、刚刚从美国的大学回来的庆龄担任他的秘书，那时蔼龄已经是孔夫人了①。不久后，也就是在 1914 年，庆龄和孙博士便结婚了②。

1913 年，袁世凯排除了国会里的反对派，成功获得五年的任期。1914 年，他把自己的任期延长至十年，并获准由他选择接班人。当然，所有这些都不过是他称帝的前奏，这是他自始至终的心愿。经过威迫利诱各种手段，他"收到"了人民要求君主立宪的请求。但在 1916 年，他迈出了更远的一步，宣告自己为皇帝。

袁世凯最终走得太远了。他用完了外国的贷款，他把他的国土上任何有价值的东西包括盐税都剥夺净尽，用作贷款抵押。他发现，如果不像以前那样随时有钱去挥金如土地笼络他的追随者，就不能保证他们对自己忠心。我想他第一次感到惶恐了，因为只有绝望的恐慌和疯狂，才可以解释为什么他在某天晚上用剑杀死了他的爱妾和她新生的孩子。

当了短暂时期皇帝之后，他被迫恢复了共和。三个月之后，他就死了，他的死无疑部分地是他的失败造成的。我想他是中国历史上最残暴自私的人。

---

① 1914 年 3 月，宋庆龄开始担任孙中山的英文秘书。1914 年 9 月，宋蔼龄与孔祥熙在日本横滨结婚。

② 孙中山与宋庆龄于 1915 年 10 月 25 日在日本结婚，并非 1914 年。

十一 尝试再次革命
——部分成功

　　1915 年，第一次世界大战期间，日本强加"二十一条"于中国，那时正在为称帝而努力的袁世凯签署了这个条约。

　　孙博士命令他在广东、湖南和其他据点的追随者起义。龙济光将军为袁卖力，杀死了大约一万名起义者①，但讨袁运动仍然继续发展。孙博士命令其他军事将领到各地筹备起义——李烈钧②被派去云南，居③去山东，朱④和陈⑤去广东，黄将军去湖南⑥，南方各省都响应参加。

---

① 龙济光（1876～1925），字子诚（又作紫丞）。云南蒙自人。原为彝族土司，后成为清军将领。二次革命时，被袁世凯任命为广东镇抚使。治粤期间，大肆镇压革命党人和残酷统治广东人民，当时的报纸揭露"全粤九十四县无一人不受其祸，无一处不遭其灾"。

② 李烈钧（1882～1946），字协和。江西武宁人。1912 年中华民国成立，被孙中山任命为江西都督。1913 年 7 月，李烈钧在江西湖口成立讨袁军总司令部，揭开二次革命的战幕。1915 年 12 月，李烈钧为反对袁世凯称帝秘密回到云南昆明，与唐继尧、蔡锷揭起护国讨袁旗帜。

③ 居：指居正（1876～1951），字觉生。湖北广济人。"二次革命"时，任吴淞要塞司令。1914 年加入中华革命党，任党务部长。1916 年，被委派为中华革命军东北军总司令，统筹直隶、山东、山西革命军，开展讨袁活动。

④ 朱：指朱执信（1885～1920），原名大符，字执信。广东番禺（今广州）人。1913 年二次革命失败后，朱执信流亡日本，参与孙中山领导的反袁斗争。1914 年他奉命返粤，在广州及东莞、阳江、雷州等处，陆续发动了一系列讨袁的武装起义，同时进行理论宣传活动。

⑤ 陈：指陈炯明（1878～1933），字竞存。广东海丰人。1909 年加入同盟会。1916 年春在广东组织民军参加讨伐袁世凯，成立粤军，自任总司令。

⑥ 1913 年 8 月 9 日，黄兴自香港乘船到达日本北九州门司港。此后一直在日本和美洲活动，至 1916 年 7 月 6 日，方回到上海。此后住在上海，至 10 月 31 日病逝。未见在此期间到湖南从事革命活动的记载。

　　黎元洪继袁世凯之后接任总统,至少在形式上维持着共和,但孙博士认识到他必须再次从头开始去解放人民。这次,武力是必需的,他打算不再在那些无关紧要的地方浪费唇舌。他为他的新革命坚持不懈又小心谨慎地工作。他的海外忠实追随者又再捐助资金,他的工作因此得以继续下去。

　　终于,在 1917 年,他得以再回中国组织军政府。5 月,北方将领发动叛乱,张勋①将军强迫黎元洪解散国会,把已经退位的溥仪重新推上皇位②,中国看起来注定要回复旧时的模样了。

　　1917 年,南方各省革命成功,孙博士再次回到广州,领导当地政府。8 月,原来的国会议员在广东汇集,再次组织国会,并决定成立临时军政府领导讨伐北洋军阀的战斗。孙逸仙被选为海陆军大元帅。孙曾向南方代表建议在南方成立一个新的、独立的政府,以便到时候取代北方政府。作为这个新政府的领袖,孙一度成为绝对的独掌大权者。

　　终于,他清楚地认识到要在任何程度上持久地把中国新、旧各种力量团结起来是一件极为艰巨的工作。他一直是崇尚和平和反对暴力的人,所以现在要放弃说理的旧办法而用战争来解决,孙感到很为难,但在中国实现统一之前,这种苦难却是必需的。对许多人来说,这是一段经受考验和放弃幻想的时期。但孙逸仙没有气馁,反而坚定了建立一个民有、民治、民享的新共和国的决心。他继续运用他的军事权威,派遣军队北伐。

　　现在,他彻底明白哪些人是不可信赖的。特别是那些军阀,就像

────────────

①　张勋(1854~1923),字绍轩。江西奉新人。原是清军将领。民国成立后,他和他的队伍仍然留着发辫,表示效忠清室。1913 年,他因率军镇压孙中山发动的二次革命有"功",被袁世凯提拔为长江巡阅使,统率两万军队驻扎在徐州一带。

②　1917 年 5 月,因是否解散国会问题,大总统黎元洪和国务总理段祺瑞争持不下。6 月 14 日,张勋以调解黎、段冲突为名,带领军队入京。6 月 30 日决定发动复辟,恢复清王朝。复辟引起全国舆论一致声讨。孙中山在上海发表讨逆宣言,并命令各省革命党人出师讨逆。段祺瑞借助全国反对复辟的声势和日本政府的财政支援,组成"讨逆军"攻入北京。7 月 12 日,张勋仓皇逃入荷兰使馆,溥仪再次宣布退位。

袁世凯一样，存心挑拨南北双方互相争斗以扩张他们自己的地盘。他们是靠不住的，然而孙又不得不利用他们。如同过去的情形一样，他的队伍中的一些人希望在进行任何根本的政治改革之前，先因袭旧制，静待时机，而那些年轻人则不愿意再等待了，他们对任何的延迟都感到恼火。孙逸仙是他们之间的调停人，也是他们能够依靠的船锚。一个优柔寡断和行事鲁莽的人常常被公众舆论左右，或者完全丧失自己的想法，但孙知道什么时候应该等待、什么时候应该行动，他的镇定自如是无与伦比的。

北京政府又发生了变化，溥仪被驱逐，他们和保皇派重新恢复共和国，推选冯国璋①为总统。他立刻被德国强迫在第一次世界大战中结盟②。

孙逸仙早在1915年就反对这种做法，他认为中国是新生的共和国，自己还顾不过来，更不要说去援助其他国家；中国内战都应付不过来，更遑论世界大战了。

南北之间继续对立，但没有什么实质性的结果。1918年，孙博士放弃广州，前往上海，在那里，他开始撰写名为《实业计划》③的著作——指出中国急需世界各国的帮助。他清楚明白中国要想得救就必须从外国获得援助。在他的著作中，他敏锐地指出在帮助中国发展的过程中，各国也将从中得到好处。这是一个借助资本主义以在中国造就社会主义的纲领。

他又一次发现他的主要支持来自于富有的华侨，他们当中有很多

---

① 冯国璋（1859～1919），河北河间县人。原为清军将领，袁世凯的追随者。袁死后，北洋军阀集团分化为直系和皖系，冯为直系首领。

② 第一次世界大战初期，北洋军阀政府宣布中立。1917年2月，美国与德国断交后，建议中国采取一致行动。英、法、日等为了各自的利益也支持中国参战。1917年8月14日，冯国璋以北京政府总统名义正式对德、奥宣战。

③ "The International Development of China"（中文一般译作《实业计画》或《实业计划》），1920年夏由上海商务印书馆初版发行全书英文本，1921年10月上海民智书局出版中文全译本。后孙中山把该书编为《建国方略》之二"物质建设"。

人奉献出自己的全部财产。孙博士继续以笔代剑，为《建设》① 杂志写了大量有广泛影响的文章，同时向人民鼓吹他的"知难行易"学说。这个学说概括地说就是做事情是容易的，但知道做什么事情是正确的就困难了。

除了写作，孙博士还忙于安排另一个军事行动为他的共和国收回广州的控制权。他得到来自海外资金的资助，他甚至把他在上海法租界的房子也抵押了出去②，这是海外会员送给他的礼物，后来这笔抵押金也是由华侨偿还的，以便有急需时可以再次抵押。终其一生，孙博士从来只是考虑革命事业，他把自己奉献给了事业，而从来没有考虑过个人或者家庭。

1920 年，他到日本长崎去考察日本现代化的造船业③。他和追随者在那儿举行了一次会议，讨论可以为国内的资源开发和交通发展做些什么，但最后都一致认为首先必须做的是实现国内的和平和统一。

经过和陈将军④的周详策划之后，广州再次得到解放，孙博士被邀请回广州。

1921 年 4 月 27 日，位于广州的国会选举孙博士为共和国总统⑤，并在 5 月 5 日为他举行就职典礼。这是他个人的胜利，也总算是向前迈进一步了。但阴谋诡计和嫉妒猜忌再次包围着他，陈将军和其他的一些人并没有真心给予他支持。

尽管如此，孙仍马上开始筹划经过广西进行北伐。

苏俄部分地出于对自己革命的考虑，一度对孙博士的工作保持着

---

① 《建设》杂志，中华革命党、中国国民党的理论刊物。廖仲恺、朱执信等主办，1919 年 8 月 1 日在上海创刊，孙中山亲撰发刊词。

② 指位于上海法租界莫利爱路 29 号（No. 29 Rue de Moliere，今香山路 7 号）的房子，此住宅由加拿大华侨集资购买赠与孙中山，1918 年 6 月后，孙中山在此居住。

③ 1920 年，孙中山一直在上海和广州，未见有到过日本的记载。作者可能误记 1913 年 3 月 23 日，孙中山应三菱长崎造船所邀请，参观该所所辖各厂一事。

④ 指陈炯明。

⑤ 作者所述日期有误。1921 年 4 月 7 日，国会参、众两院非常会议在广州举行，会上动议选举大总统，孙中山当选。

浓厚的兴趣。他们派了一个代表①从广州到广西去和孙博士会面。很多外国人感觉到，在中国实现和平的可能看起来还很遥远，他们认为应该南北分治，这样更能够得到外国对等的承认。然而孙博士不听他们这套，他坚持必须达致全国统一。

不过，他也愿意和北方政府吴佩孚②将军举行和谈，当1921年③后者提出倡议时，但就像过去一样，这个计划在实施以前就被北方政府否决了。

期间，孙博士命令陈炯明将军北进，他那时还没有看清楚陈并不是一个忠诚的支持者。当时陈反对说，军队还没有做好准备。但是总统执意要求行动，陈便假意带兵前进，然而没有真正地战斗，终于导致彻底的失败。当孙责备他不服从指挥时，他反而抱怨总统没有给予援助。4月，孙派士兵去广西解除陈的职务，但老谋深算的陈将军带着他的军队回到广州，包围并用枪炮猛烈轰击总统府④。孙和他的夫人历尽艰险分别逃离广州，在一艘炮舰上会合，这艘炮舰把他们送到上海⑤。

---

① 这个苏俄代表指马林。马林（Hendrix Josef Fransiscus Marie，1883～1942），荷兰人，马林是其化名。1920年8月，马林受共产国际执行委员会委派到中国工作。1921年12月23日，马林在张太雷的陪同下到达桂林。在桂林期间，马林与孙中山进行了多次谈话。

② 吴佩孚（1874～1939），山东蓬莱人。出身北洋，直系军阀首领。1920年联合奉系打败皖军，控制北京政府。1922年第一次直奉战争后成为北洋军阀的首要人物。

③ 应是1922年。

④ 1922年4月8日，孙中山离开桂林，4月16日抵梧州。而此时陈炯明在广州。4月20日，孙中山因陈炯明拒不来晤，下令准陈炯明辞去粤军总司令及广东省省长之职，仍任以陆军部长。而陈炯明叛变，炮击总统府是在6月16日。

⑤ 1922年6月16日，孙中山出走登上泊在珠江的楚豫舰，几日后又转登永丰舰，设大总统行辕于黄埔，指挥反击叛军。8月9日离粤赴香港。8月10日，在香港乘坐俄国皇后号邮船赴上海。而宋庆龄已于6月25日，从香港乘"大洋丸"轮到达上海。

　　1922 到 1923 年，孙中山留在上海①，为和平解决南北争端进行谈判。他再一次被北京政府邀请协助解决这个问题，但很明显，南北双方都不知道应该如何结束这场持续的战争。孙博士不知疲倦地工作，诚挚地组织了首届国会的旧议员进行会面，最后成功地说服他们回到北京召开协商会议。不过他们发现北方仍旧坚持和过去一样的旧观念和偏见，大家都感到悲观和失望。因为无法达致任何的成果，这次和谈只能又被放弃了。最初看起来还是成功在望的，因为当陈炯明叛变孙逸仙之后，北方的河北②和奉天③的地方军阀窝里斗了起来，最后直系获得胜利，把总统冯国璋赶下了台，由黎元洪取代他的位置，并重新召开国会。

　　中国的内战无疑扼杀了中国成为世界强国的希望，所有的人都认为这是无法逾越的障碍，除了它的忠实拥护者——孙逸仙，就像耐心的父亲对待顽皮的孩子一样，他再一次准备拉着祖国的手把它带向光明。

---

① 1922 年 8 月 14 日到 1923 年 2 月 15 日，孙中山在上海。1923 年 2 月底，孙中山在广州第三次建立革命政权。
② 河北的军阀，指直系军阀。直系军阀是北洋军阀派系之一，是 1916 年袁世凯死后，北洋军阀分裂出的以直隶（今河北省）人冯国璋为首领的一派。冯死后，曹锟、吴佩孚继起为其首领。主要地盘有河北、江苏、江西、湖北等省份。
③ 奉天的军阀，指奉系军阀。奉系军阀是北洋军阀派系之一，因其首领张作霖系奉天（今辽宁省）人而得名。主要人物有吴俊升、张作相、杨宇霆、张宗昌等。主要地盘在东北辽宁、吉林、黑龙江三省。

十二　俄国的影响

　　因为屡遭失败，资金短缺，支援减少，必须向各方面寻求援助。1923 年 1 月，孙博士遇见一位同情他的苏联代表越飞①，这个俄国人不是空手而来，他给予孙博士财政和军事上的援助。孙逸仙悔恨过去因拒绝外国朋友善意的忠告而犯的错误，他现在渴望得到一切能得到的援助。这标志着苏联对南中国重大影响的开始。

　　1923 年 2 月，孙博士恢复了他在广州的权力，军队一致选举他作为他们的领袖。他发现香港的态度也变得更友善与合作。

　　然而，孙回广州后，发现整个南方一片混乱，主要问题在于缺乏资金。军队领不到军饷，开始酝酿兵变，结果是在乡下到处抢掠，造成广泛的祸害。当孙博士试图处理这些新混乱的时候，另外一个俄国人鲍罗廷②从苏联来了，他被聘请担任南方的顾问。

　　他的薪水最初是由莫斯科支付的，后来就由中国南方政府负担。孙十分信任鲍罗廷，他成为南方政府实际上的总理。共和国深知来自国外的帮助和忠告对于他们取得成功是至关重要的。

　　这时内部斗争如此严重，孙中山仍然敢于梦想全中国实现真正的共和，得到世界的承认，在世界列强中获得平等的地位。但他也看到前途艰难以及失败的可能，尤其在他的健康每况日下的时候，所有的这些更是加倍困难。如果他采取最容易的道路——放弃，也不足为奇，但孙博士生来就不会放弃他的理想。他从不宽容自己，一次又一

---

　①　越飞（Adolf Abramovich Joffe，1883 ~ 1927），俄国人。1922 年 7 月，任苏俄驻华特命全权代表。1923 年 1 月，孙中山与越飞在上海多次会面长谈。1 月 26 日，《孙文越飞联合宣言》在上海大陆报（The China Press）发表，标志着孙中山联俄政策的开始。

　②　鲍罗廷（Michael Borodin，1884 ~ 1952），拉脱维亚维帖布省人。1923 年 8 月，苏俄政府与联共（布）派其到中国任驻孙中山处的常设代表。

次革命，一次又一次失败，个人的苦难、羞辱和挨骂，所有这些他都能忍受，但是要他放弃建立一个自由中国的希望和梦想是不可能的。

他统治广州最后的那些日子是最艰难的。军队对乡村实行恐怖统治，随意搜掠；这时这些强盗般的军队和城市商人之间的战斗也爆发了。孙逸仙对于独自解决这些混乱感到绝望，他认识到只有俄国人能够给他实质帮助，便越来越转向他们那边。

1923 年在广州的一次演讲中，孙说："我们不再指望西方国家。我们面向俄国。"但是，只是当其他帮助得不到的时候，他才接受来自俄国的援助。俄国的确给了他物质性的援助。在鲍罗廷的帮助下，孙逸仙建立了黄埔军校，苏联军官用最新的方法去训练军校年轻的学生。他发动北伐，成功让总统曹锟①下台，使段祺瑞就任临时执政。这时段也请求孙到北京参加善后会议，商讨就如何实现持久与巩固的和平达成协议②。

虽然敌对状态看来终于结束了，这部分应归功于俄国的帮助，但我不认为孙逸仙曾经考虑过中国应该跟随马克思主义。的确，两个通过革命而获得解放的国家有着某些共同的难题和目标，但中国在道义上和精神上都不能适应共产主义。孙博士的梦想是中国变成一个自由的共和国，这个梦想从他童年时代开始，并直到他生命最后一刻。

关于孙博士对俄国的态度，以及他是否打算接受共产主义的学说和观点，议论纷纷。事实上，在北方这些议论叫嚣尘上，分裂着我们

---

① 曹锟（1862～1938），字仲册。天津人。直系军阀首领。1922 年 4 月，第一次直奉战争后，曹锟与吴佩孚等控制了北京政府。1923 年 10 月，曹锟收买国会议员当上了总统。1924 年 10 月，第二次直奉战争爆发，直系冯玉祥反戈发动北京政变而失败，曹锟下台并被软禁。

② 此段表述混乱。1924 年 9 月初，直奉战争在江浙拉开序幕，孙中山趁此时机，决定再次组织北伐军，讨伐曹锟、吴佩孚。但孙中山的北伐计划，由于受到内部牵制的原因一再受挫。1924 年 10 月 23 日，与曹锟、吴佩孚素有矛盾的冯玉祥发动北京政变，囚禁总统曹锟，发出和平解决国是通电，并邀请孙中山北上主持大计。但在孙中山北上的途中，冯玉祥被排挤，北京成立了以段祺瑞为首的临时执政府，鼓吹"外崇国信"及召开"善后会议"，引起孙中山的强烈愤慨。

的国家。我相信孙博士的感觉在这种情况下被曲解了。

　　无疑他很感谢俄国在困难时期给予他援助和支持，但如果说他曾经有意把俄国的信条加入自己理想的中国蓝图中，我是强烈质疑的。孙博士自己的著作里面有一样是非常清楚的，他对中国只有一个心愿——以共和国的形式——民有，民治，民享——达致自由。

十三　生病、逝世、给人民的遗嘱

　　孙同意参加北京的和平会议，除了中国代表之外，他还安排了来自世界各国的代表参加会议。

　　尽管健康欠佳，离开广州之前就要忍受出血的痛苦，孙逸仙不顾个人的病痛亲自为会议做准备工作，他希望这次会议会保证他长期以来为之奋斗的持久和平得以实现。他坚持亲自安排每一个细节，并长途跋涉去日本、上海和天津发表号召人民团结起来的长篇演说。

　　在天津，他遭受疾病发作的痛苦，他被诊断患上了肝病。抵达北京时，他不得不住进北京协和医院去治疗①。化验结果证实他得了肝癌，是不治之症。他被送到他的朋友顾维钧②的家中居住，直到1925年3月12日上午9时30分去世。他去世时陪伴他的有妻子庆龄、儿子孙科和女儿。他临死前坚持把手放在被子的外面，以谨守基督徒的规矩。他的妻子看着他按基督教仪式安葬，因为她知道他会要求这么做的。

　　4月5日，出殡的那一天，他的遗体被隆重地运到北京协和医院的礼堂，背景摆放花圈和孙逸仙的巨幅照片③。

　　这张大照片稍后被放到灵车前，大批群众来到这里向他们已故的

---

① 1924年12月31日，孙中山扶病自天津抵北京，入住北京饭店506号房。1925年1月26日，入协和医院接受手术治疗。2月18日自协和医院移居设于铁狮子胡同原顾维钧宅的临时行辕。

② 顾维钧（1888～1985），江苏嘉定（今属上海市）人。1922～1926年先后任北洋政府的外交总长、财政总长、代理国务总理等职。

③ 作者所述并不准确。据记载1925年3月12日中午，孙中山遗体移送协和医院进行防腐处理。3月15日，举行大殓仪式。3月19日，灵柩移至中央公园社稷大殿，民众护灵致哀者逾十万人。3月24日，正式发表致祭，十日之内，前往悼祭致哀者达数十万人。4月2日，公祭礼成，灵柩移北京西山碧云寺暂厝石塔之内。

领袖致敬。

孙博士曾经要求丧礼从简，也不要纪念碑，但他没有想到群众对他的崇敬和爱戴，他们立刻开始集资为他建筑宏伟的陵墓。颐和园附近的一座旧寺院碧云寺，被选作临时的停灵处。

世界各地的中国人自发举行纪念仪式，哀悼他们的伟大领袖、中华民国真正的国父的逝世。

然而，即便他去世了，他也不是撒手而去，而是给人民留下了大量的教导。总言之，这些教导告诉他的忠诚追随者，他追求中国的自由和平等，而这个目标只有通过坚实而持久的团结才能实现。他指出共和国还没有达致真正的胜利，他希望他们依照他已发表的著作如《建国方略》、《建国大纲》、《三民主义》及《第一次全国代表大会宣言》去进行，直到完全实现①。

他要求他们马上把理念付诸实践，举行国民会议——也就是他这次来北京要参加的。

对家人他留下了祝福，并希望他们继续他的事业。他说他的儿子和女儿已长大成年，能够自立，因此留下他的住宅、书籍和衣物给他的妻子庆龄。除了个人物品之外，他没有留下什么遗产，因为他从来没有为自己或者家人谋过什么福利②。

当国民党建都南京时，选择了一块地作为孙逸仙的陵墓，修建资金来自于他的追随者。陵墓的建筑是中式的，墓前有一个祭堂。陵墓建筑在紫金山麓，四周环绕着孙喜欢的树，一条长长的台阶通向陵墓。

这个伟大的"纪念碑"竖立在离明孝陵不远的地方，象征着一个

---

① 孙中山国事遗嘱全文："余致力国民革命凡四十年，其目的在求中国之自由平等。积四十年之经验，深知欲达到此目的，必须唤起民众及联合世界上以平等待我之民族，共同奋斗。现在革命尚未成功，凡我同志，务须依照余所著《建国方略》、《建国大纲》、《三民主义》及《第一次全国代表大会宣言》，继续努力，以求贯彻。最近主张开国民会议及废除不平等条约，尤须于最短期间促其实现。是所至嘱！"

② 孙中山家事遗嘱全文："余因尽瘁国事，不治家产，其所遗之书籍、衣物、住宅等，一切均付吾妻宋庆龄以为纪念。余之儿女已长成，能自立，望各自爱，以继余志。此嘱！"

乡下男孩终于战胜了中国的压迫者。这个伟大领袖死后比生前更得民心，他下葬时举国悲痛，备极哀荣。

用花岗岩和大理石修建的陵墓于1929年落成。当年6月，这个中华民国之父最终安葬在南京城外紫金山的山麓。出席葬礼的有他的家人孙夫人、孙科（那时在南京担任铁道部长，正在实现他父亲发展中国交通的梦想）、近亲好友和现在中国的总统蒋介石将军①，他曾经长时间是孙中山的忠实信徒。

送葬队伍从国民党总部出发，沿着新建的纪念大道直达陵墓，两侧聚满了群众。正午12点，全中国，乃至全世界的中国人，都默哀悼念他们的领袖。

自他去世以来的四年里，孙逸仙的英名被广泛传播。在中国，他已经成为圣人和传奇人物，他的名字成为自由的象征。

他临终之时曾说："和平奋斗救中国"。很多人把这句话作为他们的口号。学校每天举行仪式向中华民国之父致敬。

孙逸仙在临终时可能还念念不忘他对于中国的梦想还没有完全实现，但他对中国的希望和他对中国人民的信任永存于他的学说中，就像他家乡翠亨村的金槟榔山不断涌出的泉水一样。

毫无疑问，现在在国内外人们的心目中，孙逸仙这个勇敢、无私的理想主义者仍然是中国崛起的最伟大的解放者。

的确，一个伟人需要的是他的事业而不是纪念碑——但孙逸仙除了在南京宏伟的陵墓之外，还在四亿五千万尊崇他的中国人心中建立起了他的圣殿，因为他是中华民国的先驱者和奠基人。

---

① 蒋介石（1887~1975），名中正。浙江奉化县人。1908年春，在日本入同盟会，参与反清革命活动。1924年任黄埔军校校长兼粤军总司令部参谋长。1928年10月，任国民政府主席兼陆海空军总司令。

十四　今日中国

　　今天，世界的目光比历史上的任何时候都更加注视中国。在最困难的环境下，中国进行了长期和艰苦的战争。中国人民的坚毅、特质受到了考验并被证实是杰出无疑的。

　　这不再是孙逸仙和我少年时代的中国了。它不再是在清政府束缚下、重文轻武、沉醉在昔日辉煌美梦中的睡龙。相反，今日的中国是一个完全清醒的国家，改革思潮方兴未艾，也完全认识到她在世界事务中的地位。如何善用这个地位则是另外一个问题。

　　荷马李将军有一个在目前看来很有见地的看法："一个强大的中国意味着我们在东方得到保护。"因为，正如他在其军事著作《无知之勇》中证实的那样，他预见到日本在远东的侵略野心。但这个教训来得还不算太迟，我想，特别是西方国家，从未像今天这样清楚地认识到中国在东半球所能发挥的均势的价值。无论是战略上、资源上和根本上，中国都扮演着东方和平守护者的角色。然而，要它接受和履行这个任务，它必须能够胜任并好好装备。

　　很少革命者会像孙逸仙那样，不辞辛苦，为人民留下完整的实施纲领，使新政府继续运作。在他的《建国方略》、《建国大纲》和《三民主义》中，他订定了实现政府政策的最完备的细节。这些规定尽管在不同时期有各种争论，仍然是中华民国的脊梁。

　　一直以来，很多人认为，中国要成为世界各国重视的竞争对手，必须先整治好国内的秩序，但到现在，这样的想法还没有实现。中国仍然没有真正统一——虽然在抗日战争期间她已经差不多迈向统一了。孙博士逝世以来的最近二十多年，纵使外界看来中国发展缓慢，但在国内也确实取得了一定的成就。

　　中国始终是一个难管理的、发展缓慢的国家。这部分是因为中国的民族特性，部分是因为那些孙中山曾经斗争过而又从未完全克服的老缺点，也就是国民教育普及的缓慢，没有统一的语言，资源缺乏充分的开发，以及大规模交通的发展仍是困难重重。同时也必须认识到，朝这些方向取得的些许发展，也在十年战争中破坏殆尽。因此，中国的重建和恢复，必然比其他大部分国家需要更长的时间。像大多数因战争而千疮百孔的国家一样，中国目前需要援助以开展今后的工作。不过，与其他很多资源匮乏的国家不一样，中国拥有自己的资源，中国拥有丰富的尚未开发的资源以及无限的人力资源，这两项资源就能够及时拯救中国了。

不过，时间却成为了世界上最短缺的物资。美国刚刚够时间投入到最后的战争中，英国也一样。保持警惕和做好准备被证实是安全的最佳保证。因此，中国不能够利用它历史悠久的处方——世界也未能允许中国这样做。从纯粹自私的观点出发，必须帮助中国发展并维持它的实力，这样中国才能够反馈它的帮助者。

很多人觉得，因为持久的内战，中国已经没有重建国家的能力。对其他国家来说，中国似乎混乱和政治无能。外人认为，这其实和孙逸仙活着的时候的情形是一样的，中国除了宣告自己为共和国，并没有为建立共和国而奋斗。然而，这样的评论，实则上忘记了恢复简单的秩序所需面对的巨大障碍。

孙逸仙去世的时候，只有少数人知道一个自由政府的根本原理——而这些人中并不是所有都可以被信任的。当时政府官员流行面对任何形势都要充当胜利者以及各家自扫门前雪的风气。孙逸仙提倡个人奉献、无私地投入事业的精神，显得非常不一样，因而需要花费时间去理解，更遑论要遵照实行了。

然而不管旧的还是新的障碍，从孙博士去世以后，中国不论在民族或政治方面还是有进步的。在三十年代，中国的货物入口量创新高，它漂亮地扑灭了鸦片贸易，在制造业特别是棉纺、丝绸和面粉方面都有了飞速的发展，它的运输系统至少已经成真且确实地运作。比起日本来说，中国现代化的步伐似乎比较缓慢，但应该看到中国和日本两个国家，大小相比就像大象和老鼠一样。

在抗日战争中，中国广阔的距离和范围就是自己的避难所。中国从不需要真正害怕侵略。一次又一次，敌人来到中国的国门前，不是看到其幅员的辽阔就被吓得绝望而退，就是即便取得临时性的胜利，却随着时间的推移被中国同化了。中国就像动作缓慢的巨龙，把许多侵略者吞没了。

　　无论如何，中国在将来一定会完成统一大业的。这是一个巨大而又缓慢的工作。统一中国很像统一欧洲——只是这是个更巨大而散乱的欧洲。人们接受新想法的速度很慢——但一旦他们接受了，他们便非常坚持和忠诚。遗憾的是，由于缺乏教育和沟通，他们常被或好或坏的领袖所影响，这不是人民的错，错在那些总是掠夺大多数人的肆无忌惮的一小群人，所以，中国首先的工作应该是给所有的人民一个真实和清晰的现状描述。当这件事完成之后——不管是现在还是百年之后，中国人将肩并肩地跟随着最英明的领导，其他问题也将迎刃而解。那时，世界将无法批评中国，一个负责任的世界强国；而孙逸仙建立一个自由平等中国的梦想也将完全实现。

　　在中国革命开始努力的期间，世界各国必须要有信心、耐心和信任。虽然战争使革命的步伐缓慢下来，但斗争已胜利过半了，今天的中国以前所未有良好的状态坚持走自己的路。

　　不久，我自己将会回中国，重访我的出生地，在孙逸仙为了人民的自由而立下最初誓言的小村子里漫步。我知道我将看到这片土地上所表现出的混乱和困惑，我的心将深深为战争带来的苦难和剧变而伤心。但如果我的老朋友孙逸仙的精神伴随我旅程的始终，我知道他会的，我对中国的信心便不会稍减。

　　对很多人来说，第一次革命似乎已经很远，但对我仍历历在目。我怀念第一批敢死队员对革命的渴望、奉献、昂扬的热情与勇气，我很庆幸我能够在孙逸仙一生的伟大事业中扮演过一个即便是次要的角色。他也许会平静而谦逊地对我说，我讲了太多不重要的琐事，而重要的事情则说得太少。但我想本书就是要介绍一个伟人一生的琐事，因为我相信，这个人物和他的事业一样重要。像我们这些从童年时代就开始熟悉孙逸仙的人如果都离去了，这个人物就将在传记和历史中消失了。我自作主张地认为，至少会有人想了解他的全部背景，以更全面地认识他的贡献，即使我所做的这些，只是部分填补了孙中山生平传记的某些欠缺，我也心满意足了。

　　中国完全实现共和的道路可能很漫长，但只要孙逸仙始终被铭记在中国人民的心中，中国不可能会失败的——因为把他整个生命都奉献给了解放中国人民的事业的孙逸仙，其一生是没有"失败"二字的。

孙公中山事略

陆　灿

国父出世

　　孙公讳文，原讳帝象，字德明，号中山，一号逸仙，生于民国纪元前四十六年，阴历十月初六日寅时，即阳历十一月十二日。籍广东省香山县翠亨村，在新改中山县东镇第四区，距城六十里，水道达金星岛，由香港经零丁洋税关至泮沙湾，由崖口湾登陆，乘人力车，可到村间，计程不过四里。村前有一林，由沙岗仔至竹头园，树林葱葱，碧绿可爱。左耸犁头尖山，公之祖墓在焉；右近金槟榔山泉，乡人咸在此取水作饮料。远瞧牛头山，环绕西南至东，过半村之山门溪，发源五桂山，离村略远，多产草药，特产乃吊钟花，冬令落叶，取梢浸养，初春发叶开花，远近到采。村面背皆向禾田，烟户不过百家。户口皆东向，惟孙公住宅则西向，陆皓东祖屋亦然。孙公薨逝时，翠亨旅檀乡人，咸赴檀侨哀悼会举哀。

　　公父讳林①，字达成，号道川，业农，为村中忠厚长者，公母杨氏，皆享高寿，终时俱在八旬外②。公兄讳眉，字德彰，号寿屏，尝在檀香山茂宜岛畜牧，积资数万，前后尽交其弟经营国事，几至破产，乃回中国，在九龙再业畜牧，藉此联结党员，运动新起义。辛亥三月廿九日，黄花岗先烈起义失败，被解出境③，遂往

----

① 孙中山父亲孙达成，名观林。
② 孙中山父亲孙达成生于 1813 年，1888 年去世，享年 76 岁。
③ 此处叙述有误。黄花岗起义起事于 1911 年 4 月 27 日（农历三月二十九日）。而孙眉于 1910 年 9 月 28 日已被香港政府驱逐出境。

广州湾经营商业，召集旧党。迨武汉成功，公被选为临时总统，眉公又回澳门，组织卫队，随行就任①。民元回乡，民三在澳门弃世②。

孙公未降生前一月，其母杨氏太夫人，夜梦乡之所谓北帝者，披发现形，惊醒后诞公于翠亨乡之里第，故以"帝象"命公也。

少年居乡

孙公幼时，在乡冯家祠书塾读书，其师为赖桂山及程直生③诸先生，馆规甚严，循循善诱。其中学童性多好动，公其一也，常与同学列队争斗，故绰号为"石头仔"，遇不平等事，如乡人之畏盗畏差者，常挺身干涉。

由檀山回乡后，凡乡政如教育、防盗、街灯、清道、防病，皆为筹办。及学医后回乡，凡来求诊治者，皆不受医金，活人无算。一日在乡，见有患脚痛者，向一流民而冒行医者求治，该医先索十余金方允下药。公曰："医者父母心，彼勒索如此之巨，必非良医，何就医为？"该医手出飞铊，叱曰："汝若倒我饭碗，吾当以此铊死汝于一击之间！"公即奔回家中，取得手枪，向医曰："汝冒医行骗，吾将以枪死汝于一击之间！"该医懊恼避去。后公示患者一方，以白矾猪膏埋药，竟获痊愈，所费无几。

孙公居乡，书席前中西文咸备，医科、格致、游戏，每日均以时间表定之。余暇即从乡中宿儒陆星甫、杨汉川④潜修国学。又常带青年到山门溪作泅水种种游戏，及学枪法、习体操等事。公与乡人陆皓

---

① 孙眉并无组织卫队，随行就任。1912年1月中旬，孙眉才与黄仕龙等坐船到上海再转赴南京与孙中山会面。

② 孙眉于民国四年（1915年）2月11日（农历甲寅年十二月廿八日）去世。

③ 程直生，一般作程植生（1860～1932），名步瀛，字守坚，号君海，又号籍笙，广东香山（今中山）南朗人。

④ 杨汉川（1856～1902），名锡京，字礼华，号汉川，广东香山（今中山）翠亨村人，"清敕授修职佐郎，候选训导，廪贡生。"

东、杨鹤龄①、杨心如②常谈革命，出入与偕，乡亲目之为"四大寇"③。

留学檀香山

孙公在乡间，见乡人由广州、香港、澳门、金山、檀香山而回者，经济丰裕，并谈洋务，故有出洋之志。其兄旅檀业农，已有积资，能助入学。公遂于一八七九年夏抵檀香山，寄宿于意奥兰尼学校，时年十三，与殷商钟宇④、唐雄等同学，向学甚勤。当时每学生学费约百五十元，便足一年之用，因其时檀岛生活程度甚低故也，别校所收学费更有廉于此者，惟其兄爱弟心切，不吝资助，故始终无转校。

土人骂夏乌刺初教英文字母。校长威利士牧师，乃由英国新派来檀治理校务者。学生朝晚须到教堂祈祷，并令在校长住所用餐，拜上帝，读圣经，同学华生概为信徒。公意欲洗礼，以告其兄，不料兄闻之怒甚，且悔令入校，大有用夷变夏之忧，责骂备至。时有翠亨乡人杨鲲池者，晤其兄曰：此子有大志，信外教何害？不可过于束缚。其兄怒仍未已，暗禀太公，促他回乡，加以严训，公以有志未遂，旋下埠求助于同学钟宇君，且留居其府上。

---

① 杨鹤龄（1868～1934），名仕年，字礼退，广东香山（今中山）翠亨村人。1921 年 9 月，孙中山曾聘请杨鹤龄为总统府顾问。1923 年 4 月，孙中山任命杨鹤龄为港澳特务调查员。

② 杨心如（1868～1946），小名帝镜，名兆蓉，字正乐，广东香山（今中山）翠亨村人，曾参与广州起义、惠州起义及黄花岗起义的策应。广州起义失败后，转赴台湾。1897 年，陈少白到台湾通过杨心如结识当地爱国志士，并于当年 11 月在杨心如家成立台湾兴中会分会。此后二次革命倒袁、护法运动等，革命同志来往南北，多以上海、台湾、香港为联络所，台湾方面，杨心如是实际的主持者。

③ 据《杨心如事略》，孙中山、陆皓东、杨鹤龄、杨心如曾被称为"翠亨村四杰"。而"四大寇"一般指孙中山、陈少白（新会人）、杨鹤龄、尤列（顺德人）。

④ 钟宇，即钟工宇。

一八八二年七月廿七日举行毕业礼式，来宾甚众，在座有檀香山国王架剌高①、王后奄麻②、宫主利利奥兰尼③。英文法科，由国王奖赏，公为第二名。公于三年前英文未识一字，竟获二名奖赏，足征其敏而好学也。

毕业后决意回国，未有旅行费，同学华生每助数金，并由华人教士化冷爹文与西商波云士等助资回港。钟宇君雇艇送公开船，缘当时檀港尚浅，轮船寄碇海心故也。一八八三年到乡，具有中外学识、文明思想，其成就伟大之事业，即基于此矣。

破除神权

公由檀抵乡，受父母所责，依然不易其志。尝与其友陆皓东等巡视庙宇，将北帝神像手指折断；后过左廊，将金花夫人神像面皮刮破，一耳坠下；独留右廊天后，未受损伤。乡人见之，大生鼓噪，谓将一乡所敬奉之神像毁辱，必罹大祸。召集乡老会议，诉诸太公④，谓其子如此举动，大碍乡规，若神降灾，惟伊是问。当时太公当众认错，应允从［重］新再塑神像，众怒始平。公有此出人意外之举动，其超群志向，改革思想，乃革命之起点也。由此观之。此等毅力精神，比诸一八二四年檀香山王后架比阿兰尼在车娄威琉璜山诋毁琉璜神尤为勇敢。盖王后至尊，世上无有能罪之者，而公则一介乡曲少年，乃能不避灾害，敢入庙中拆毁偶像，且又不惧众怒，是诚难能可贵者也。公以故乡之人迷信神权，骤难改革，知广州有一基督教堂，必能觅得知己，可以暂借枝栖，公遂离故乡而赴羊石⑤矣。

① 架剌高（David Kalakaua），或译作"架剌鸠"，1874 年被举为夏威夷王（1874～1890 在位）。
② 奄麻（Emma），是夏威夷王架咩霞咩霞第五（Lot Kamehameha，1863～1872 在位）的王后。
③ 利利奥兰尼（Liliuokalani），架剌高之妹，架剌高去世后被举为夏威夷王。
④ 太公，指孙中山父亲孙达成。
⑤ 羊石，指广州。

维新发轫

公自抵省后，往广州英美教会之医院帮工。此院乃嘉医生①主任。后嘉医生见公非常勤学，略授以医术。当时教会正拟开医学校，以为教授华生学医之所，公乃立意学医。行年二十②，奉父母命与本邑外壆乡卢耀显公女公子慕贞结婚，生一子名科，即哲生君，又生二女，次女于民国二年离世，三女琬配戴恩赛博士。卢夫人税居澳门。

公入香港雅利士医院③学医，此医院乃何启博士④所设立者。博士前在苏格兰得医博士衔，及在英京⑤再得大律师衔，与英妇雅利士结婚，夫人旋在港弃世，故博士创办该医院以纪念其夫人雅利士也，今已归并香港大学矣。民前十六，何公见中国国事日非，皆因泥于守旧，作《新政论语》⑥一书痛陈变法，意欲平售普及国人。公与各有志之士，皆踊跃代售。编者回国亦买百本遍送亲朋，惟时势未至，接受者视若闲文。

公从学康特黎⑦博士五年，一八九二年始在医学堂毕业，所领凭照予权用内外科行世，公即往澳门设医馆。澳门在香港对面海湾，乃葡萄牙租界，一五五七年由中国租借开埠，概限制外国人经商。至一八四二年五口通商后，商务始盛，大开烟赌，以收饷为行政之资。埠中华商设有医院，乃用中药治病，该院请公用西法行医，常有剖割大症，即请其师康特黎由港过澳同施剖解。公因是救活多人，口碑载

---

① 嘉医生，即嘉约翰（John Glasgow Kerr）。
② 作者所述应是虚龄，孙中山与卢慕贞于 1884 年 5 月结婚，时年 18 岁。
③ 雅利士医院（Alice Memorial Hospital），今一般译作"雅丽氏纪念医院"，何启为纪念亡妻雅丽氏，在伦敦会的帮助下创办，1887 年 2 月 17 日开幕。同年 10 月 1 日，香港西医书院宣告成立，并以雅丽氏纪念医院为教学和实习场地。
④ 何启并未获得过博士学位。
⑤ 英京，指英国首都伦敦。
⑥ 《新政论语》，所指或是何启著、胡礼垣校的《新政论议》，该书分上下二卷，全二册，光绪二十一年（1895）香港初版。
⑦ 康特黎，即康德黎（Cantlie）。

道。乘间招集党人，图谋革命。后葡人忌公医术，谓未有葡国医照，不准在澳行医。遂往广州博济医院（今改名中山医院）悬壶①，常有政界踵门求治，藉此知官场腐败。公遂撰革旧维新一书上李鸿章，署名《孙文上书记》②。旋与陆皓东等作京津之游，李相见书不纳，再到檀岛组织兴中会。

陆皓东

　　孙公在乡间结识陆皓东，称为道友，曰：得一知己，可以无憾。皓东亦谓孙公脑满，称为再世拿破仑。是以二人相得甚欢，饮食起居必与共焉。

　　陆公讳中桂，字献香，号皓东，生于民国纪元前四十年③，在上海出世。父讳恩，字廷汉，号晓帆，在上海业商，驳艇运货，善画工，稍有余资。公甫十岁，习见其父书画，甚有心得。一夕他父见其帐眉，画有最精美百鸟归巢，责他年纪尚少，岂可费许多资财购此精致物品。他云：自画者，不过买白地而成之耳。父不之信，速他再画一幅，不料公不数时竟再画成第二幅矣。翌年公父弃世，扶柩回乡，时年十二。在乡冯家祠与孙公同学，读书慧敏非凡，每日熟读百行。群童读书，他即看《三国志》，阅毕一回，即自描写一图以示书友，编者亦与焉。背书则先朗念。凡听音乐，回乡则将谱教人。晚间所携灯仔，内藏自制抽力机器，水甀一热则在内活动。乡人称之，曰"奇人"也。

　　十六岁时，广东办团防，钦命阅兵大臣方耀④到县阅操。当时县

---

①　1893年底，孙中山离开澳门回广州开业，初悬牌于双门底圣教书楼，后在西关冼基开设东西药局。孙中山1886年秋曾入广州博济医院学医，但未见有1893年后在该医院行医的记载。

②　此文在《万国公报》月刊第69、70册（光绪二十年九、十月上海出版）连载时题目为《上李傅相书》，今一般称为《上李鸿章书》。

③　此处有误，民元前四十年，则是1872年，但陆皓东生于1867年9月12日。

④　方耀（1834～1891），又名方辉、方照轩，广东普宁人。出身行伍，以镇压太平军发迹，官至广东水师提督。

官所报皆虚额，惟向各乡抽丁当勇。当时陆公欲窥军事，与乡人陈爵、陆帝焕等到濠头郑家祠①操演。阅兵大臣高座祠中，发令点兵，唱名应号毕，只令各勇在祠外放枪。所谓勇者，大半是烟精、乞丐，衣冠不整，有碍观瞻。放枪则参差不齐，或横身，或背指，亦算额兵。陆公返乡，将情形报与孙公，互相轩渠，谓若有革命健儿五六十人，则可夺得虎门炮台矣。

十八岁再往上海，习洋文不数月，在电报局翻译电文。因闻日本将与中国开战，约孙公同游京津，窥探军事。后孙公来檀，陆公则留沪运动党事。

至甲午年回粤，与乡人杨鹤龄、杨心如、港商杨衢云②、陈少白、尤少纨③等设乾亨行于香港，以运动革命，外观如洋行，内实为革命机关。编者到会多次，是时已绘成青天白日旗矣。因谋攻袭广州，遂与孙公回省，运动文纶堂绅商署名条陈粤督，批准举办农务学堂，设机关于咸虾栏④，在此招集党员。惟急需军火，陆公回乡将田变卖，及夫人首饰换资，带往省城行事。时遇省城芳村福音堂起造，在港办有短枪藏入水泥桶里运省。不料在天字埠头为桶破露出，被搜充公，后又为巡勇侦悉机关。乙未九月九日事前之夕，陆公报告孙公，此事已泄，须要迁避。不料翌午到围，陆公因未检齐文件及人名部等物，是日往返数次。此次被拿，一同殉难被杀者陆公、朱贵全、邱四。被捕七十余人，多数省释，惟广东水师统带程奎光⑤狱毙。就义时陆公廿九岁。孙公方回机关不远，党员将被围事报知，奔往水鬼潭埠头，

---

① 濠头郑家祠，即香山县（今中山）濠头乡郑氏大宗祠，距翠亨村约 20 公里。

② 杨衢云（1861～1901），福建海澄（今龙海）人。1895 年 2 月 21 日，与孙中山等在香港建立兴中会总部。10 月 10 日被选举为兴中会会长。

③ 尤少纨，即尤列（1866～1936），名其洞，字少纨。广东顺德县北水乡人。

④ 广州东门外咸虾栏张公馆，为兴中会招待各方同志之分机关。

⑤ 程奎光（1863～1896），字恒敦，号星堂。广东香山县（今中山）南朗田边村人，民国海军总长程璧光之弟。1893 年，常与孙中山、陆皓东、郑士良等相聚于广雅书局抗风轩议论时政。广州起义中任运动水师之责。

用程启敬之旧煤汽艇，驰到唐家湾上陆，直到前在檀山同学唐雄君家，坐轿落澳门，转往香港。若当时搭轮船直往香港，必为两广总督所派驻港侦探在埠头拿获无疑矣。此乃孙公首次遇险得脱也。

陆公被捕，美领事到署取保。惟公当南海县官李徵庸审讯时，义愤填胸曰："我本想杀尔，今被尔杀我，还有何言！"命取纸笔，直认革命，图谋维新，洋洋万言。审官见之为之下泪，吩咐解差不得脱其长衫，送至较场斩首。亲属不敢领尸，惟寻有他遗下一牙，持此安葬于犁头尖山下迳仔亭①。乙未年春编者回国，陆公由省返乡，必到舍下，每日不离，忽闻噩耗，痛哭无已，事后亦梦哭公焉，感其首次为国流血也。孙公为临时总统回乡，给与陆公家属银三千元，以安其家。

考察历史之革命

孙公自上书与李鸿章不纳之后，其革命思潮愈加炽烈，决意直接推翻专制政府。公每日手不释卷，遍阅英、法、美革命书，参以中国历史所言历代变政。有法国著书者言：公熟读卢骚②战史，深知人类解放之大进步，及铲除暴虐，革命乃第一法门。若变中国，必先驱逐满人，去其阻力，然后可以维新，而使中国在世界上与诸雄国齐驱并驾。渴望民主政体施于民众，决定三民主义矣，五权宪法之所由来也。盖其在檀岛及香港见闻中之善政，居民安居乐业，是以蓄意为一革命领袖，竭其毕生之精力行之。附从者望之如泰山北斗，尽心护佐。中国革命事业见于历史者，凡二十四次。孟子曰："民为贵，君为轻。"此语为民权之嚆矢。惟国人向被满州政府笼络，智识昏暗，

---

① 陆皓东衣冠冢原在故乡翠亨村附近之山门坳。1937年，中山县县长杨子毅主持，耗资六千三百七十元，修建陆皓东烈士坟场于翠亨村犁头尖山南坡。

② 卢骚（Jean - Jacques Rousseau，1712～1778），一般译作卢梭，18世纪法国启蒙思想家、哲学家、教育家和文学家。但卢梭并无著作名为"战史"，所指可能是他的《论人类不平等的起源和基础》，书中提出了以革命推翻暴政的结论：暴力支持暴君，暴力也推翻暴君，一切都按照自己正确的自然行程前进。

其明达者又不敢纵谈国事，以免有危及身命。盖自洪杨革命由一八五一年至一八六四年告终，二、三年后孙公出世矣。

洪杨与孙公之革命比较①

太平天国失败之后，广东人多有知其底蕴者，盖当其将届成功之时，清廷乞助于外人，将洪剿灭，自是排满之思想，翠亨乡人感之最深。洪秀全生于花县，与孙公同省，洪自幼勤学，稍长执教鞭，未几游庠，适应乡试于广州，途遇宣传耶苏②教士，受洗为教徒，嗣因屡试不第，郁抑无聊，自称为天王，一时慕道来归者百人。洪杨变法与孙公之革命言论，如出一口。一八四六年洪秀全遇一美国教士罗拂士③，授以道理，回至乡间，组织一拜上帝会，一年之间，入会者二千人。该会友到处毁拆偶像，县官将其领袖二名监禁，同道者大抱不平，疾呼天父天兄谕旨，布告洪秀全为圣神，由此起事。至 1853 年得南京，1861 年又得宁波，欲由宁波北上歼灭满人，因不利于广东及上海商务，英人遂议决帮助清廷，遣戈登将军助其平乱，说者谓死于战事者，二千万至四千万人。

太平变法与孙公革命，其宗旨相同，皆欲解放中国于满人束缚中也。洪秀全则谓奉上帝之命，其事必成；孙公则谓合世界潮流，其志必达。其同志大都由少数而成多数，其组织则由秘密而开明也。

革命之株连

陆公皓东为革命先觉已如上述矣，在世允为一革命首领，他不独深通中文，学普欧亚，品性勇敢，牺牲一切以助教，欲建一良好政

---

① 此节所述洪秀全与太平天国史事，与史实多有不合，请读者自行鉴别，整理者不再一一注明。
② 耶苏，即耶稣，指基督教。
③ 罗拂士（I. J. Roberts, 1802~1866），即罗孝全，美国人，为浸信会最早来华的传教士之一，亦是中国基督教浸信会的创始人。洪秀全与罗孝全结识于 1847 年上半年，当时洪从家乡到广州罗孝全的教堂处学道。

府，其名应留于青史。盖其先代民众流血，播其种子于后继者，使之一跃为中国维新作事，或死于此道。

陆公有叔字星甫，乃翠亨乡正，当其闻陆公被拿时，恐被波累，惊慌不已，后因斡旋幸免。

戊戌年，编者先父陆兰谷，亦兴中会员之一，在乡间田亩中被广东水师提督何长清①、兵弁何天保督队拿往省城，谓伊与孙文同党谋乱，讯毕下狱。初年备受苦楚，后幸因通晓文字，管监委帮理文案，宽宥相待。编者在檀多方运动，禀保数次，废〔费〕去六千金。嗣后禀称"父困囹圄已有六年，祖母年近七旬，病在床褥，无人侍养，恳恩开释"等语，此禀呈请驻美公使伍廷芳咨文回粤②，由总督德寿③允准押送回乡。倘家严不懂文字，不得狱官优待，必与他犯同毙于狱中矣。

逃亡之孙公

一八九四年冬④，孙公到香港匿于友人家，知侦探窥其行动，及悬赏缉拿，公遂往问律师，英政府可以保护他居留在港否。律师答云：若有人告发或可成案，不如暂离此埠。公乃往神户，费用由其友人供给。所到之处，交友众多，且得人信仰。一八九五年三月中日和议之后，国人竞尚维新，青年辈纷纷往日本留学。惟当时尚有提犯之约章，若被本国政府行文购缉，可由中国领事递解回华。因此，公剪去辫发，一则可以脱离满洲制度，二则可以办〔扮〕作日人。他对西报曰："我剪去一生长成之辫发，先不剃头，又长起上唇之须，往衣服店买得一套最新日本装穿好，对镜一照，惊悉如许之大变相，方知天佑我也。因我较平常华人略黑一点，皮色象于母亲，故有人谓我有

---

① 何长清（？～1909），号榆庭，广东香山县（今中山）小榄人，武进士出身，光绪二十二年（1896年）授广东水师提督。

② 此处叙述有误，见本书36页译注。

③ 德寿，广东巡抚，曾三度代理两广总督一职。

④ 1894年冬，孙中山尚在檀香山。因而此处所述应是1895年冬，广州起义失败之后。

马来岛人血脉，或有人谓我在檀出世，其实皆非，我乃一纯正中国人。日本自战胜中国后，世人以礼待日人，我办［扮］日人，亦出入相宜也。若无此举，则不能逃脱数次之危险地位矣。"

公太夫人、夫人及其子女因公首次义举失败，不能安居于翠亨，遂迁居香港。一八九五年编者回华娶妻于翠亨村，熟识孙家，复檀时并代他带家属来檀，与其长兄眉公同住。眉公在茂宜岛商牧，又设店于架贺雷埠①，稍有余资，建筑大厦，俾其母、弟妇、二侄女及其侄孙科居住。

游历檀香山

孙公游历檀香山前后凡三次②，多住郑照③家。檀岛华侨皆属广东籍，与公有同乡之谊，且吸受自由风气，思想文明，知中国非实行革命，不能达自由平等之目的，故公攘臂一呼，响应者众。公到埠未久，适英人康特黎医生回国，道经檀埠。常例，过往船客必登岸游览一天。康医生夫妇带一日本女佣同乘马车游埠，公遇于途，上前招呼。康医生错认为日本人，令日妇为之传译。公以英语向康医生回答，说及姓名，方能认识。及畅谈已毕，握手言别，康医生谓公曰："若到英国，请在我家居住。"公诺之。

留檀数月，忙于运动，招集党员，开会于何宽君家，何君现尚居檀埠。当时会众不过三十名，议决立兴中会④。入会者须要宣誓表其忠诚，不能泄漏会中机密，并服从首领命令。檀侨先后入会者甚众。按曾当该会书记者云，该会记录已于一千九百年火焚华埠时失去，惟

---

① 架贺雷埠（Kahului），或译作姑哈禄、茄荷蕾，檀香山茂宜岛上市镇。

② 据记载，孙中山曾六访檀香山，时间分别是 1879.6～1883.7，1884.11～1885.4，1894.10～1885.4，1896.1～1896.6，1903.9～1904.3，1910.3～1910.5。

③ 郑照（1875～1959），字有章，广东宝安县（今深圳）人。檀香山出生。檀香山兴中会首批会员，与刘登专任招揽会员及筹募义捐等工作。

④ 此处叙述不准确，兴中会成立于 1894 年 11 月，广州起义之前。

其主席乃刘祥①公，理财黄华恢②君，书记程蔚南③公，顾问李昌④公。李公乃前在香港皇后书院毕业，与侨商程蔚南公同学，李公学贯中西，檀山政府聘其来檀充当衙署通译，乃革命党中之握要人物也，入会誓词，由他布告。孙公首先行之，其法，左掌上置圣经，右手向天高举，恳切求上帝监［鉴］察。后一一照誓词宣誓，誓后或遇危险，甚则至死不变。会员大都青年有志之士，后有遵孙公号召回国者。其尚留檀山者，皆名望商家，及热心之基督徒，或在银行及大商店当职者。该会第二次开会则有百人，三次则更多矣。

众以将来或须回国作战，乃选出会员一班，请一丹麦人，曾当中国南洋练兵教习队长名柏者，在化冷爹文⑤先生书院教以兵操，每星期操二次，系用木枪。编者亦与焉。爹文先生生于檀岛，学成往中国传教多年，是时回檀，设学校教授华童，故到场习操者，先生多相识，惟其秘密用意，则先生尚未深喻也。当时中国人尚垂辫发，独意奥兰尼学生短发易服。

孙公在檀时募集会款美金六千元，当时作为巨数，因华侨财政非厚，惟恪守党纲，尽其能力以助之耳。

游历美洲

一八九六年六月，孙公以檀山华侨赞成革命者十居其九，遂取道

---

① 刘祥，生卒年不详，广东新宁人，檀香山华侨，兴中会初成立时被推为主席，以后无所表见。
② 黄华恢，生卒不详，广东南海人，檀香山华侨，兴中会成立时被举为司库。己亥梁启超到檀时，曾列席保皇会。
③ 程蔚南（1858～1908），名锡燎，字守亮，广东香山县（今中山）南朗安定村人。曾在檀香山中国领事馆工作，协助到檀的华工。亦营商，在檀香山开设糖厂。在兴中会第一次会议上被选为书记。
④ 李昌（1851～1912），广东清远人。在香港皇后书院毕业，与程蔚南为同学。1882年到檀香山，担任政府机关译员。1894年兴中会成立时，在李昌家宣誓。
⑤ 化冷爹文，即芙兰蒂文（Frank Danon）。

美国金山①。该埠亦多粤人，大开欢迎会，慷慨捐资。由金山遍往有华侨居留各埠，招集党员。公到美西某埠，有一洗衣工人将其二十年之积蓄奉献，公不敢受，惟该工人意最坚决，公乃纳之。因该人听公之演讲，仇满非常热烈，当以身作则，令他侨踊跃输将。孙公谓欲改造中国，非实行革命不可，美国亦是如此，然后后方可脱离英国束缚，听者皆心悦诚服焉。

当日孙公在美国，闻中国出使华盛顿之钦差欲尽力诱拿，将公解回中国。数月后，有月报访员问公，若俾拿提解，以何刑法处之。公曰："或先将脚镣夹实，用锤击碎，割下眼盖，将肉用小刀削为细件，死后不能领尸安葬。"中国古律对于国犯无稍体恤，访员甚骇诧之。

游历英国

一八九六年九月，孙公由纽约往英国。抵英京时，践在檀之约，寓于康特黎医生家②。英京华侨罕少，无招募党员之必要，惟欲与英政府筹借款项，待中华民国成立然后偿还。并欲结交英国义士，或可补助中国之解放，因知英人曾有帮助波兰及匈牙利等国谋自主之战事矣。孰意目的未达，反几罹杀身之祸，则非孙公始愿之所及料者矣。

被困于英京中国使馆

孙公在美时，已知有侦探尾之，但公之智谋，允能趋避，凡写船票，皆临时改名，故在英京无虞有危险之事。不意于十月十一号礼拜日，竟被人诱困，几遭不测。事后公语西报曰："我向地温些街欲往教堂，遇有一中国人问我是中国人，抑日本人？我答曰：'中国广东人。'他认为乡亲。后又来一人，强我同往他等寓所吸烟。对以未暇，因康特黎医生在教堂等候。后又来一华人，先遇者离去。其后我等行至一住宅门口，双扉大开，两人分立身旁，强我进去。讵知足甫入

---

①　金山，指美国三藩市（San Francisco），位于美国加利福利亚州（California State）的西部，华侨一般称之为"旧金山"或"金山大埠"。

②　孙中山初抵檀香山，并非住在康德黎医生家。见本书 29 页译注。

门，即被关禁，不胜惊骇。后察知该处为中国钦署，缘该署已接到华盛顿消息，饬令侦伺于我。该署使人往康特黎医生住宅取我之文件，康宅以我外出却之①。若由文件中搜出党员名单，则国内有许多人不免矣。该署又议定办法，在船赁妥船位，载我回国，将我暂时隐藏在此候船。"

公又对某报访员云："我被困于一房十二日，看守严密，候船将我作狂疾人解回中国。若无我之教师康特黎医生住在英京，断无逃脱之望。经数次失效，始能通出消息。"

一九十一年②十二月九号上海《大陆报》登录孙公被困事曰："初写信数函，用银为坠。由窗门抛出，不料被钦署工人拾得一封，报知主人，立将各窗封固。后卒用银贿买一英国工人代其通讯，将未搜出之名片上书数字与康特黎医生。"

康特黎医生所著《孙公小史》云："凡遭难必有女界营救，是为常事也。中国钦署衙役之妻闻其夫言，谓钦署困有一中国人，情殊可悯，该妇人即缮一函曰：'你有一友于前星期日被困于中国钦署，意欲载他回中国，若果解回中国，必遭大辟。予对于此不幸之人，不胜怜悯，今特致函阁下，请速援救。此信不敢署名，惟深贡实诚，仰为信我之言，即速办理，以免延误。此人姓名乃孙逸仙也。'"此信于十月十七号夜十一点半钟放在康特黎医生门隙，当时康医生闻门钟一响，下楼到门捡得该信，递信人经已去了。得信即速往苏格兰差馆③通报，差头置之不理。明日再到该处告诉情形，总不动听，反谓医生发了神经病。医生着狂，又恐过时，迫得往外交部见其友人，将此事直达沙里士卑厘侯④，即令将被困人释放。若非如此，二十四小时之后，孙逸仙则下船向中国回去，与其被执之党人同受刑戮矣！"

《大陆报》登录孙公言曰："英国人不能直入钦署释放犯人，惟在

① 公署曾有意图取得孙中山之行李，但最后未有行动。
② 作者文中公元纪年均用中文数字表述，如一九一十年，即1910年；一九零四年至七年，即1904~1907年；一千九百年，即1900年，下文不再一一注明。
③ 苏格兰差馆，即苏格兰场伦敦警察厅。
④ 沙里士卑厘侯，即索尔兹伯里（Salisbury）。

外遍布侦探及巡警，免被暗中藏犯下船。最后钦差见得不能再为隐瞒，乃将他释放。"

孙公逃难多次，以此次为最危险也。英国报纸即日将此事长篇纪载，环球上通英文者，莫不知孙公之名①，及景仰其人矣。公又不忘与其通讯于康医生之署役夫妇②之恩，致书眉公③，谓该署役被除。眉公汇数千元以酬谢之。释放后，语于英京《泰晤时》西报④云："烦赐篇幅，代传予之诚心，感谢英国政府出力出予于险云。"

孙公随［遂］在康医生处居住数月⑤，并考究欧美政治，以为将来改造中国之师资也。

孙公之游历及其预备之运动

孙公自离英京，即往法京⑥作短期之游，遍览欧洲各处名胜。惟其心志欲在东方办事，遂渡洋过星加坡⑦。星人闻公之名久矣，故一到埠，欢迎者塞途中，有多数殷富者。惟公则不分贫富，一体待遇。每逢集会，皆以其热诚布告，谓欲放光明于中国，非实行革命推翻满清政府不可。并本其一生之志向，游历之见闻，招集党员，照其前在别处之方法行之。该处华侨非常信仰，随即募集巨款，星加坡变为一革命得力之机关。嗣后孙公往返该埠凡数次，或为筹款，或为避难。侨民对于公言听计从。且深知未改革以前，须从宣传入手，惟中国地方辽阔，如欲宣传普及，非经数年之运动不为功。

---

① 此处，原稿删去"因此拐诱受报纸之宣传乃知满州政府之专制行事，孙公英雄奋斗以取自由皆在世人眼光之内"一句。
② 所述有误，见本书 31 页译注。
③ 眉公，指孙中山长兄孙眉。
④ 《泰晤时》西报，即《泰晤士报》（The Times），英国的一张综合性全国发行的日报，1788 年创刊。
⑤ 1896 年 10 月 23 日，孙中山伦敦蒙难获释后，孙中山暂居于康寓。1896 年 11 月 2 日，迁回葛兰法学院场八号。
⑥ 法京，指法国首都巴黎。
⑦ 此处所述不确，见本书 34 页译注。星加坡，即新加坡（Singapore），亦译作星嘉坡。

革命领袖之奔走

海外支部虽散各处，惟公常时通讯引导之、联络之，故成绩甚佳焉。组织总机关于日本，因横滨华侨甚众，东京亦有许多留学生，内有习化学者，可利用其制造炸弹，秘密招之入党。最奇者，党员虽众，无不忠实者。惟有一次，日本人名拿既唔刺者代买军械，将公所交银币骗清。此事难对捐募者说明再科，迫又往星加坡再为筹款，不料所得逾于前次。

公由星回国，假扮苦力、工人、小贩或日本人周游数处，其时政府已悬重赏侦辑，而公并未遇难，常在茶楼私宅对人谈论国事及满人之政治不良。惟遇知己者，则通其真姓名，播下种子，联络小团体以为后应。后虽数次起义皆遭失败，此盖时机未熟，无可如何，然革命思想潮已深入国人脑海中矣。

得道者多助

孙公又出游美洲，在金山用中、西文演说。散会时，有一美国少年往见公曰："我愿将我之所长贡献于你，我深信汝之运动必有成功。"此人乃咸马里①，曾在士单佛大学②毕业，彼为军事热心家及中国之好友也。从此二人研究将来军事，公用之为军事顾问，在金山训练预备革命之救国青年，学习兵操及技击等。此事传入别埠，小吕宋埠③亦照此办法。清政府闻之，行文禁止，无效。自此以后，公对美人曰："汝等首先将西法输入日本，因汝等乃信基督教国家也，我们意欲照汝模范组织一新政府，盖汝乃自由平等之先进国，我望汝们发现多数喇化拉日将军。"向来西人皆以华人性主自守，不欲与外间交涉，至此始知不然，盖此时国人已多醒悟者矣。

---

① 咸马里，即荷马李（Homer Lea）。
② 士单佛大学，即美国斯坦福大学（Stanford University）。
③ 小吕宋埠，即菲律宾（Philippines）。

孙公斥清朝官吏

清例，国内每省设一总督，以下官职甚多，然无法律之可言，每一官之意旨即法律也。判事虽有不公，或政令之暴虐，民众亦无从申斥。税收并不公开，用途若何，民众全不知晓。其不肖之官吏，则更剥民肥己，枉法营私，则尤为地方之巨害矣。

革命导师

孙公之提倡革命，与前代之反正不同，前者不过易姓而治，依然君主制度也，至一八九四年始于更换国体，建设四万万人之共和政府。只以民众无一定方言，又多数人不谙文字，交通不便利，币制税课不统一，其他总之，内政、外交有待于改良者，奚止千百，公特为此毕生奋斗，务欲达其目的也。

革命时机

欲知革命毕竟之成功，须追溯一八七四①年以后大事而言之。是年既平太平天国，北京政府穷乏，定有新税曰：厘金②，由内地设卡将来往货物抽收，国民之负担綦重。加以西后之天性暴戾无道，厉行专制，以阻维新，凡深通外国学问，及与洋人洽熟者，皆深恶之。初中法启衅，西后悬赏杀害洋人，平常人一百两，领袖五百两。迨同治崩，光绪继位，他［她］更垂帘听政，大权独揽焉。

迨至甲午中日战争，中国败衄，国人亦以为彼知觉，中国之积弱在于泥古，须急行新政，以稍救之。孰知彼乃冥然闷觉，上下酣嬉，计中日之役，已募外债三万万元，此数逾于北京所收入国课三倍，吁

---

① 应是 1864 年。
② 厘金，亦称厘捐，源于咸丰三年（1853）江北大营筹措镇压太平军的军饷之时，至同治元年（1862）除云南（同治十三年设）和黑龙江（光绪十一年设）外，厘金制度已遍行于全国各地。

可嘅〔慨〕也！

一千九百年，义和团之乱，西后纵容拳匪，仇视洋人，他〔她〕以为拳匪果有神灵，张我国威，在此一举。迨八国联军长驱直进，乞盟城下，所赔之款，比之中日战事借款，又加一倍，国事日非，其愚不可及矣。

倘使拳乱定后，痛定思痛，深知大局危殆，锐志维新，未必不可转弱为强。无奈此顽梗性成之老妇，一意阻止，此中殆有天意焉。天意为何？即所以助革命成功也。盖满清若能维新，则人民不至失望，则革命不能得举国之同情。惟满人日以假面具向人民，人民忍无可忍，故革命风潮，一发而不可复遏。

革命筹款

孙公〈因〉当时星加坡等埠华侨虽踊跃输将，惟不能达到二百五十万之数，遂到欧洲往谒银业家，商酌借款。有一法人欲取抵押品，孙公毅然却之。后经奔走多处，巨款遂成，宣传费及军械费于是有着。

孙公筹款定有一种办法，乃发行金币。著者藏有一票额为中国银拾元，乃中华民国所发第一八六二九号，印有青天白日旗一面，谓民国成立后，由国库还回金银拾元，署名总理孙文、财政司李公侠。各埠环球上有华侨，多有出资换此金币者，足见当日华侨之渴望革命成功也。

外人之阻力①

一千九百年预备起事，党人多受过军事操练者，其统带亦谙西操，并有洋人为坐教，因有欧人、日人欲助公成事也。其所需之大帮军械，尚属缺乏。且公由横滨往香港，船一到港，港政府已接到北京政府消息，不准公登岸。此时，革命健儿〈已〉经聚集于三州〔洲〕

---

① 本节所述与当事人回忆颇有出入，见本书43页译注。

田①山寨路口，严密坚守，以候领袖。及知公不获登岸，众皆失望。该党之财政司先公搭船到港，亦不准登岸，遂将原款载往星加坡。公亦转往该埠矣。

其后，公再往香港，此次登岸无阻，惟英官监察甚为严密，不能接济其党人，惟用书信报知党人移营别处，然后得以接济之。惟延迟既久，无机可乘，各人遂散回乡里。

檀报之言论

一九零三年十月，公在檀时，西早报云："一千九百年九月，孙医生欲造成一新中国，由南省起义，倾覆专制政府。先生所统带不过六百人，先在香港附近地方发难，意欲攻占惠州，并约别处齐举，取福建省为根据地，以数百民军与四千满洲兵对敌，初获胜利，后因所约之党人同时在别处起事不果，遂令先生之计划不成，殊可惜也。"

外人之革命观

革命事业自一千九百年失败，在他人多失望矣，惟以公之坚忍锐志，信其有望焉。盖凡事只恐立志不坚，如果专心一志，不论成败，冒万险以赴之，未有不成功者。公及党人之坚［艰］苦卓绝，外人论者亦决其必能有成焉。

一千九百年之起义，其中坚分子乃留学东京之学生。因该学生等留居日本时，吸受东方文明空气，愤中国之酣睡，回国宣传革命道理。有一留学生名唐才常②者，在汉口组织一会。革命事业得唐君之力固甚多也。

---

① 三洲田，原属广东惠州，今属深圳宝安区。
② 唐才常（1867～1900），湖南浏阳人。1899 年夏秋间在日本横滨与孙中山会晤，"商讨湘、鄂及长江起兵计划"。1899 年 5 月，与梁启超等人在横滨创立自立会。1899 年 12 月，唐才常在上海发起组织正气会。1900年在汉口设立秘密机关，组建自立军，计划在湖北、安徽和湖南同时起事。1900 年 8 月 22 日，清军破获汉口自立军总机关，唐才常被捕就义。

檀侨之特性

一九零四年，有卜舫济①夫人者（乃美国牧师法零西士这普地士，华名卜舫济，上海圣约翰书院校长之妻也）同校长到檀，向大多数中国及外国人演讲，云上年檀埠有许多中国青年往圣约翰书院肄业，因有夏威夷学生三十五名，其父母亲属聆言甚切。他云檀香山学生有改良书院之精神。著者问他何故？答云："该学生由夏威夷返沪者，乃在此同美国青年，在于公家或私家〈学校〉毕业预备科，有爱国热诚。到上海则初次见其古制之困难，甚为奋勇，欲一时废除之，而登诸新世界，常将其爱国热诚贡献于同学，欲唤醒其爱国之精神也。盖其在檀香山时，已为足球或野球队也，其带有运动之精神，而教本校之青年学生运动。本〈校〉学生尚以为失却其斯文体态，后训练纯熟，大有裨益于卫生，体操亦大有进步矣，有此功效。"至于一九一五年，在上海买有一大游戏场，该款乃由募捐而成，因校长与牧师向纽约教会筹款无效，盖教会中人鲜有知此项体操输入中国及日本等处之有益也。

圣约翰书院毕业生，有为外交总长、内阁总理、全权大使，又有许多大名鼎鼎之医生、律师及政府部员。论及圣约翰书院，则顺言其它学校，如广东之岭南学校、山东之教会大学、中英书院、长沙之湘雅大学，各校毕业生遍布中国，大放光明，改良政府，革故鼎新，此等学生，虽不全然信服孙公，惟其热心改造中国，则咸有同情矣。

一九○三年在檀事略

一九零三年十月七号檀西早报云："著名革命家孙逸仙博士，由横滨乘西伯利亚船，五号到埠。在本埠秘密运动或公开运动，侨民深信革命真理，多趋向之。"十二月十四日又云："昨日下午，著名革命家在荷梯厘街戏院演说，勇敢而言曰革命唯一法门，可将中国救出于

---

① 卜舫济（Francis Lister Hawks Potts，1864～1947），美国人。1886 年获纽约神学院学士学位，后到中国任圣约翰书院英文教师，1888 年起任圣约翰书院校长。

国际交涉之现时危惨地位，甚望华侨赞助革命党。听者接纳，表示热诚。先生身穿白麻衣服，头上短发，恰似小吕宋人，其言论举动，显出有感化人群之力，加以态度温柔，秩序整肃，真乃天生领袖。彼谓首事革命者，如汤武之伐罪救民，故今人称之为圣人。今日之中国何以必须革命？因中国之积弱已见之于义和团一役，二万洋兵攻破北京，若吾辈四万万人一齐奋起，其将奈何！我们必要倾覆满洲政府，建设民国。革命成功之日，依照美国法制选一总统，废除专制，实行共和。又在利厘霞街华人戏院演说，听者亦座为之满，无插足地。何宽君主席。公演说雄辩滔滔，徵引历史，由古及今，谓汉人之失位，乃由不肖汉奸助满人入关征服全国。他深信不久汉人即能驱逐满人，夺回国家。又谓中国人分党太多，非如日本人之能一致爱国。中国政府派出日本留学生千名，多属汉人。惟少数之满洲人结一会党，窥探其同学，若谈国政者，指为冒犯，随时禀告朝廷，不准学生入武备学堂及所忌之大学。驻外之中国钦差，又不准中国人谈论国事。我等如无国之民，若在外国被人殴打，置之不理。今日所拖辫发，乃表示尊敬满洲，若有违令，即被残杀。观于昏昧之清朝，断难行其君主立宪政体，故非实行革命、建立共和国家不可也。"

孙公留檀至一九零四年三月三十一号，搭高丽船往金山，拟游美国各埠，由东道回国。公之往来皆守秘密，惟此次对西报访事说出行程，谓他望于夏间可到中国大起义举，倾覆满洲。惟在何地点，他则谨慎不言，但谓革命事业大有进步，中国人已醒悟矣云云。访事祝曰："我望有日得了消息，你被举为中华民国总统。"公莞尔而笑。

孙公在金山亦非常之活动。五月间，该埠《益三文拿》① 西报刊有中国总领事因公到埠遍贴告示云："为晓谕事：照得现闻华侨中来有一反党首领，用虚言煽惑人心，有识者明知其目的系在敛钱供其挥霍。惟恐愚民无知，受其所骗，本领事有保护侨民之责，为此示谕侨民知悉，切莫受其所愚，并约束其子弟勿为所惑，致贻后悔，切切特示。总领事钟示。"

公从前五星期搭高丽船到埠，被关员扣留。因政府接到通讯，谓

---

① 《益三文拿》（The San Francisco Examiner），美国三藩市西文报刊，或译作《三藩市调查报》。

溥伦①贝子于高丽船抵埔［埠］后，约两星期前来金山。当时公预备
上船，关员谓其护照不妥，将其困于移民局三星期，待溥伦到后，方
准自由登岸。闻说该埠领事馆照会华盛顿外务部，请派暗差多名，保
护溥伦至圣雷②埠，免生意外之事。因溥伦乃满洲皇子，前往观览一
九零四年所开之世界展览大会。美政府不虑公有行刺皇子之举，知公
无用此手段打击其仇敌，且信他能制止党人用此等过激办法，谓他只
知攻击满洲政府，并不加害一皇子或一爵位人员。

　　孙公既离埠，往圣雷、华盛顿、纽约等埠，继至英京。因举义在
即，不便逗留，复由苏彝士运河③往星加坡回国。此时党务发达矣，乃
语人曰：各党部已有主任一人，共同一班领袖，乃秘密集议，照党规公
举。每省均有分部，集议皆在私宅，常换地点，现有三十至四十部。党
友一时号召便可从公，每部皆有千人。可在就地管理政务，消息亦属灵
通。军人预备联络。其所最难者，欲令一般平民均知宪法意义也。

　　处此境况，如何使其民众能知宪法条理，成一问题。无怪当是时
少数民众及外人评公为作乱者，又目为理想家、浮说无济于事者亦有
之。惟有法人科宁花诸那曰："此无定之理想家，在一九零四年已定
合格之计划，实行之，可能倾覆满洲政府。七年后，此浮说无济于事
者，于一九十一年，其回国不过四日，即有布告其为一国全票所公举
为一国之元首之事④。"又云："我与孙公谈话，可定伊为一大运动首
领精神代表之模范。"若该法人者，其可称为公之知己矣。

创立同盟会

　　自屡年预备，至一九零四年，以为时机已至，再起推翻满洲清廷
而创立民国。革命党已得大批军火，各支部正在静候号召，横滨大机

---

① 溥伦（1874～1925），字彝庵，爱新觉罗氏，清道光帝嗣曾孙。

② 圣雷，指圣路易斯（St. Lours），是美国密苏里州最大的城市。1904年世
　界博览会在此举办。

③ 苏彝士运河（Suez Canal），即"苏伊士运河"。

④ 孙中山并非全票当选临时大总统。1911年12月29日，17省代表在南京
　选举中华民国临时大总统，每省一票，孙中山得16票当选。

关及各分会亦得通告，其时至矣。一九零五年秋，公返日本东京，与黄兴、宋教仁、张继及留学生等组织同盟会，推公为首领，黄兴副之，颁布决议文，海外内后定制三色旗。

领事密禀

一八九九年，驻檀中国领事官咨文回广东总督，谓檀香山革命党非常活动，不利政府，将会员名姓及在中国住址列出，请查拿究办。檀岛入党者，对于家属咸有戒心，因知古例有波及父兄亲属之条，接到此等消息，恐广东有此案发，即株累多人矣。又无法补救，盖其父兄亲属皆不知其子弟在檀有此志向也。

郑照君言①

孙公在檀香山设兴中会时，中国青年入会者甚多。中有郑照君，年仅二十，乃夏威夷土生者，实心赞助入会。时公言："我与汝誓为兄弟，若有号召，汝即回来。"郑照乃客籍人，惟其能通晓本地言语，与诸华侨在会内皆能彼此明白也。一九零四年他得接号召，着伊回国。郑君即往横滨总机关见孙公，并偕一群中国学生，旋往香港。彼知一切计划：欲占夺一衙门，内有军械局所存枪枝及子弹等物，守衙军界经已运动联合反正，各股党人皆已预备听令，若可联合大举，则乘势北伐，宣布合众国。此等计划甚为乐观也。

郑照君与其党人乘夜火船，次早由香港到省城，登岸则往机关处，即现时之救主礼拜堂，乃英国教会所设者，此机关乃各领袖聚集之所。一九零七年，郑君与公同处一室，所有机密事宜及关于大举计划，他尽知之。由香港将短枪子弹藏于水泥十桶，寄往省城。租火船

① 此节所述，与史实多不相符。如孙中山1904年主要在檀香山和美国大陆活动，年底赴英国，未见有曾回广州或到新加坡之记载。所述的起义，应该是1903年1月，洪全福、谢瓒泰等人策划的广州起义，这次起义最终事泄失败。"惟此次计划，兴中会干部概未与闻，中山时在越南，仅由港友函告，略知大概"。文中所述起义过程，与史实亦颇有出入。

载三千武装党人，意欲占领衙门，即派人驻守。又载苦力七百名，预为搬运粮食等物。不料船员见如许多人一齐搭船，恐生意外，拍电回港，后得香港来电，武装党人不能落船。即时电港停止苦力勿来，不料船已启行，苦力到省无人招呼，只得四围游荡，被拿者数百。惟审问时，多属不知实情者，概已释放。短枪亦因桶破露出，关员尽行检去。是役被杀者数人，囚毙者亦数人。首次由檀回粤党人李杞、侯艾全、夏百子、西人威林库力（制炸弹者）皆幸免。公与郑君暂避于横巷，直往埗头雇一小舟，出金钱买疍妇衣服二套，改办［扮］女装，及用包头布盖了短发，令他直向沙面而行。遥望一间大礼拜堂，由此登岸。此教堂乃德国柏林所设，其中有党人五百名预备过城，内有中国教士梁慕光①乃革命领袖，及其会众华人乃属党人也。公一到，众人谓此事泄漏，各人须自行逃避，以保生命。

公与郑君假办［扮］疍妇，在埗头见有一中国明车火船，搭大仓到香港，在党友家居住数日，孙公即往星加坡，郑君亦回檀矣。

此乃公第三次之失败，惟每经一次之失败，则多一次之进步。首次勇敢行事，有实力居其间者不过五百人。二次其计划略大，若港政府准公登岸，举事之后民众投归旗下，或可成功也。三次既经完备，惟遇险阻，其计划亦归失败，党人奔避星散矣。

设公因此灰心，其党人亦萌退志，则革命前途不堪问矣。惟其坚忍不馁，努力前进，故主义终能实现也。

第四次革命

一九零四年公由广州避难于香港二日，动程往星加坡及南洋群岛，该处党友甚多。因香港太近省城，布满侦探，且悬赏缉拿。赏格定七十五万元，久居恐有危险。在星则甚属安稳，此处有华侨百万皆赞助其主义者。所奇者，有此大赏格，其从者未有通奸卖其首领，所到之处亦未闻有此不义之消息。惟有为其担任理财者，有不义于公。钟宇君云有一代理人收款二千元，终不知去向。会众仰望大公无私义

---

①　梁慕光，广东博罗人，兴中会员，博罗等地的三合会首领。三洲田起义时，是孙中山、郑士良部署在博罗的起义军首领。

勇之领袖，周游环球，或东或西，旋转革命精神之动机，以成将来之大志愿也。

　　一九零四年至七年，此三年，公用其全力宣传革命道理，及勉励其当地之党部，将来必底于成。或遇有望清朝立宪者，公谓欲望中国变政，须行革命，设立共和政府为唯一法门。自知戊戌变政不成，光绪被困，劝进者被杀，何以为之？中日未开战以前，有外国教士大声疾呼，设法运动中国维新，其一乃美国正教士胡兰雅①先生，其二则英国李提摩太②博士。此二人所著作论说，登于《万国公报》或编成书，意欲将其诚意，直陈中国积弱形状，达于社会，望其改良，并指明日本变法自强，因用西法治国，盖日人志愿求学，中国人则坚守古法也。当时有数省总督，如李鸿章者，读此真正言论，感激靡浅矣。一八九八年，康有为文士因在上海及香港地方见得维新文化，所读改良论说，被化为恳切信徒，及国中多数青年、官场亦被感化焉。其计画［划］乃上达政府官员，使知有改良之必要，若中国图强，则列国位于各大强国之中。康北上见其幼帝，光绪亦信其言，盖光绪已读过前一八九十年有基督教会中国妇女一万名所进与皇太后《圣经》一本③，略谙西法，又读维新书籍，发起维新感想。故三月中连颁上谕，力图维新。接此上谕，政府各部皆以普及，将成例科举考试完全废之，勉励学西法，或留学，或出洋考察政治，又设学校，以学洋务。当时英爵赫德④，代中国办理税务者，税关乃中国唯一之正当条例之部分也，读其上谕，谓：

---

①　胡兰雅，所指应是傅兰雅（John Fryer，1839～1928），英国人，1861年受英国圣公会派遣来华。长期在江南制造局任编译，参与创办上海格致书院。

②　李提摩太（Timothy Richard，1845～1919），英国传教士，1870年由浸礼会派遣赴华传教，1890年到天津任《时报》主笔，鼓吹维新变法。

③　所指应是慈禧太后六十生辰，中国基督教的女教徒呈献一本《新约全书》（1894年上海美华书馆版）以为寿礼一事。此事发生在清光绪二十年（1894年），而非作者所述的1890年。

④　赫德（Robert Hart，1835～1911），英国北爱尔兰人。1854年来华。在中国任海关总税务司长达四十五年（1863～1908），势力广涉中国的军事、政治、经济、外交以至文化、教育各个方面。

"我不信此生可见及此"。因彼及他人见变法行于太速，非可试办于三月内，遍布此事，应要数年为之。

维新党人预料若行其计画［划］，必须废除寡后，意欲将其围困。惟以不能干涉国政，故其策不行。维新党人求助于袁世凯，故知有此事，以告西后及各大臣，大加反对变法，谓中国之大，乃由古法而成，其他各国皆野蛮思想，不足效法。有此决心，此由于西后奸险成性，不懂外国事务，虽有中日战事及义和团，乱后未尝开其眼界。他［她］则带兵进宫擒拿光绪，困于瀛台，又拿获维新党羽，将青年者斩决六人，并将赞助维新官员降罪。西后特别注意缉拿劝进领袖，惟康已平安逃到青岛，再搭英国船往日本①。康虽逃脱，惟其亲属亦被株连，祖坟亦被毁掘。所有维新上谕作为废除无效，当时西后与各大臣见此若欲保全朝廷，须事挽救，报到一九零四年，革命起义，四处民心摇动，略有恐慌，至日俄之战，日本操胜，盖其用新法也。

其后西后颇有改良心志，乃于一九零五年选定官员，游历外国考察政治。至一九零六年各员回报，拟以应允立宪，修改法律，整理财政，海陆军取用新法制度，设立警察，各大都会令学西法，使国人关心于国事，并颁布新法，表面上见之亦有乐观。有谓照此法则或可维新，定有成效，惟满人之嫉妒尚存，非易行也。

公与其党人不信其诚意，若满人势力不除，终为专制，因公等素抱民国主义也。清政府以维新党人激奋人心，预备发难，故假意立宪以愚国民，惟民党知其狡计，进行革命不懈。故一九零六年萍、醴之役，二处皆有战事发生，惟党人欠缺子弹，亦难成事，刘道一②等死之。一九零七年公自信其筹备完善，筹划进行在广东举义三次，皆失败。其目的在于直陷行政机关，因内有军械存焉。是役战事乃由河内机关主之。是年春初，黄兴将军带领党人发难于湖北

---

① 变法失败后，康有为由北京逃沪转港，又离港赴日，旋抵加拿大。直到1917年10月康有为才第一次到青岛。

② 刘道一（1884～1906），湖南衡山人。1905年参加同盟会。翌年秋，回国筹组萍浏醴起义，旋被捕，英勇就义，时年22岁。

失败，黄将军逃走①。五月，清官发难，亦遭失败。七月，在汕头起义不成。虽属无济于事，惟可表示民意矣。

是时通讯各党部，谓人心经已固结矣。一九零七年八月一号，郑照君在檀爹比士燕梳②部雇工，十五号接公电报一"来"字，当时即向司理辞职回国。司理人甚为烦闷，谓伊初到，干事甚好，何不预早通知。郑君谓有要事，接到电报，不能稍延，是以即日离弃职守。是日十一点钟下船，虽不便告人以此秘密要事，惟知举义之时不远矣，自知其必有用于领袖，盖其曾在意阿兰尼学校肄业，善操英语及熟识西人习惯也。郑君至横滨总机关，已知计划系委任以统带青年学生之职，共二十人，均谙化学，能制炸药及炸弹等物者。齐往香港，及到，又令同搭火船往东京海防。是船先抵北海，乃中国广西地方，有一水师提督下船查验，各搭客在船面排列成行。郑君猜得该北海官员必接有报告调查党人行动，不禁惊异，恐被拿获。公之从者，凡遇党友须用暗号，提督行将到郑君之前，郑君无意中将右手盖于心中，欲停其跳动。提督视之，亦伸手摸心，还其暗号，则表示他亦党人也。初以为用计拿他，不信提督乃兄弟也。惟见其直行无语，又无举动。当时郑君口干，说不成语。在船党人互相环视，不信无意外事端发生。船到海防，取河道至东京河内。见孙公到时，将在船所遇提督所还暗号〈以告〉。公出纸示之，谓水师经已入党，惟待岸上起义，则连［联］合一致反正。该领袖知陆军亦预备响应，党人虽有勇敢，惟未经训练，难胜经练军队，须俟数年方成效果也。

九月间起义，不数日已得数市镇。惟清兵太多，众寡不敌，又欠子弹，是以败走，逃入法界。当时各寻生路，公与郑照君逃入村落，遇乞丐二人，公即用大金一圆与二乞儿，换着衣服。此二乞丐所得大金可换通用银四十六元，敷其数月费用，又得新衣，何乐不为。四人同至一茅舍，孙公与郑君穿上旧衣，取泥涂面，至河边坐船，至香港

---

① 1907年，黄兴在日本、香港、越南河内等地策应革命，没有带领党人发难于湖北一事。

② 燕梳（insurance），保险业初传入中国时的译名。

平安登岸①。

至此失败后，孙公非常忧闷。郑君劝他无庸再起，因每次失败，皆丧失人命。公答谓必要由此做去，至战胜则止，或需时日，惟其主义必有决胜之日也。前苏格兰王布鲁士②不受英国束缚，与英国战争失败七次，奋斗二十三年，卒达目的。公鼓动革命，令国人齐起反对其压迫者，亦同此理也。

一九一一之预备

一九零八年，西后逝世。应允预备立宪开议会，尚隔一年。其议员乃由有限制选举者公举之，此等假面议政院，上议院人员由摄政指出，意欲笼络革命党而和平之，公已洞见此怪剧也。

当时报纸，如日报、月报非常发达，逐日增多，故国人阅之，已觉受满人残虐，有改良之必要。一八零七年中国始创办新闻纸，乃在上海发刊。革命报名曰《中国报》③，乃一九百年在香港开办，后设《民报》于日本横滨埠，《少年报》④于金山，《自由报》⑤于檀香山。至一〈千〉九十年全国统计，日报月报馆约有五百家。人谓国民不识字者占多数，报纸何以普及于民众？有答曰：凡绅士公所、秘密社会、乡间茶馆及家内，凡人所群聚之所，可由识字者宣读关于变政条理者，与有志者听之。

清廷欲兴教育，广开学堂，惟办理甚为腐败。惟外国所设学校，中学、大学，其学生获益甚多。外国中学共五十七所，美国所办者占二十五，英国亦然。各学校之创办及其供给，皆赖新耶教会为之。天主教有中学五所，二所乃杂科教授，如香港大学与焉，其他则医学

---

① 此段或是作者误记。1907 年下半年，孙中山一直呆在越南活动，12 月和黄兴、黄明堂等发动镇南关起义，但起义失败后仍在越南活动，直至 1908 年 1 月 24 日才被河内法国殖民当局驱逐出境，前往新加坡。
② 布鲁上，即罗伯特·布鲁斯（Robert the Bruce）。
③ 《中国报》，是革命派报刊《中国日报》和《中国旬报》的合称。但作者此处所指应是《中国日报》。
④ 《少年报》，即《少年中国晨报》，1910 年 8 月 19 日创刊于旧金山。
⑤ 《自由报》，即《自由新报》，1908 年 8 月 31 日创刊于檀香山。

校，附设于医院者数处。留学生往美国及欧洲留学者颇多，中国人有志求学入此等学校就学者不胜其数，且入该学校肄业者，参以国学，有大增其势力，皆能代其教会效力，虽有大反对及误会亦可平之。中国人等毋忘教会人之毅力，因此等学校，能将正理传播于中国青年。公对于美国人云："吾等之大希望，乃承《圣经》及基督教育。因我等来欧美得而知之，盖改良中国之根本。"他认为民众所需者，不独通晓新艺，及政治条理更有裨益于新生命也。

公怀教育普及民众之心深切，所到各处皆鼓吹兴学，在檀香山则有华文学堂之设，今改中山学校；翠亨一隅，亦有培正分校。故今日广州大学以及其他学校多有改名中山，以留纪念。孙公之令名，泗万古不朽也。

崛贞一牧师之言

由一九零七年至一九十七［一一］年，在星嘉坡、南洋①、东京、香港、日本、檀香山、美国、英国、法国，由苏彝士河回国。于此四年中，孙公尝到日本，有时居留数月，因他与日本人相似，惟不谙日语，所晓者乃酬酢通用数言耳。一九零六年，横滨埠有大多华侨在此设总机关，与内地各党部通讯。当时是有崛贞一牧师在横滨日本教堂主讲（现在檀香山督理日人基督教堂）在日本与公及革命党人相遇之事迹，令人注意者，谓"一九零六年公离日本之后，有一美国讲经会代理携其友人到舍，介绍孙公书记陈少白先生，乃公嘱其留居横滨代维新会党办事。不久见有华文信件一封放在舍下书席，拆读之，谓其有难，须一友人帮助，请往见之。即到其住舍，访闻中国领事官报告日本政府，谓其在埠运动革命，引诱日人及中国人，日政府令他离境，任其自由往别处。陈先生既知吾表同情于孙公及其理想，请余指示帮助，他居留日本，在此有要务斡旋。二人商酌，余定意同他星夜到家，将陈先生办［扮］作日人，令吾妻即缝日本衣服与之更换，因当时埠中日人多服日衣也。穿上日衣，不再留于吾家，余即带他就

---

① 南洋，指南海附近的东南亚诸国，包括马来群岛、菲律宾群岛和印度尼西亚群岛等。

近旅馆居住。馆主乃余相识者，谓此青年朋友，乃自幼出外，忘记祖国言语矣。陈先生在旅馆居住约四月。后孙公由美而来，留日六月，常到家中，与余结为好友。公对余且信且感，常有畅谈大事。公谓有大希望，上帝相助，必底于成。此乃孙公自用之言，因伊对余云，他乃一基督教徒也，他或未到过日本教堂，盖他不谙日语故也。孙公迁往东京，结识早稻田大学教员多名。又常［尝］遇大偎伯爵①，亦甚器重，惟不能表示其同情于大事。日本基督教徒甚仰佩之，因教徒等信公为民请命，反对压迫残暴之满洲政府也。"

一九一〇年，牧师在檀埠，闻公在科街福音堂听书，特往访问。后到牧师家中畅谈，问及革命事业，答云："递年则可起义，一切计画［划］均已筹备，此次自信成功。"又云前次回国，西部可以自由行动，因军队均已疏通，准备联合革命党，公往来皆得彼等之护卫也。是年公将近离埠之时，华侨开欢送会。化冷爹文牧师为主席，因牧师佩服公之主义，又知中国人有此毅力。当时，其友人见欢送者之非常热心发现也。

崛牧师大加器重于公，赞羡其志向、能力及其宗旨，惟意料公未知艰苦，只信倾覆满洲，则容易设立中华民国。公表示其理想，若民国一成，弊政则化为乌有，渐达光明矣。牧师心中谓公一人可建设巩固政府尚属疑问，因中国现状之贪赃、压制、妒忌成性，行政者可一但扫除之与否，惟不敢对公言之。

崛牧师谓日本变政，乃次第仿行新法，中国之不识文字及愚蒙者多，须先行准备，然后可立共和政府。前总统威尔逊②有云："欲行共和政体，必须多数人民晓然于共和真理。"此言实属真情。惟公心志已决设一民国，自信中国之弊政皆因此而廓清之。

崛牧师称赞公之理想，甚表同情，最重者乃以教育大放光明于中国。

总而言之，崛牧师之羡公，信其乃一高尚、诚实及恳切为［之］

---

① 大偎伯爵，即大偎重信（1833～1922），曾任日本内阁首相。1897 年经犬养毅与流亡日本孙中山相识，与革命党人有往来。
② 威尔逊，即伍德罗·威尔逊（Woodrow Wilson，1856～1924），美国第 28 任总统。

人，甚赞羡其有为民众大领袖之志向，及其爱国之心。既知公已在一教会学堂意奥兰尼肄业，又在教会医学堂毕业，谓常与公多次畅谈，其言论与理想皆合与基督教宗旨。或近年忘其故志，不得而知，惟该牧师深仰公之行事云。

一九一十年公离檀香山，往何处不欲人知，因恐传出消息，即有电报中国政府。惟未知因何泄漏，六月二十九号西早报云：公在檀内岛轮船公司扣娄甸船，将启行往茂宜岛，时欢送者回埠，他即过蒙古船，该日乘之往东方。七月东京《朝日报》报告，谓来横滨搭客中有一孙逸仙，改名"亚罗霞"①，在日本则用"达艰奴"②，在东京作客于一友人家，待查知其真确住所，日政府即将其递解出境。因政府不允窝藏革命党人，故劝他离境。《朝日报》谓他已离去往新加坡，在该埠如前次之逃避，作客于友人家中，乃得平安。

当公之奔走时期，黄兴将军在广州起义，一九一十年之广州新军兵变，惟二次皆无实效。一九十一年，黄兴将军准备在广东候令，已知各省均已预备，一呼响应矣。

公再游美国，语其友人，谓其时可望从速成功。一九十一年游历金山、斯亚度③、斯波近④、坚沙时埠⑤、圣雷、芝加咕⑥、纽约等埠，各埠皆有党部及军队，由咸马里将军训练者，此项军队甚有勇气，惟未编成队伍回国效力疆场。

公在美洲得有消息，谓在武昌宣布中华民国。公即在美国发行布告文，详论革命主义，及希望美人表同情于新中国，因其政体乃效法美国，各省权限统归中央政府。各报纸访员争先恐后来见孙公，惟其紧守秘密，住于纽约附近咩地臣公园之旅馆，其华友亦不报访员知之。公已预备搭茂利天尼亚船，惟因不及下船，再作逗留两星期，此时访员亦不能遇面。惟最后在火船定位，用其在纽约所改之名。到了

---

① 亚罗霞（Alaha），或译作阿罗哈。
② 达艰奴（Takano），即高野。
③ 斯亚度（Seattle），今译西雅图，美国西北部太平洋沿岸最大的城市。
④ 斯波近（Spokane），今译斯波坎，美国华盛顿州的第二大城市。
⑤ 坚沙时埠（Kansas），今译堪萨斯，美国中部的农业州。
⑥ 芝加咕（Chicago），今译芝加哥，美国第三大城市，仅次于纽约和洛杉矶。

英国，无人认识，直到英京。

又作客于其师康特黎医生家，公对医生谓欲借债五十万磅［镑］，有事要用。公未尝有失望在欧美之表同情者可以借款，因有最后之成功也。公之筹款，皆赖华侨踊跃输将，外国人亦间有捐助。惟其冒险为国筹款，资本家皆避之。一九一一年，前后既经数次向外国人借款，皆无成立，欲向本国人商借，则中国内地殷富者不敢表同情于作乱之事也。

孙公在康特黎医生家中得接电信，信面题英京孙文，盖此名乃交电报局来往电信之用。康医生谓此电信乃报告孙文被举为中华民国总统，盖于此或有误会。因公于一九十一年十二月二十七号到上海，后四日被举总统①。十二月二十二号，孙科在檀埠对访员谓其父接有电信，由江苏巡府［抚］程德全②请他即速回国，或因此误会也。公对康医生谓若被举总统，暂承其任，俟有贤能则让之。此语对于康医生所云，已知有作中国将来总统之设想及建设时期，惟满洲朝廷尚未倾覆，预料清廷必然自倒也。其所对康医生言让位之语，其友人非常反对。

一九一一年之革命起义时，公正在外洋起程回国，在美国接到武汉起义消息，在英京接到设立民国之布告。因四川省反对政府借外债以筑该省之铁路，收为国有。当时革命党四处运动，炸弹、子弹皆已制定，正候机关号令行事。因在汉口俄租界制造炸弹，意外爆发，引起疑问，事机将泄，革命党人逼得随时起事，即由北自南，各省沿下杨［扬］子江③，清兵连［联］合反正，东南数省，归于革命党范围，布告民国，电召公即速回国。是次反正，伤损人命甚少，若比较太平天国反正，死者二千万；又一八五七至七十四年，回教起事战亡者，一千二百万；此次则至少流血也，只有数千人战死在于西安府、

①　孙中山到达上海是 1911 年 12 月 25 日。
②　程德全（1860～1930），四川云阳人。1910 年任江苏巡抚。1911 年武昌起义后，于 11 月 5 日宣布江苏独立，被推为江苏都督。
③　扬子江，长江在江苏省扬州、镇江附近及以下江段，因古有扬子津渡口，得名扬子江。扬子江原本只是指长江较下游的部份，但在外语中也泛指整条"长江"。

武昌、福州及南京等处，由十月十号起义至十二月二号宣布民国①，甚少损伤人命。十一省脱离满州政府，各领袖会议报知孙公将举为临时总统。

公离英京用回原名孙文，革命首领候补中华民国总统，用假名时期过矣。公往巴黎，取道苏彝士河。至星加坡，该处华侨喜其首次凯旋，开会欢迎，非常热闹，欢呼救国伟人。有一班青年女子，散花于其所行路上。及到香港，公发一布告书，谓中华民国成立，望美国从速承认，寄与华盛顿外务部。公意知前者美国人表示同情及承认民国，盖美国人心里，见有第二共和国出现，与其国之政体相同者，则便合于人类行为，不论其有无筹备也。

公于耶稣诞后一日到上海，欢迎者尤盛，沪上国人皆欢呼孙公为中国救主。民国现已统治中国，各省份之一半将其军队预备北上，驱逐满人。到上海四日，南京参议院开会公举孙公为中华民国总统。孙公本一乡民，屡年为国奔走，成为国事犯，今其希望成为事实，中华民国成立矣。在民众欣幸之中，自知有大责任之对付，因满人尚在北京，未被驱逐，秩序尚待维持，需以时日用其智慧、忍耐及政治才干，战胜其古法之贿赂、勒诈，南北之妒忌，及军阀之纵横。公则发现疑心可否破除此等难事。公既为一成功之革命家，可为成功之建设家乎？此一疑问，实皆未深知公者也。

中华民国大总统

一九一一年公预备回国掌理武汉起义，惟因汉口制炸弹爆发，逼得举事。武昌既已发难，无可停顿，且广州、南京、武昌皆可和平投入各处军队反正后用以北伐，北京军队半数已归化革命矣。

反正战事毋容多述，因有详细之著作者纪述之矣。惟补录袁世凯承命出山，充满清总兵元帅②，他认识革命之潮流不可遏抑，劝清廷退位，故孙公即以中华民国总统大位让之，不听其友人阻止之言论也。

---

① 1911 年 12 月 2 日，江浙联军占领南京，"东南大局，从此救平。"
② 1911 年 11 月 1 日，清政府任命袁世凯为内阁总理大臣，掌控军政大权。

一九十一年十二月十三号檀香山西早报访员见孙科君,登诸该报云:"'顷者,江苏巡抚程德全电促我父回国。'访员问曰:'乃父将有中国总统之望乎?'答曰:'未知。若有选举权,吾当投筹也。'并谓民国旗式非新制成者,前十六年已为首次起义在国内飞扬矣。此旗乃陆皓东所定,系用青天白日,表示自由日光表射寰球。"是时孙君尚未毕业,谓意欲再往美国嘉省①求学也。

一九十二年元月一日,南京参议院公举公为中华民国总统,报告建都南京,定成临时约法②。孙公传递国书于各友邦,谓满洲政府不良,设立民国乃独之一良药,请承认之。公应允外国,前与满清所立和约继续有效,及尊重各租界,所有外人财产保护之。其希望乃在造成巩固国家,得享和平,以图强盛。

或谓孙公欠于建设才能,惟其理想计画[划]皆绝妙,其诚意欲实行之无疑矣,自信由条理上而达于大进步亦无疑矣。一九十二年二月十二号因何告辞大位③?有谓公与袁世凯密约,内情不得而知,并未见其别项理由。公之不纳其从者之申说、在南京之反对言论、并由美国各埠檀香山各电信之反对,或因既经许袁为总统,公为人践言,意欲谨守之。因公之许,可免至生灵涂炭,盖公只望倾覆满清而已,今目的既达,故无他恋也。

编者与孙公同乡及世交,自幼仰慕其为人,公之自少而壮而老所行之事,皆系于怀,先父被囚亦为其主义。乙未年首次举义失败,受公之托,带其家属杨氏太夫人、卢氏夫人、哲嗣科(即哲生君)及其二女④来檀香山,与孙眉公同居。船到横滨,陈少白先生下船安慰一番。编者到埠当《隆记新报》⑤翻译,凡关于国家消息,与香港《中

---

① 嘉省,指美国加利福利亚州(California State)。

② 1911年12月29日,各省代表选举孙中山为中华民国临时大总统。《中华民国临时约法》于1912年3月8日由临时参议院正式通过,3月11日公布。

③ 孙中山请辞是在1912年2月13日。

④ 此时孙中山幼女孙婉尚未出生,"其二女"之说或是作者误记。

⑤ 《隆记新报》,原名《檀香新报》,1881年在檀香山创刊;1883年改名《隆记报》;1903年改名《檀山新报(隆记)》,成为革命派与保皇派笔战的重要阵地。

国报》陈少白先生主笔互相通讯。

一九十二年在檀香山得闻武汉起义成功，孙公被举临时总统于南京，立意回国。因平夙关心国事，当务之急，欲大发展维新农务于国家，求新立民国设立试验场及农务学堂，因念及首次举义，公与先叔陆皓东曾条陈两广总督设立农务学堂也。檀埠农务试验场主任衣委威厘确士博士及次长开夜学教授种棉、种禾，曾从之研究。檀侨开恭祝民国成立大会于亚了剌公园，同二师到听演说。散会后，从中运动威厘确士博士回华办事。对编者云，博士方毕业时，钦使伍廷芳欲聘伊回东三省设试验场，惟知日本人在满洲之势力，恐有破坏其用心教中国人，故辞之，自愿来檀就职。当时闻中山公被举为总统，政事焕然一新，故允回中国，不居官位，惟欲中国给以费用，将其三、四年之时期，可以遍布各省试验场，交回国人自理，伊即回美，嗣后农业发达，皆知威厘确士博士之名，即满意矣。编者在南京时曾将事达于孙公，谓给与使费邀他回华，惟让位与袁世凯后，国事变迁，是以未果其行也。美国与德宣战，威博士调部使理种植军粮，前数年辞职休养，在美京《缙绅月报》充当笔政，著书二本，一为《百科农学》，一为《查验畜类》，行世甚广，每年日本售去数千卷。

编者一九十二年元月十六号回国，同行乃公之哲嗣孙科君及美国同志青年者十二人，皆搭"地洋丸"轮船回国。路经檀埠，登岸游玩，本埠同盟会接船欢迎，并同乘自由车游览檀埠名胜，下午设筵欢送，午后启轮东归。到横滨时下碇，公之日本友人数名，内有一名由南京回来者，与横滨同志下船关照，《新报》访员及照相者络绎而至，登岸时欢迎者甚众。甫入日本旅馆，日本政府派来暗差四名，皆穿礼服，在旅馆守候一夜。翌晨搭火车往东京，下车时又有礼服暗差二名立于车站，跟随入日本旅馆。编者询其来意，谓保护重要人物，免生意外之事。后下船再往神户，华商在埠头欢迎者多人。正午统一会请赴茶会，席上有山东商人演说。大意谓彼乃北方人士，在座粤人占多，现今民国成立，本该通融南北一家，何以粤人常言北伐？盖伐者，因有罪而伐之，我乃北人，自问有何罪而须伐也？寄语诸君若到南京，代求大总统须以和平统一中国，是所厚望。

翌晨动轮往上海，在船上得接无线电报云：北京党人谋炸袁世凯，弹击马车前部，轰毙马夫，惟袁幸免，下车时尚口含纸烟。刺客被获，真不幸也，留此权奸，以祸中国。数日到沪，同科君寓法界宝昌路陆军分部，每阅沪报如《民立》、《民权》等报，无日不骂袁贼。当时民国代表伍廷芳与袁世凯代表唐绍仪①议和，因政体问题与唐不合，遂与伍直接电商。在沪闻卢氏夫人偕二女同南洋男女党人十余名来沪，英商哈同②预备舟车，着编者下船欢迎。是日设宴，以饷同行者二十余人，并请留宿其家，后因人多各自寓栈。翌日同往南京，与孙科君同寓总统府，即故天皇宫③地址。

当时袁贼代表清廷下议和条件于总统府，交参议院认可，不允更改，惟将第一款"大清帝号相传不废"，只改"相传"二字为"仍存"字耳，余皆照全文通过④。南京报纸揭破袁贼奸计，大骂不已。孙公曰："袁世凯老于政治经验，经过如许艰难，逼清廷退位，既知吾等让权与他，岂有不照良心维持国家?"孙公特设报纸名《中华民报》，日以恭颂袁贼功德，大总统非袁莫属⑤。谁知袁早已谋夺大位，使其部下将官上表清廷促其退位，后即谓须要有政治经验者为总统，方可息战。编者闻孙公意欲让位与袁世凯，党人极力反对，因恐袁老奸巨滑，终属难靠，若为私利，则无所不为也。

各省党人在南京讨论孙公退位，编者亦与焉。盖护助孙公者，反对此意见甚力，党人不信袁氏可能行孙公数十年之奋斗主义，咸谓孙

---

① 唐绍仪（1862～1938），字少川。广东香山县（今珠海）唐家人。武昌起义后，充当袁世凯内阁全权代表，与南方代表伍廷芳在上海举行议和谈判，磋商关于清帝退位的优待办法，以及孙中山的辞职和由袁世凯继任的各项问题。3月，袁世凯就任临时大总统后，提名唐绍仪为第一任内阁总理。

② 哈同（Silas Aaron Hardoon，1851～1931），近代上海的一位英国籍犹太裔房地产大亨。

③ 天皇宫，指太平天国天朝宫殿（天王府），孙中山在南京的临时大总统办公室位于天王府的旧址。

④ 《关于大清皇帝辞位后之优待条件》是南北双方多次协商后的结果。

⑤ 一般所知的《中华民报》，1912年7月20日在上海创刊，由邓家彦主办，以"拥护共和进行，防止专制复活"为宗旨，猛烈抨击袁世凯的北洋政府。但陈旭麓等主编的《中国近代史词典》（上海辞书出版社1982年10月版）"《中华民报》"词条，则说在民国初年在北京也曾出版《中华民报》，但语焉不详，作者所指或是此报。

公过于信重。而公则谓袁世凯既已宣誓，何不信之。并谓袁能使清廷退位，弊政可以告终，又免生灵涂炭，不然率师北伐，财政困难，事之济否尚未可知。退位问题议论良久，无法挽回孙公之意，因其心信退位有益于国家，藉此可以统一南北。黄兴大元帅为公主义奋斗多年，此次战胜成功，及咸马里将军（孙公之军事顾问）皆云：务须北伐，若下次行之，更难十倍。后黄元帅闻孙公决意，在元帅府恸哭失声。

编者熟识孙公，与孙科君同居一府，数次语于孙公，要求不可让权于袁，自信袁不能践约。又留欧美诸学生亦同意劝谏。孙公谓："汝等久居外国，不知中国情形。"孙公又对党人曰："现因经济困难，不能延久战事。"党人云："有十数省代表在于南京，可以筹款。"惟无法可以转其志向，无奈预备与袁交代。二月十二日孙公退位，编者尚在南京，自知不能行其志，迫得回广东省亲，后复回檀香山。

孙公让位于袁，特派唐绍仪、汪精卫、蔡元培①、宋教仁②为特使往北京，请袁世凯到南京接临时总统大任。谁料袁用奸计，使其部下河南军四千人，就在特使所寓之六国酒店附近市场放火抢劫，有谓特使行李亦被回禄。藉口谓北京军士闻袁将离京，故此生变，袁果离去，不知伊于胡底，须在北京镇压方可无事。盖官僚蛇鼠成窝，岂肯离却老巢，受南方监视？其后不得已在北京交代。

民元二月十二日，清太后代清廷罪己逊位，颁布诏书，大意谓天下大势，民众趋向共和，天意显然，岂敢不顺数万万民众之观念而自荣一家，今与皇帝等将政权交回国民云。

清廷既退位，孙公往祭明孝陵。盖明太祖乃汉族明君，循中国古例，每次易朝均有布告于已故英灵者，故孙公虔肃往祭，告以中国已归汉人治理。有一秘书员宣诵祭文，谓中华民国总统前来报告设立民国，废除满洲制度，望中国得享荣光。礼毕回府，众人欢呼而散。到府接客，孙公演说谓将以南京为首都，及袁世凯等将到视事，并谓袁已应允

---

① 蔡元培（1868~1940），字鹤卿，号孑民。浙江绍兴人。近代民主革命家、教育家。1912年1月任南京临时政府教育总长。

② 宋教仁（1882~1913），号渔父。湖南桃源人。近代民主革命家。1912年1月任南京临时政府法制局局长。

服从我们主义，有如党人，若他前来将受民众之欢迎，我则隐退闲居为一平民，与你等无异，惟尽我能力以尽国民一分子义务而已。

二月十四日，下退职书于参议院，谓袁世凯有政治经验、建设才力，中华民国交其治理，可望国利民福。孙公荐袁自代，谓本该不干涉参议，惟因满虏退位，袁有大功，前曾布告满虏退位，则功成身退，凭汝等选举贤能。参议院遂举袁世凯为临时总统。

孙公若醉心利禄，则无退位之思想，今淡视荣利，则真正爱国可知也。

一九十三年，袁世凯请往北京，居之以宫殿，而授以帝皇之待遇，无非欲诱孙公以利禄，听从其诡计①。此奸狡之袁世凯，度孙公有如中国多数官僚，受其诌媚。孙公全然背之，并质问为何谋杀武汉首义元勋方维②、张振武③。反遭其忌，收回铁路总办职位。袁氏之奸，自此国人皆知矣。

有一久居中国之美国人对编者曰：当时北京官场报告，瓜分此款三千万元。此时编者尚在南京，日本某公司乘北伐需款孔亟时，欲贷款三千万元，惟取地方作抵押。孙公拒绝之。英人修夫希炉在广州行辕谒见先生，誉之曰："透明诚实，正直忠良，俭朴坚忍，为国事不辞劳苦。"又云："破坏家少可邻比，惟建设非他所长也。"此盖因孙公预备计划离时尚远，国势之阻碍，难以急速行之也。

孙公与袁世凯之比较

民元二月十四孙公罢职，翌日参议院公举袁世凯为总统。当时报纸亦有评判，《大陆报》云："此奸狡小人，阴险图谋，隐伏数年，由

① 1913年，孙中山主要在日本、上海及港澳等地活动，并未到过北京。1913年3月，宋教仁遇刺身亡。4月孙中山致电袁世凯，因办理"宋案"不能应邀进京。7月，"二次革命"爆发。
② 方维（？～1912），湖北随县人。武昌起义参加者之一。1912年8月随张振武入京，一同被捕遇难。
③ 张振武（1870～1912），湖北罗田人。武昌起义参加者之一，和孙武、蒋翊武并称辛亥三武。后招黎元洪忌恨，设计诳之入京，复密电袁世凯将其捕杀。

地底孔中摇摆而出。外国人谑戏之曰：'虚伪魑魅、一夜间发现奇遇之袁世凯。'孙公发起数次革命，每次效力皆胜于前，末次未知由何处运动已成功。孙公名盛一时，北京政府悬赏七十万两缉拿，而公目的终达。其进行方法除其亲密党人外，无以知之。将来北京必有遭扰。因其过信于袁世凯，自行辞职故也。"

法人花诸那在南京谒见孙公，与之同食，笔述〈云〉："所遇中国人太多，惟公表出其无虚伪，及具忠诚。有著者谓公奸狡阴险，与我所见，其神色完全反对之，其颜容实有表示一种忠诚态度。"花先生知孙公最深，及常与言论，且深知其历史，因其时常亲近以研究之。至于讥诮孙公者亦有之，西人有毁孙公为一游说串谋者，又谓理想无济于事者，不合于有何重大担负者。花先生见孙公乃深精伦理于国事，及于改良社会，孙公不独为一理想家，实一经国之实行家也。

当时外国人最亲近孙公者，乃访事著书者佛烈打力麦哥灭，往中国为访义和团乱事，报与英、美杂志，在中国及附近地方经已十二年矣，其评论最为真实者。笔述云："孙公虽未从学政治学堂出身，而能激动民意，结合党人以行革命。孙公显有天演特授精神，而为中华民国元首，世人眼光多未能测公之万一。公乃一显明、忠直、恳切之人，具有高尚心志，数十年来无稍畏惧。及见于事实，其大功德被举为总统时，民众认识矣，其先觉在其祖国崇拜矣。当时告辞总统大位，令举袁世凯，其维新党人为其后盾者反对之。公心信袁氏，同外国通达人亦表同情。公辞职后，为一平民之孙逸仙，将所收复之国权还诸民众，并建新政府以垂久远。"

孙公退职之后，为铁路总办，因知中国之退化原因，乃欠交通之弊。除通商口岸附近地方之外，皆崎岖道路，铁路只数千英里。满洲政府反对筑铁路，初筑铁路数英里时，政府购之，将铁轨起出废之。惟公非属于工程师，其铁路计画［划］甚为草创，又无款项以行此极大之工程，故计划终未实现。

孙公信其能向欧西各国借款，供其政府以行其计划，对于此事，已同花诸那商议。花先生答云："法国资本家皆属谨慎，借贷非敢冒险也。"正在言语中，前清摄政王入见。花先生曰："见此王子来见平民之子，大有可观，此人为颠覆清朝者。"是晚袁士［氏］请宴，皇子同公在座，花诸那亦与焉。是晚之宴会，诚为服从民国之意也。

　　袁氏特请花诸那调查政府财政部。他察得其泥用古法，及非常混乱，即呈其新计划，欲代改良，但袁氏顽锢，不能用其议。此法人乃公开中学之教习，及一通达之旁观者，其判断人才甚有诚力，其判论袁氏，方知孙公之举动光明也。伊云："袁世凯性情阴险，举动残暴，令人莫测云。孙公深知袁之历史而反信之，成〔诚〕一奇事。"有一美国人在高丽识袁者曰："其骄奢僭妄成性，惟其能练成中国军队，得下属心，此乃其善用权术所致。"又云："袁氏时常斩决华人赌犯及其他犯人，常将高丽良民下狱，充公其家产以为己有，并无畏惧之心，惟能真心待其恩人及其朋友耳？"

　　麦哥灭论袁乃纯正中国人，谓他有才能，堪以管理国事者，惟不谙别国言语、文字，未出过洋。革命党视之为狡猾背信者，当受职行礼时，宣誓谓保守约法，一有实任总统选举，他则告退。

　　孙公退职荐袁自代，外国人信袁为中国有势力之人，能巩固政府，预料可以利中国及永享其商务之权利，而不至民众之反对，屡年加增纠纷也。孙公未久自知信袁之错。俄、法反对承认民国，因此有碍袁之外债计划。袁尽用其财政，以编散南军，而增北军。未得参议院之认可，乃违背约法，袁与其顾问向五国银行团议成大借款二千五百万磅〔镑〕。五国银行团既得其本国政府允准，参议院奋起反对，欲废去此借款约章。真正民党议员主张尤力，布告谓未得参议院同意，何以同五国银行团借款于袁，因此结成革命反对最力精神，乃知袁由刻虏伯炮厂承买枪炮子弹，此款用徒〔途〕不依原议，实属非法也。

预料袁氏称帝

　　孙公再宣布袁氏之尊〔专〕横，求外国停止交款，因其实知袁氏用款推到民国，以遂其称帝之野心。当时花诸那适在中国，怨恨欧洲列强允准借款，因他信此能置中华民国于危险地位。伊赞羡威尔逊总统有先见之明，此等政策于合众国宗旨不合，故美人不加入银行团。花曰："民主声浪犹如潮涌，小论好恶，卒成事实。此主义发行于全亚细亚洲，在印度，在法属东京，在日本帝国，由此而达于中国。若用力以压抑之，徒增反响也。"

孙公欲免内争，实属无效，故有一九一三年七月武昌讨袁战事①。八月时，袁氏之精锐军队平之，多数民党被擒斩决，另悬赏侦缉领袖。此等专制手段，乃照满洲之旧习而行。

孙公此时已离中国。因是年五月，知袁欲用计加害，布告缉拿。及其逃脱后，对访员曰："有人语我，谓袁世凯开秘密军机会议，决定缉我及伍廷芳、李医生等，称为逆犯。伍廷芳同周在英租界可保平安。我在李医生院子，有人报告谓有一班兵士由上路而至，顷刻敲院门甚响，兵士骑墙而入。我认得管带余浩（译音），因知他乃一凶悍强暴之徒，在上海工务局当警长者。是时方知报告乃属真情。若被拿获，即拥至北京秘密审判，定为斩决矣。李医生前往开门，未启门时，摇手使我离去。未离住宅之前，袁世凯嬖人将李医生捆绑，饱以老拳。我因熟识地方，由后门山路走出。馀二人亦被拿，照李医生一样待遇。次早尚未天明，逃到南京住宅。该夜在途中有人语我，谓住宅夜间必有侦伺，故先到河南路友家。访得昨日下午有兵到住宅看守，并向夫人查问一回。

我之十三岁小女②往探外婆，在中途截问。我之受此欺压，比之英京使馆被困尚有过之。至此自知前数月手创成立之政府，今竟无功也。三星期之久，常欲与黄兴将军通讯，易屋同住，夜间往来南京一次。变相回家团住［聚］，至天明而出，夫人谓我出后，常有侦探看守。一日，有一上级军官乘醉施以横暴，将带病小女扯出病床，用枪头刀毁坏其床及家具等物。兵官谓若不说明孙公在于何处，即要提解夫人往北京。无奈下跪，表明千真万真不得而知。一九十三年六月十三号末次回家，夫人语我不可再回，须往黄兴将军处，免被陷害。

孙公逃回香港而至珠江，一星期内用去百三十五镑英金。由港搭中国船，船主熟识孙公者，因前在港澳行医时代，与他医病不受医金，他反索船费五百元。由港载至珠江，于言语中知伊为袁党，惟彼此熟识，方能心信。船至猪栏登岸，再雇艇到广州，船主及其同伴皆认识睨视于我也。该船主乃挑夫头目，在广州城报告地方官，谓我住

① 1913 年 7 月，李烈钧在江西湖口宣布起兵讨袁，标志着二次革命爆发，期间江西和江苏是主战场，宣布独立各省并无湖北或武昌在内。

② 孙中山幼女孙婉生于 1896 年，此时已 16 岁。

在省城。一日我在写字房休息，见他与巡警同行。我在武州黄兴将军营处，此人前来见我，欲照西式握手，我既见他在省城与警卫军司令龙济光同行，故见他一到武州，斥之，黄兴发令将他斩决。我欲见家人，黄将军帮忙寄信，助以款项，并取回音。未离该埠之前数日，我们往来埠中皆穿敝衣，在河中同下流社会同居。我知必有人思疑，因操口音不同，常觉不安，因有大偿［赏］格侦缉我也。黄将军同我落在沙艇，以为不能再遇黄，给船资三两，我给四元预备伙食一包，约八、九磅粮食，用旧衣包裹，以敷数日之用。当时约我们欲往美国，亦有人供给费用。若被艇家知之，断难逃生。在河陵，黄将军觅得船位，乘汽船而至香港，我则乘渔艇至澳门。未离之前，议妥再会。经十二日之拂郁，我喜欢到了日本门司，又喜闻黄将军依议五日前到了长崎，即时相会于内地海旅馆，此处乃约同避难之所也。"

孙公致书与袁世凯，谓他叛国奸贼，告以声讨颠覆袁氏如倒清廷也。

讨袁时期

孙公离国后，一九十三年七月武昌起义讨袁①。不二月，被残暴如前清所用以平乱手段胜之。当时，孙公知讨袁，其党人心志不如前时革命之团结，盖革命经已成功，其奋斗精神未免略为涣散。孙公征求北京行政及南方党人之进步非常关心，惟待东南各省预备，然后大举，若有能力则恢复约法，因见袁氏欲毁灭之。留居日本数月，复回上海，居于法租界②。

袁氏向来不信共和条理合用于中国，故由其得举总统之日，着手设法收集权势于中央，不计其应允以南京为首都，利用兵变，照旧在北京立政府。袁忧日本之野心图谋中国，又提防俄国在北方之行事。袁自信其权势足以镇压中国，故设法增长其势力。一九十三年十月，能令参议院举他为五年任之总统，排斥异己之议员，解散国会，专权自居。一九十四年，布告修改之约法，延长总统为十年一任，并授权

① 武昌起义，应是李烈钧在江西湖口起义。
② 孙中山于1913年8月到日本，两年多之后，于1916年5月才回上海。

委任继其职者。一九十五年，其将官表示决心拥袁氏为皇帝，袁氏遂运动数省劝进，求将民国改为君主立宪国体。袁用巨款，在国内外鼓吹，谓民众欲行君主政体。袁之美国顾问古德诺①博士谓共和政体不合中国国情，写成通牒，颁告各国。此人在德国学习宪法，因此论调带有专制气味。至于末段语曰："我实无疑谓一君主制度合于中国，胜过共和制度矣。"该博士之议论，或出于诚心，及居中国之外人亦以为然。北京英国钦使乃袁氏之老友，亦信之，惟其公使馆对于此政策无甚轻重。列强质问袁氏，详解其计划。拨文威卢深知中国大事者，谓以袁氏之品，虽居高位，亦不能有益于国。此诚深知袁氏者矣。

康有为曾作长篇论说反对古德诺博士，袁氏出全力以阻止其刊印，无效。其文一出，远近咸知。惟袁氏既已决心，于一九十六年春，谓顺承民意，改民国为君主，遂开洪宪新纪元。

西南各省反袁热烈，云南致一电云："若不取消帝制，即行革命。"并将袁之宣誓保全民国誓词，示知西南各省，与袁脱离，在广东组织讨袁机关。当时四川省报告讨袁，袁世凯积怒发狂，入房见其爱妾同新产儿子卧于床上，拔剑刺杀二命。后知计划难行，称帝不过数星期，于三月二十二号出上谕，取消帝制，仍为总统。袁氏之死，盖因征讨南方革命，以致财政支绌，忧闷而死。一九十六年六月一号袁世凯弃世②，黎元洪升任总统。黎乃不赞成帝制者之一分子，当其登位，串谋帝党者咸逃避焉。

留居上海

欲知孙公之由一九十三年至一九十六年六月在中国所经过之事实，须从简单上言之。在此时期，离去日本之后，乃留居上海，静候

---

① 古德诺（Frank Johnson Goodnow，1859～1939），美国政治学家、教育家。1913 年被袁世凯聘为总统府顾问。次年回美任霍普金斯大学校长。1914 年 11 月发表《中国新约法论演说》，认为袁世凯的《中华民国约法》更符合中国国情。1915 年 8 月发表《共和与君主论》，鼓吹"中国如用君主制，较共和制为宜"。

② 袁世凯去世于 1916 年 6 月 6 日，而不是 6 月 1 日。

时机。其于衣服、饮食，中西参半，惟极朴实，一生不吸烟、不饮酒。当时已患肝痛之病。有问其使费款项何从而至，因其时常款客，用款良多。当时有一美人在邮政局当职者，谓至少亦有担保信二万五千张经过信馆交孙公收者，此信件乃环球各处如美洲、澳洲、星加坡及别处而来者，料内并有付款。中国人反对孙公者，传说袁世凯授以一百万两以讨好孙公让位与他。又说日本人供给款项，俟其操权时然后酬谢。反面则有外国人及中国人谓孙公乃一谨慎忠诚者，不纳贿赂。此等谣传，往往对于大人物各处有之。因中国官场习惯，利用职位而行敛钱，及其通例之勒诈，当权者上行下效，无怪有此意见，谓孙公设革命之谋以敛钱。多数中外人皆信孙公高尚，断无敛钱之理。有一中国儒者，谓孙公及其从者为作伪棍徒，其实厚诬孙公耳。

地理学家富列度力高炉文于一九十六年八月往谒孙公，在上海法租界住宅内，此宅乃仿欧西款式，孙公亦衣西服，办事甚忙。当时广东讨袁起事，与之谈论革命之将来，约有两句钟。孙公云："革命事业虽有希望，惟大改革中国惟时尚远。"言语中露出有望日本帮助振兴中国，盖因此所生谣言，谓日本人供给孙公款项也。公曰："中国政事无所谓失望，惟我等或无生命见此。从根本上之大变政，实有此日也，因国民爱国精神已甚为发达矣。民众已了解此事，犹之种子已布，必有发生结果之日也。"

编者承孙公之命运动社会，在檀香山当隆记报馆翻译时，创设中西旷［扩］论会。闻公为国事奔走，第二次来檀，欢迎登岸，在隆记报馆设立机关，由此合集开设兴中会，创办寰球学生会檀山支部、四大都会馆、夏威仁①华人公所等会馆。曾当中西旷［扩］论〈会〉主席三任、记录五任，四大都会馆主席十任、英书记六任，学生会理财一任，华人公所主席六任、英书记六任②。历年厕身社会，皆欲提高

---

① 夏威仁，即夏威夷。
② 据郑东梦编：《檀山华侨》（第一集，檀山华侨编印社1929年版）"檀山华侨闻人录"载，陆灿曾当中西扩论会主席六任、记录五任，环球中国学生会理财员一任，四大都会馆主席十任、记录六任，夏威夷华人公所主席十任、记录八任，万那联义会书记十六任。

侨胞人格，奋起爱国精神，勉励青年学习中西文字，令入大学专科，以期报效于祖国也。孙公每于筹款，必有通讯，四大都会馆拨款及集众捐款已达万元，华人公所亦达五千元。此皆在檀岛对党国事务大略经过之情形也。

SUN YAT SEN——AS I KNEW HIM

(Memoris of Luke Chan, boyhood friend of Sun Yat Sen)

by

Luke Chan and Betty Tebbetts Taylor

"Overseas Chinese are the mother of the revolution. "

——**Sun Yat Sen**

Dedicated to the memory of my beloved uncle, Luke Ho Tung, first martyr of the revolution, my beloved father, Luke Lan Kook, who suffered six years imprisonment for the Cause, and all the sacrifices of the dare – to – die patriots.

CONTENTS

FOREWORD

All of the societies in Honolulu elected me as Chairman of the China Relief Association during the China – Japan war to serve without pay until August, 1946. At times I received letters from Mainland writers requesting the biography of Dr. Sun Yat Sen as I knew him. During this time, however, I was too busy raising relief funds to undertake such a large job concerning the life of this great man.

After V – J day the Relief Association dissolved. I then collected the data and pictures necessary to compile a book. On my visit to the Mainland, I called on Mrs. Betty Taylor at Los Angeles who had written to me through the San Francisco and Honolulu Chinese Consuls requesting what information I had concerning General Homer Lea. During my visit I furnishedher a short story which I remembered from Nanking, and she volunteered to help me write the biography of Sun Yat Sen.

In view of China's calamitous situation at present, caused by internal war, drought, floods and inflation, the funds derived from this book I willingly send to China to relieve the sufferers.

I have long thought that the real story of Dr. Sun Yat Sen should be told by a Chinese, for the benefit and better understanding of the Occidental world. Many books have been done on Dr. Sun, but always from either an American or European point of view. The Chinese are aware that many of these works are incorrect as to statement and in the picture they give of Dr. Sun, yet nothing has been done to substitute the truth for the fiction.

Like all great men of whom the truth is obscured by legend and mystery, the character of Sun Yat Sen has become to the Occidental world, a combination of George Washington – of – China and mystic rebel. It is to dispel these half – truths that I have chosen to present this work. I am, perhaps, little better suited than many others to do the life story of Dr. Sun, but at least the facts I make use of are based on my own experiences and memories of past actions, and not merely on hearsay. For the Sake of China, as well as the rest of the world, I feel that this book, giving a clearer, truer picture of the first president of China, can fill a definite niche in the more complete understanding between the Occident and the Orient.

Luke Chan

I
Birth and childhood in the village

Sun Yat Sen and I were born in the same village, Tsuei Heng ——
meaning Transparent Jade Green —— a small Cantonese village in southern
China, located midway between the Shek Ki and Macao roads and the wa-
terway to Gold Star Harbor, forty miles from Canton and the Pearl River.
We were five miles from a market, depending on traveling peddlers for
trade, and ten miles from a village of any size, Tong Ka, which means of
the " Tong family", a settlement of some two thousand houses. We were
all more or less related, my grandmother being of the Tong family. Her
brother, my grand – uncle, was chief elder of Tong Ka.

Our own village of a hundred brick houses with tiled roofs, surrounded
by the usual low Chinese wall, with a sprinkling of mud grass – thatched
farmer's huts on the outskirts, enjoyed, due to its remoteness, a certain self
– goverment even under the Manchus.

Now and then the mandarin and Manchu collectors appeared to harass
us with their harsh, high – handed methods, sometimes setting fire to a
thatched roof merely for sport, but more often they left us to pay the district
magistrate a yearly tax on the rice fields and let it go at that. We were too
small for them to worry about. There were hundreds of such villages in
Kwang Tung at the time.

Because of this call upon our own resources for self government, the
people of Tsuei Heng, developed an independence of spirit very marked
amongst the younger men. This was to be reflected most strongly in the
character of Sun Yat Sen, and no doubt was the beginning of his rebellion
against oppression and stagnation.

Tsuei Heng was an ordinary agricultural settlement of the Fragrant Hill district, and was later renamed Chung Shan in honor of Dr. Sun. Surrounding it were the mountains Plow Point, Buffalo Head, and Five Spice, which brought the live – giving streams from Golden Betel Spring and mountain Gate to water its rich rice fields. Most of the rice farms of three to five acres, were owned by landowners either in our village or in one of the larger cities, but were worked by tenant farmers who lived on the soil with their families.

One of the tenant farmers occupying the mud – lined house of a ten mow farm, about three and one – third acres, on the edge of the village, was Sun Tat Sung, father of Sun Yat Sen. He eked a modest living from the soil to support his wife, two sisters – in – law, two sons and a daughter. One of the boys died quite young, leaving only the son, Ah Mi, about fifteen years old, and a little girl. It was a house of hard work but one of intelligence and forbearance. This it itself was unusual, particularly at a time When China, under the yoke of the Manchus, was steeped in tradition and backwardness.

Being seven years younger than Dr. Sun, I cannot of course recall the day of his birth, but I believe that I can picture it for you correctly. It was the month of November, in the year 1866. America struggled in the aftermath of a Civil War; Europe marched blindly towards the Franco – Prussian war, which started four years later, while China basked in her ancient traditions, a sleeping dragon under the iron heel of her Manchu conquerors.

In the village of Tsuei Heng, the mountains stood stark and barren. It was crisp but not cold, a wind from the north scattered dead leaves round the temple door. Inside the temple, the three village gods sat in stolid silence, two female idols with the male god between them. He was Buck Dai, North King, chief god of the village. A formidable idol, clasping a sword in his hand with one thumb up thrust towards heaven. Here the villagers burned their incense sticks and offered their prayer papers in the hope that fate might be kind to them.

Buck Dai had been much in the thoughts of the family of Sun Tat

Sung, of late. The farmer, his wife and two sisters – in – law, had discussed him late of an evening, While the two children of the house listened in awed silence. The wife of Sun Tat Sung, a dark, small – footed Punti woman, about to bear another child, had had a disturbing dream.

She explained to her husband, " In my dream, Buck Dai came to me in sorrow. He wept with his long hair about his face, as if the child I carry shall bring him harm. We must avoid such catastrophe, and appease the god by dedicating the child to him. We must name him Tai Cheong —— Image of the god. "

There was some argument with her husband on this point, but she insisted so strongly, that on November twelfth (not second, as so many books place it) when a son was born to Sun Tat Sung, he was given the milk or first´name of Tai Cheong, in the hope that being dedicated to the god, he would not harm him. Fate, however, had marked Tai Cheong, to oppose not only village gods, but nations and dynasties as well.

Tai Cheong, who was to become Sun Yat Sen, grew up in the village living the usual life of a farmer´s son in a remote Cantonese settlement. He was small and well – formed, with the round face and dark coloring he inherited from his Punti mother. He was quiet, studious, sincere, but even as a child rebelled against convention. Most of us were not required to do much at home, but Tai Cheong had small chores to perform for his father. When sent with a long bamboo pole supporting two earthenware jars to fetch water, he is known to have broken the jars, wipe water and mud along his sleeve, and tell his family convincingly:

" I fell and broke the jars, so I could not bring the water. "

This worked very well until his elder brother, Sun Mi, unknown to Tai Cheong, watched the performance one day from behind a tree.

" It is better," said Sun Mi, catching him by the scruff of the neck and wielding a bamboo rod with vigor, " to make sure no one witnesses your deception before you practice it!"

The village maintained two co – educational schools in the Chinese fashion in the clan temple. Here every child attended from dawn to dusk, with only a break for breakfast and dinner. We were presided over by a middle – aged male teacher, of a decidedly strict disposition, who marked our daily lesson to be read aloud by the entire class and then individually, by memory, with our backs turned towards him. The wealthier pupils each brought their own small writing desk and seat. The rest sat on the worn ones provided by the school. There is much to be said against the slowness and monotony of the Chinese scholastic method, but though it teaches little in the time alloted, it does teach that little very well, and a boy having learned his three word classic in this manner is not likely to forget them. Years later, Dr. Sun told me that he still remembered the early exercises of the village school.

There was not much free time for any of us, but what entertainment we found during our recreation had to come from our own initiative. On the Festival days of New Year, Decoration and Full Moon, which were our only days off from school, with the exception of a month on Chinese New Years, we played two games with great gusto.

One, Jumping Frog, was similar to the American hop – scotch. Tai Cheong, liking anything requiring quickness of wit and limb, took a leading part. Four boys each place a shoe, two feet apart in a straight row, first hopping on the right foot completely around them, next going in and out between each one, and finally over the shoes. The winner must hop to the last without touching or making a mistake. Tai Cheong was good at this, for he was unusually agile and quick.

Another prime favorite was Sugar Cane Splitting. We placed a long stalk of cane (after first buying one) perpendicularly on the ground, with a small knife on top. In turn, each boy would take the knife and in one stroke, attempt to cut off as long a strip of outer skin as possible. The one with the longest strip got to eat the cane as a reward while the rest of us paid for it. Tai Cheong often ate the cane, which I seldom did, I am sorry to relate. Other games are flying kites, kicking a feather shuttlecock, and batting sticks.

About this time a relative of mine died in Shanghai, and his remains, according to Chinese custom, were brought back to his village, Tsuei Heng, by his son for burial. The boy, Luke Ho Tang, was an uncle of mine, though merely a few years my elder, and at the time was about twelve or so. He remained to go to school in the village and he and Tai Cheong became fast friends.

Luke Ho Tang was something of an oddity to the rest of us. He had been born in the great city of Shanghai, and was quite experienced compared to the rest of us. He was a fine scholar, a clever artist, and something of a musician. He was extremely progressive in his views, and shared Tai Cheong's discontent with the fear and apathy of the village people in regards to the Manchus. He was a quick, active, bright – eyed boy with an insatiable curiosity, and was capable of a fanatical loyalty once aroused. This was to be proven beyond doubt later, when he made himself the first martyr of the Revolution. The mutual attraction between Tai Cheong and Luke Ho Tung grew into a close friendship that was to last throughout the life – time of both men.

At this time there was much talk in the village, of Hawaii, where many of her sons had gone to become merchants or land – owners, and where, from the glowing letters received in Tsuei Heng, life was much better and easier. Among those who had prospered in Hawaii was Sun Mi, elder brother of Tai Cheong. When at last a letter arrived from Sun Mi, asking his father in most respectful form, to allow young Tai Cheong to join him in Honolulu and there attend school, he was delighted. Ever since Luke Ho Tung's arrival, with his tales of the outside world, Tai Cheong had been anxious to travel. Sun Tat Sung outfitted his son, and there was a sad farewell on the part of parents, aunts and school chums —— especially on Luke Ho Tung's part. But to Tai Cheong it was all high adventure! I think that he always liked to travel, even under the harassed and uncomfortable conditions of his later life.

A boy of thirteen, still small and dark, with a quiet but eager inquisitiveness, he journeyed to Macao to sail on the English steam – and – sail ship, S. S. Grannock, in 1879. He said that he meant to miss nothing on this, the beginning of his journey through life, and he was as good as his word. On board ship, he spent most of his time asking questions of the people who spoke his language, and visiting the engine room to view the mechanical monsters working there.

Three weeks later after a thoroughly enjoyable voyage, he landed in Honolulu, dressed in his Chinese garb with his queue piled up neatly under his round silk cap with the red button on top. He was met at the dock by his brother, Sun Mi. Again there were new sights everywhere for a Chinese village boy. The buildings, the palm trees and pounding surf, the white people with their light skins and blue eyes, speaking such a strange tongue, and the colorful Islanders themselves.

Tai Cheong, busy watching the sights before him, barely listened to Sun Mi, explaining that the school he was sending him to was called, Iolani —— an Anglican Mission School, presided over by Bishop Alfred Willis. It was unfortunate that Sun Mi lived on a distant island, Maui, where he had a cattle ranch. This made it necessary for Tai Cheong to board at school, and so he visited his brother only now and then. If the truth were known, however, Tai Cheong was just as well pleased to be on his own away from family dictatorship.

Bishop Alfred Willis, later my own teacher when I went to Hawaii, was an unselfish and unusual man. He took great interest in the young Chinese he gathered about him, and the education he gave them was sound and thorough. He had purposely made it easy for them to come as boarders, charging $150 per year for everything.

Bishop Willis took a great interest in Tai Cheong, who spoke no English, but applied himself diligently and seriously to his studies. Needless to say, the education he obtained at Iolani, was entirely different from our monotonous recitations of the Chinese classics in our village school. Everything was new and fascinating to Tai Cheong, and for the first time he began to get a complete picture of the world and its affairs. This inclined, however, to make him even more discontented with life such as it was lived in China.

He made excellent progress, so that in 1882, three short years after entering Iolani, he was awarded second prize in English grammar. The prize, a book on China, was presented to him publicly by the King of the Islands, Kalakaua.

By this time he spoke fluent English, and maintained an avid interest in everything about him —— perhaps too much so, for on one of his visits to Sun Mi, he informed his elder brother that he wished to be baptized a Christian, with the rest of the pupils at Iolani.

Sun Mi was shocked, naturally, for in his wildest dreams he had never imagined such a turn of events. He sent his younger brother to school for one purpose only, to get an education. Furious at Tai Cheong's suggestion that he wished to abandon his native gods for a new one, he forbade him to give it another thought. Sun Mi also wrote at once to his father explaining the matter fully, and orders came by the next post to send Tai Cheong home immediately, Where, Sun Tat Sung added, " l will take this Jesus nonsense out of him. "

Tai Cheong departed with reluctance on the first steamer sailing for Hong Kong. On the journey inland to Tsuei Heng, he boarded a native junk that passed the little island of Cap Suey Men. Before reaching the island the captain called for each passenger to submit to a search by the custom officers. If any argument arose, of course, it would go hard with them.

The officers were greedy officials and in some cases demanded presents as a bribe. After the first inspection, Tai Cheong repacked his baggage. Shortly a second set of officers appeared and demanded that he open them again. Again Tai Cheong submitted wordlessly. It was adding insult to injury when still a third set —— this time opium inspectors came up with swords rattling, to request another search. Hardly had he closed his bags when a fourth set, armed and dressed in uniform, explained that they were Kerosene inspectors and must again search his bags. This was too much for Tai Cheong. With some asperity he told them that his bags had already been examined three times, and that if they would glance at the size and shape they would see clearly that there was no room to pack any such large item as kerosene.

The officers promptly turned on their heels and marched off.

This action threw the captain and the other passengers into a panic, " Any show of resistence," they wailed, " will only make trouble for us all! The ship will be detained until they feel like issuing us clearance papers! Now we cannot start in the morning. "

Tai Cheong replied calmly, " I will appeal to a high officer for you, when the ship makes port. "

At this the captain and passengers laughed. They told him, " There is no such thing as appeal here. If you do go to a higher authority it will only make it harder for us. "

The captain told him of an incident in which a passenger brought some sausages from Hongkong for home use. Twice, in passing the greedy inspectors, they were taken from him as a forfeit. The third time he put poison in the sausage, and the same inspector, taking it for himself, was instantly killed.

This gave Tai Cheong an excellent chance to preach the need of reform. He told the people that such measures should not be necessary —— that a sound, free government would give every man equal rights and liberties. It is questionable whether he made much headway with this frightened little group, but in any case he had made his own bid for freedom against unjust authority, and had spoken his mind to his people. Oddly enough there were no repercussions as far as the inspectors were concerned. The ship was cleared and went on its way.

In the village we knew of Tai Cheong´s being sent for, but the seventeen – year – old Tai Cheong who returned reluctantly to remote Tsuei Heng, was an entirely different young man from the boy who had left some four years before. Westernization had left its indelible mark. He was full of new ideas, and more than ever dissatisfied with the old ways of his people. Where before there had been signs of personal independence and determination in him, there was now open rebellion and defiance.

Everything about the backwardness of village life dis – pleased him.

He realized poignantly, how little freedom and opportunity his people had, when compared to the rest of the world. Tradition and narrowed education, he saw, coupled with the harsh Manchu rule, held his countrymen in iron bonds which seemed all but unbreakable. He was by no means the first or the only young Chinese to feel this way. China was honeycombed with secret societies who hoped in one way or another to bring about a reform, or to overthrow the present government. And there had been sporadic but futile uprisings even, the latest and most nearly successful being the Taiping Rebellion of the forties which lasted fourteen years. But all had ended in failure, either due to the Manchu vigilance and censorship of all press and communications, or through foreign intervention. It seemed to most intelligent Chinese that a successful revolt and overthrow of the Manchus was almost impossible.

It is, perhaps, important to get a small but clear picture of China's political history, in order to understand what brought about the Revolution and its aftermath.

Under the Mings, who were truly Chinese, China enjoyed for the most part a benevolent rule of some two thousand years. There were of course good rulers and bad, as there have been in every land, but more often than not they were able and vigorous men who tried to the best of their ability to help the country and their people, and rule China in peace and prosperity. The system was a good one, for the times. The trouble was that it grew outdated, and the Manchus, who had by this time adopted it as their own, refused to change it.

The old system of rule consisted of the Emperor, or Son of Heaven, who resided in Peking, and was regarded as the spiritual and moral head of his people —— but it was supposed to be more of a father – children relationship. There were to be certain freedoms and duties of the children towards the father, but he in turn, was to guide them and protect them from harm. The Son of Heaven was an absolute monarch, but there were certain 'strings' attached to his power.

Each province had either a governor – general or a governor, who was a mandarin, and who ruled his own area as completely as a sovereign. He was merely required to send the revenues and reports to the Throne and otherwise was left alone. Public offices were filled through competitive examination, which meant that a high official was not able to ‵sell′or bestow ‵an office on someone at will. Promotion was on the basis of an unbiased review of his service record. All of these things were supposed to restrict the Emperor by lessening his control by patronage. There was also a Board of Censors, whose chief duty was to supervise the Supervisory officers and regular administrative officers, thereby imposing further limitations on Imperial powers.

In reality, it was a personal – relationship commonwealth of self – governing provinces, under the titular head of the Dragon Throne. Actual rule in the provinces was in the hands of provincial officers. Cities were run by merchants and craftsmen through their guilds, or chamber of commerce. Villages were run by aldermen or selectmen, or elders. Over each province ruled the governor, or perhaps a governor – general ruled several provinces. He was a mandarin, and directly responsible to the Throne, but he was not invited nor expected to take an actual hand in local government unless the necessity arose. Over him, of course, ruled the Emperor.

To the masses of the people, therefore, government was a matter of little importance. It flowed along as water, here turbulent for a time, there peaceiful and quiet. But under the Ming ruling, the people had a perfect right to rebel against and replace a bad or weak leader. This applied not only to local rulers, but to the Emperor himself. This right was a right of ‵rebellion′but not of ‵revolution′. It meant that in time of dire stress, they could replace a leader or ruler who had proven unworthy of office, but it did not mean they could over change the form of Empire or government itself!

Under this system, however, it is quite understandable that even when the Manchus from the north conquered China and took over the rule at Peking, the masses of the people were hardly concerned with the change in the beginning.

The Manchus were crude but clever. They recognized the main worth of the old Ming system of government which had worked for over two thousand years, and they decided to keep it, with a few additions of their own.

It was these additions, that at last brought the Chinese face to face with the bitterness of their defeat and incurred their undying hatred for the Manchus. From the beginning, the Manchus offended the Chinese by ruling in force instead of by moral authority, as had been laid down by the Mings. Afraid of losing their newfound power, the Manchus kept their army intact and placed armed garrisons in each province. Everywhere possible, they put Manchus over the Chinese m andarins and officials. This was fortunately not always possible, for the Manchus lacked enough able men to go around. Still the humiliation of those scholars and mandarins called to serve at court was a lasting one.

The Manchus put a strict censorship on the press, and on all communications. Eternal vigilance was the price they knew they must pay for victory. Their spy system was elaborate and far – reaching. It is no doubt partly responsible for their rule of 268 years.

In spite of their changes in the Ming system to suit their own convenience, the first hundred and fifty years of Manchu rule were not particularly bad years. In the beginning, there were several strong and able Emperors, such as Kang Hsi and Chien Lung, grandfather and grandson, who were shrewd, good businessmen, and indefatigable workers. Women were kept strictly out of politics, the Emperor took care of State matters personally, and there was a certain vigor introduced by the first Manchu rulers, that was good rather than bad for China.

The real faults of the Manchu rule, began at home —— that is, within the Palace itself. In order to insure their upbringing according to Manchu style, and keep them from corruption, the Manchu Princes lived a life of narrowness and solitude within the confines of the Forbidden City. The tutors were supposed to teach the young rulers all that they needed to know of the world and affairs on the outside, but one man cannot teach another the exact meaning of life. Life must be lived, to be fully understood, and the later Manchu princes were never given the opportunity of being more than robots of the Court. Chia Ching, Tao Kuang, were both weak, extravagant, licentious men. Under these later rulers, the Court became more dissolute and corrupt yearly. Women were beginning to interfere in politics, and with their own limited views and education, to add to the misunderstandings. Eunuchs, those wily creatures who had always lain in wait for falling power, were swift to seize it once the opportunity presented itself.

Next came the rule of children, Hsien Feng, nineteen when he became Emperor in 1850, Tung chih only five when he mounted the throne, and Kuang Hsu, a baby of four. This was a rule of regency, actually, and put into the hands of the Dowager Empress, Tsu Hsi, the power she had long been seeking.

The Manchus had slowly proven themselves unable either to control China or protect her, by a series of political fiascoes, first the humiliating and nearly fatal Taiping Rebellion which lasted fourteen years, next the opium wars resulting in the concessions to the 'barbarians', and lastly, the Russian demands for northern territory which had been met in 1860. All of these things had caused loss of face, not only in China but all over the world. The degeneracy of the ruling family, and the mounting tyranny of the Empress Dowager, by this time a ruthless and power – hungry old woman, completed the Chinese disgust with their system of government.

It is little wonder, therefore, that Tai Cheong, with hundreds of other active – minded young Chinese, saw the complete folly of the system and wanted to change it. I do not think that he wished to bring about the change himself, at this time, but he did hope to help stir others up to the pitch of doing so.

He often discussed the subject with my uncle, Luke Ho Tung, for they were equally interested. Luke Ho Tung, in fact, want so far as to volunteer his services to drill with the Manchu troops, who came from the yamen at Canton to gather recruits. When he returned from his outing, he drew Tai Cheong aside and told him in disgust:

" Fifty well trained soldiers could rout an army such as this one, and storm the Tiger Gate Port which guards Canton. "

" Why isn´t there such an army, then?" asked Tai Cheong thoughtfully. " If there were, we could seize the government and China would be able to take her rightful place among the world powers. Why isnt there a man to start this thing?"

Luke Ho Tung laughed, and said, " Perhaps you are the one for the job. "

They were merely words spoken in jest, on Luke Ho Tung's part. But in the progressive, idealistic mind of young Tai Cheong, they implanted the germ of the idea that there was a job to be done for China, and that the game was well worth the prize.

Revolt, any kind of revolt, was now uppermost in their minds. Discussing the fruitless Taiping Rebellion, a movement started in 1846 by Hung Siu Tsuen, as a Christian movement, but which later grew into an organized revolt against the Manchus, the boys remarked that the Rebellion had begun with the destruction of ancient idols.

Tai Cheong got an inspiration from this. He decided he would, with one sweep, cut the ties that bound him to gods, family and tradition. He drew a few of us aside, including Luke Ho Tung and myself, and said since his return from Hawaii, he had been forced to burn incense in the temple, but he had done it simply as a ´gesture´, that he didnt believe in it. If we were shocked, we were too excited to show it after we heard his next proposal. He said that he would take us to the temple and wipe out some of this superstition by despoiling the very god, Buck Dai, to whom he had been pledged at birth. This was a tremendous step for a Cantonese youth in a small village of southern China, with nothing to back him up but a great ideal and a grim determination that what he was doing was for his people —— for China.

We went to the temple in broad daylight, but there were no people there, merely a guard asleep outside. Leaving two of us to watch the guard, Tai Cheong and Luke Ho Tung entered the temple. Luke Ho Tung carried a pocket knife, and while Tai Cheong broke off the upraised finger of the god,

Buck Dai, he in turn scraped the paint from the cheeks of the one goddess.

Of course my companion and myself were so curious about what was going on inside the temple that we failed to see the guard wake, and at once the alarm was given and we all fled to our homes. Tai Cheong had been seen, however, and recognized as the ring – leader. From the background I have given previously you can imagine some of the consternation that spread through Tsuei Heng like wildfire. This dastardly, infamous act was without parallel!

The elders rushed to the home of Sun Tat Sung to inform him what his bold son had done in the temple. Sun Tat Sung was full of excuses and humility for Tai Cheong and his entire family. He did not know what had made his son act in this manner. He explained that he was abashed, humiliated, angry and completely bewildered. The elders argued in turn that the gods could not be appeased, might even destroy the whole village unless Tai Cheong was banished. The defenses and arguments of his family were of no avail against the strength of the entire village. It was certainly not how any of us expected our prank to end, but Tai Cheong was forced to leave Tsuei Heng in disgrace. I say that none of us were prepared for the final result of Tai Cheong's defiling the gods, but Tai Cheong himself was quite aware of the danger when he planned and executed the move. I was to learn in later life, that he never did anything without first weighing both cause and effect against the final result. Perhaps that is why he was perfectly cool and collected when he left the village in disgrace, and started out on his own at last. I have never known him to be confounded by any event, no matter how momentous, and he began his journey to Canton, though alone and without funds, in exactly the same calm manner in which he later accepted the first presidency of China.

II
Education for Medicine—
Marriage—First Revolt

I will no longer refer to him as Tai Cheong, for the milk – name only applies to his childhood and youth in the village. Since he left Tsuei Heng with a new ideal and principle —— almost a new character, I will anticipate his own action myself, and call him Sun Yat Sen.

He arrived in Canton without funds, friends, or even a trade. He realized that he possessed one valuable asset, however. He spoke excellent English due to his Iolani training. Young Sun Yat Sen approached one of the heads of the Anglo – American Hospital in Canton, and was able, due to his linguistic abilities, to apprentice himself as general handyman and interpreter. Though his duties were many and of slight importance, he realized once again how outmoded were the ways of his own country's doctors with their superstitions and inadequate cures, when compared to the skill of modern methods.

Dr. Kerr, one of the staff doctors, became a friend and admirer of the serious, industrious young Chinese. One day he told Sun of a medical school for Chinese to be opened soon by mission society in Hongkong. Dr. Ho Kai, who graduated as barrister and physician in Scotland, came back to China with a Scotch wife, whose death left him some funds and he sponsored a hospital with the aid of Hong Kong Missionary. The school was named Alice Memorial Hospital after Dr. Ho Kai's wife. At once young Sun Yat Sen was inflamed with the idea of helping his people through advanced medicine. " I want to attend that school," he told Dr. Kerr, who was delighted to secure such an avid student for the new venture.

Back in our village, however, certain events were taking place that would also effect the life of young Sun. His father had died a year before, and his mother, according to custom therefore, since her son had now reached the age of twenty, wrote him that it was time he married. She had selected the daughter of a neighboring villager, Lu Szu, a Punti, like Sun's own mother. Because it would have been unheard of for even such a rebel as Sun Yat Sen, to refuse to obey his mother's wishes, he dutifully returned to Tsuei Heng for the marriage. He did not know the girl, had never seen her, nor would be until after the wedding ceremony, for this was also according to custom. It was an attractive wedding in the old Chinese style. As soon as he was married, however, Sun Yat Sen returned to Hongkong to prepare for entrance into medical school. While awaiting the school opening, he decided to have himself instructed for baptism by an American Congregational missionary. His life at this time seemed to be a combination of the old and the new.

In June 1887, Dr. James Cantlie arrived from England to open the Chinese Medical College. The students began their classes in the fall, and from the start, Sun proved himself a capable, sincere, and hard – working student. He attracted the attention of Dr. Cantlie, who seemed to take great interest in him as a person as well as a student and potential doctor. As with most of Sun Yat Sen's friendships, this one blossomed into a loyal and lasting one.

Sun made few close friends however, amongst the students. Those that he did draw to him, through his intense yet outwardly calm feeling for China, he told of his hope for a new government, and the crying need for proper education and agricultural advancement. These young men began to see, through Sun's eyes, the demands that their country had a right to make upon any group that governed her. Such thoughts were radical in the extreme. Yet the basic principle as Sun explained it, was simple. The people must be fed and educated. Through intensive agriculture he would accomplish the former, through advanced educational methods and modern equality, the latter. After that there was no reason why the people should not govern themselves. It was a stirring thought to these young students

—— as always the receptive hot – bed of revolt. But no one knew what to do about it. No one seemed to have a workable plan for action, not even Sun Yat Sen, at this time. He felt passionately, as they all did, that something must be done, but he was in the dark as to how they should proceed. Sun, therefore, continued to absorb his medical education with the quiet fervor of which he was capable. He still thought that he could best serve his countrymen through the medical profession.

All of China was honeycombed with secret societies of one sort of another. They had long been a fashion´ in China. But most of them were long on talk, while short on action. One active younger group though, the Triad Society, was headed by a classmate of Sun´s, named Cheng. Also active in the group was my young uncle, Luke Ho Tung, and because of the close friendship involved, Sun Yat Sen also took an interest. Various historical events spurred the society on to greater effort in spreading their Revolutionary doctrine. For one thing, the Japanese succeeded in annexing Formosa. This proved to the interested young men that military strength and ´modernism´ was essential to national safety. In the spirit of their new nationalism and military interest, Luke Ho Tung designed a flag, a white sun on a blue sky, later to become the Chinese Nationalists flag. When Chiang Kai – shek led the northern expedition from Kwang Tung to Peiping the nation was united and then adopted the red ground with white sun and blue sky in the left corner, as the national flag of the republic of China.

Studying day and night, Sun succeeded in being the first graduate from Medical College in 1892. That same year in Hong Kong he was baptized a Christian with Luke Ho Tung. He continued slowly but surely to discard the old ways of his people, mental, physical, and spiritual. He formally dropped Tai Cheong now, and called himself Sun Yat Sen. Sun, of course, was his last name —— such as Smith or Jones would be. Yat Sen, translated roughly into English, carries the meaning of a genii (genius?) of freedom, or in the broader sense, one who dares to follow his own dictates.

Going into practice however at this time, was not easy. In the first place the Portuguese at Macao, where Sun chose to start his practice, were jealous of the young Chinese with modern methods who was a threat to their own business. On the other hand, the Chinese themselves had to be won over to a Chinese doctor who forsook the ancient methods and practiced in a modern way.

Business was very poor, from the beginning, but Sun proved himself an excellent doctor and surgeon on the few cases he did attend. To while away the time in Macao, Sun discussed politics and government with members of the various secret societies. He was amazed to find so many young men who seemed to share his own thoughts and hopes for China. Many of them were former missionary students like himself, who had broadened their outlook through travel and occidental education. It was natural that they should see the shortcomings and backwardness at home upon their return, and want to do something about it. What young student even today, returning from a big college city, does not find ill comparison in his home town? And in this case, the contrast was so great that there could be no comparison at all. There was no use in appealing to the government in this case, for it would net them nothing but imprisonment and severed heads. Nor could they expect aid from the older people, for they were either too steeped in tradition to consider changing things, or they were heartily afraid of the Manchus.

Although the Manchus had lost 'face' in the Japanese war and in the Russian and British demands, the Dowager Empress was still a complete power in China. Dr. Sun Yat Sen found that he was more interested in finding a way to make the wily old Empress do something for her people that he was in his medical practice. As he told one friend: " If I am only a doctor I can hope but to cure one patient at a time. If I help China to free herself, I can cure 400, 000, 000 at once!" And so the die was cast. Dr. Sun left Macao and his medical practice without regret, just as he had left the village of his birth, and for the same reason —— that he might help his people.

He returned to Canton with his friend Luke Ho Tung. Sun was a natural orator, and they soon pressed him into service. Many were reached through his voice. Though a calm, quiet speaker, his voice was clear and convincing to the listener. It was not easy for him at first, however. He practiced long hours to perfect himself. But like everything that he wished to master, this came to him in time. Besides being a fine orator, Sun was born leader, and his friends were quick to recognize it. They wished to do more than just make speeches about their dreams; they wished to bring them to reality.

Dr. Sun returned to Canton, setting up his headquarters in a drug store, using this as a 'front' for his activities. In 1893 he made a brief journey with Luke Ho Tung from Hankow to Peking to personally view the Manchu system of government. He found it corrupt and stagnate. The young revolutionists decided then and there to petition the government through Li Hung Chang, for a more progressive educational and agricultural program. The petition was instantly turned down by him.

The refusal of the government however, proved to Dr. Sun and his followers that peaceful ways could never accomplish their objective. They realized at last, that force ——revolution, could be the only answer! Now the Young China meetings were held in secret. They gathered money for arms. Everything was done in the strictest privacy.

The next year, 1894, Dr. Sun saw a chance for revolution due to the fact that the Manchu Government was busy fighting Japan. Funds, however, were vital to his cause, and he decided to go to Hawaii and ask Sun Mi for help. His brother was at last convinced of the worth of the new cause, and with Dang Yim Nam, another Hawaiian Chinese, became the first well – to – do merchant to join the cause. They both offered young Sun every cent they possessed and helped him win other local members to his new Hing Chung Hui party —— or China uplifting Society. So that when he left Honolulu in 1895 there were a little less than one hundred members for the new society.

Dang Yim Nam returned to China with Dr. Sun to help him set up a society headquarters in Hong Kong. They planned to use Canton as the springboard of their revolt.

At Hong Kong the society opened a false Kin Heng Hong, or Import Office, as a front —— while using an 'Agricultural School' at Canton.

On September 9th, due to a careless shipment of arms, a Customs official at Canton discovered six hundred pistols. Spies of the government had also notified the Imperial soldiers to surround the Canton headquarters where they arrested Luke Ho Tung, Heu See and Chu Kwei Chuan. Dr. Sun, on his way to the headquarters was warned off just in time to escape walking into the hands of the police.

I was in the village at the time where I had returned from Hawaii for my wedding, and though I knew what was going on, the rumors that reached the older villagers were disquieting. Luke Ho Tung gave himself like the zealot he was, to the Cause, even selling his young wife's jewels to aid the Movement. I had an Aunt living in Canton, and her letters concerning Luke Ho Tung disturbed the village very much. None of them, of course, had any idea that these reckless young men, whom no one in the village understood, were planning a revolution.

It was a sad beginning for the brave little party. And it had swift and frightening repercussions upon our village of Tsuei Heng! My Aunt wrote at once that Luke Ho Tung had been taken prisoner and that Sun Yat Sen had been forced to flee.

Dr. Sun, I learned from him later, had gone inland from Canton to the home of one of his Iolani schoolmates, Tong Phong, and roused him at midnight, asking him to secure a sedan chair so that he could travel to Macao and get a ship for Hongkong, where he might be safe in the British concession. He said he, wished to go to the United States Consul to see if they could help Luke Ho Tung.

Luke Ho Tung had steadfastly refused to give any information to the Manchus.

In Tsuei Heng, however, where I had just celebrated my wedding, we were having a small revolution of our own. The letter from my Aunt, which was received by a granduncle of mine who was elder of the village had completely demoralized the old man.

He kept jumping up and down from his chair – seat in his agitation, quoting from the letter, saying that those young men were crazy, that they would cause the loss of all the heads in the village! He wailed that warrants were out for both Sun Yat Sen and his followers, and since he was the elder of the village they would hold him responsible! He was so thoroughly frightened that he did not know what he was doing. I am afraid I was young enough to think it was very amusing to see him jumping about like a puppet in his long robe wondering when the blow would fall.

" Arent you afraid?" he asked finally. I replied that I wasnt. I added that Id bet my other grand – uncle, who was also the head of the village, Tong Ka —— and a much larger village, would not be frightened either. I suggested that he go to see this relative, if he were in a quandary as to what to do, and ask his advice. This seemed to please my grand – uncle and quiet his fears, but he begged me to go in his place, saying that he was old and infirm. He was in such haste that he offered then and there to go and get me a sedan chair for the journey. But I told him there would be plenty of time in the morning.

As a results (result?) I arrived in Tong Ka in my sedan chair early the next morning. Since grand – uncle was a mandarin, I must pay certain court to him in the old way, so I was decked in my best robes for the event. It seemed rather strange to me to go through all this ceremony after my free life in Hawaii, for I had been away at school also, and had just returned long enough to marry.

Grand – uncle's house, situated on a hill, was very impressive. His two brothers had houses on the same hill, and the three of them ran the village of Tong Ka, which had about two thousand houses and was the market town of our district.

Twenty – one steps led up to grand – uncle's house, and a lovely garden lay about it like a mantle. I was received at the door and went to salute grand – uncle with folded hands, bowing three times. He was an old man in full mandarin robes, with long thin moustaches which he stroked or yanked as the case may be, to show his emotion. When we were at last seated in the parlor we began according to polite custom, to discuss such things as the weather, the garden, the seasons, until as a signal that I might begin to discuss the real purpose of my journey, grand – uncle said shrewdly, " Now, why did you come to call upon me so early in the morning?"

I countered politely by saying, " Just to see how you were, grand – uncle. We don't see you often, and grandmother wishes to know how you are. "

Grand – uncle smoothed his moustaches and said, " You do not come this far, so early just for that reason. Come, tell me why you are really here. "

Thus bidden I could really get down to brass tacks as it were, so I told him the whole story of my village's woes, adding that the elder, my other grand – uncle, did not know what to do.

At first he was slightly amused at the antics of a few students, whom he considered upstarts but harmless. But when I came to the details of my Aunt 's letter concerning Luke Ho Tung, who was her nephew, that he was imprisoned and might soon be decapitated, my mandarin grand – uncle yanked both of his moustaches and jumped up from his chair, saying: " How dare you little villagers have the nerve to handle such a big business as the overthrowing of a government without money, soldiers, and warships? It is a rebellion! Treason!" He went on for some time, but I remained meekly silent until his rage had passed and he again sat down.

" You have had great experience," I said, " you must tell us how to proceed, and how to receive the Manchu soldiers when they arrive seeking Sun Yat Sen and the house of Luke Ho Tung. " We both knew, of course, that the houses and families of these two rash young men would be seized if available. They had gone however. Dr. Sun had sent for his family, who were now hidden in Hongkong.

Grand – uncle sat jerking his moustaches, first one then the other, while he thought. At last he asked me if the elder had a book on police – procedure. I said I didn't know. Grand – uncle got his book and said that the elder was to read the passages on dealing with warrant – servers. He added that the chiefs of the village should meet the soldiers politely and show them every courtesy, escort them around on their search (leading them as much out of the way as possible) and that we would find a passage in the book saying that these soldiers might be 'paid off' according to the number of miles they had come to serve the warrants. This seemed all that he could suggest. If the soldiers were paid off, and found nothing to 'seize' they would probably leave at once.

I returned with this comfort to my other grand – uncle, who received the book on police – procedure, reading it avidly. He proceeded to carry out to the letter, all the suggestions. But I took a few precautions of my own, putting men with guns in the surrounding hills, just in case we were in for a wholesale seizure or slaughter of the village. As it happened we had no trouble. Our soldiers were rather indifferent men who accepted their 'pay' and allowed us to lead them to Sun Yat Sen's empty house, and finally left us in peace. The Sun family had of course, move to Hongkong upon receiving word of the revolt.

Meanwhile Dr. Sun worked tirelessly in Hongkong to save his friend, Luke Ho Tung. He approached the American Consul, who interceded for him. He also got Luke Ho Tung's employers a Cablegram company, to swear that he was only a student engaged by them, and could not have been serious in his revolt activities. But all his friends had reckoned without the zeal of the young revolutionist himself. When the Consul went to the Yamen he discovered that Luke Ho Tung had confessed in writing! He explained to friends that he wished to become the first martyr to the Cause, adding that the Manchus could kill one —— but not the millions to follow the Revolution. He was beheaded fifteen days after the failure of the first revolt.

Dr. Sun sent word asking me to meet him in Hongkong. He was much upset at Luke Ho Tung 's death, yet determined to carry on for the revolution. He told me that he was going to take refuge in Kobe, Japan, and work from there until ready for another revolt. He asked me if I would take his wife, mother and three children with me back to Hawaii, and leave them in Sun Mi's care. He said that it was no longer safe for them in China. I agreed readily, and our party embarked shortly for the Islands.

I felt, when I left him there in Hongkong, that this was a new Sun Yat Sen —— passionately determined, yet cool and calculating as a general. Gone was the impulsive boy, Tai Cheong, and in its place was the shrewd, inflexible leader we had all been waiting for.

A thousand failures could mean nothing against such a dauntless spirit, in spite of the puny effort that had ended in black despair for so many close to me, after talking with Sun Yat Sen, I felt for the first time a definite hope for China and I was determined to help in any way possible.

III

In Japan and Hawaii

After our ship reached Honolulu, later settled Dr. Sun's family with his brother, Sun Mi, on Maui. We heard of course, directly and indirectly of Sun Yat Sen's activities in Japan.

Dr. Sun's friends had provided him with funds to reach Yokohama. He said that he had settled on Yokohama as a place of exile because it was close to China and would make and excellent point from which to conduct future operations.

The Chinese – Japanese peace made in 1895 enabled Sun to go to Yokohama. Yet even with peace he had to use every precaution to elude the Manchus who had placed a huge reward of $100, 000 on his head, and whose spies were thick in Japan. Besides this, the extradition law was in effect between the countries and, if caught, he could have been returned by the Chinese consul to China for trial and execution.

Early in his public career, however, he got used to these constant threats to his life, and if anything they seemed to stimulate, rather than intimidate him.

Since disguise was important at this time, he adopted western dress, grew a moustache and cut off his queue. Because he was very dark, he could easily pass as a Japanese. And indeed, in later life, people often said he resembled a dapper Frenchman, with his neat, dark clothes and clipped moustache, rather than a Chinese.

Dr. Sun stayed in Kobe for a year setting up headquarters to carry on his revolutionary work, with the help of his Chinese friends and Japanese sympathizers. He found the Japanese alert, and helpful and extremely interested in his plans. This was to have repercussions later, but at the time their aid enabled him to set at least the groundwork for future revolution activities. There was tireless effort on the part of Dr. Sun and his little band in isolation at Kobe, to carry on the work.

Hawaii was especially fertile as a field of sympathetic support to Dr. Sun. To begin with, we were all Cantonese and closely allied to him and to the first outbreak in Canton. Interest in the revolution and speculation as to Dr. Sun's success ran high in Honolulu in those early days. Because most of us had enjoyed a western education in Hawaii and the freedom of new ways, we were unusually aware of the need for a change in the old Chinese regime. We had all seen what progress and modern methods could accomplish, and we were anxious to help bring this change about for China —— in spite of herself if necessary. Dr. Sun realized the importance of this support from the progressive young China across the Pacific. He knew that he must have help both moral and financial, and nowhere was he more likely to find both than in Hawaii.

We learned that he planned to come to Honolulu early in 1896. When the Chinese Consul learned that he was coming, he tried to arrange a great reception. Then word reached him that Dr. Sun was the revolutionist leader wanted by the Manchus! At once he changed all of his plans and did not even greet Sun.

There were plenty of us to receive him, however. A great respect was already felt for the young revolutionist who had dared to defy the Dragon Throne. Those of us who had enjoyed the advantages of Iolani were acutely aware of the need for a change in China. But more surprising and more moving to Dr. Sun, was the honest interest and loyal support of the Elders who had come to Hawaii. Under the old system it would have been strange indeed to find men of venerable years following blindly such a youthful and radical leader. More than that, however, in this case, was the fact that Dr. Sun was revolutionist and a fugitive from their government. Their support was unanimous and unfailing —— indeed the new order of aroused thought had already taken hold and produced tangible results.

After visiting with his family and close friends, Sun began the real work of organization for the Cause. Even with the unflinching support of his countrymen, it proved to be slow work, yet Sun was untiring in his zeal and effort to place before all, his creed and his plans for China. He went about it much as a new missionary might go about instructing his first class of converts. He explained slowly, painstakingly, in simple language that they would understand. Not once did he adopt a flowery oratory, keeping instead to the simplicity of well – known symbols and everyday expressions. Yet his audiences, because of this honest simplicity were more moved than they would have been if he had ranted and raved. Always a quiet, convincing speaker, he developed into a powerful one as well.

After some months of speech making, during which time he laid a sound groundwork for complete understanding of the Movement, he called a meeting of some thirty men of standing, at the home of his friend, Ho Fon.

It was a most interesting meeting. Under Dr. Sun's guidance, it was decided to form a regular organization to be called Hing Chung Hui —— China Uplifting Society. Each member took a simple oath of allegiance in that they would keep faith with the society and its doctrine, be ready to aid the leader as requested, and at all times work to the best of their abilities for the Cause.

Dr. Sun was himself the first to be sworn in, placing his hand on the Bible and quietly asking God to witness his oath. The others quickly followed suit. For the most part they were young men, capable, vigorous and intense. They were the product of at least partial western education, and ideal compatriots of the zealous, progressive young leader —— Sun Yat Sen.

The next few meetings of the newly formed Hing Chung Hui saw a steady swelling of the rank of followers. But these young men wanted to do more than give money and listen to speeches. They wanted to personally take part in the freedom of China.

It was suggested that since actual fighting would be inevitable, some military training was essential to their cause. Without further ado, a young Chinese captain and a lieutenant, W. Yap and C. K. Ai, were selected from the ranks of the society, and a Dane, Victor Bache, was hired to head the instruction. He had been an army man, and though he trained his young Chinese, with sticks in the yard of Rev. Frank Damon, there was no lack of true military precision. The wheels were at last moving across the seas, for the Chinese Revolution.

Dr. Sun continued to gain support in the Islands, and money poured in for the Cause. Some $6000 had been gathered by June of that year, a large amount for those times, and much of it represented the entire savings of certain donors. Sun was exceedingly pleased, and decided to try the same methods of organization in San Francisco, where a large population of Cantonese had settled during the gold rush. He hoped to find the same enthusiasm and loyal support amongst the wealthy merchants and traders of California as he had found in Honolulu. He was cheerful and optimistic about traveling abroad alone, with the danger of Manchu spies still waiting for a chance to capture him. He seemed only to have one thought in mind ——the immediate and complete success of the Cause. Like Robert the Bruce, his failures only made him try again and again with renewed vigor and determination.

IV
California and England

During the first part of his visit to Honolulu, Dr. Sun met quite by accident, his old instructor —— Dr. James Cantlie. The Dr. and Mrs. Cantlie were on their way back to England, and had just stopped for a day in Honolulu. Dr. Cantlie had taken his wife and her Japanese maid for a carriage drive around the island. On their way, they were hailed by a man on the sidewalk whom they took for a Japanese. His hair was cut short, he wore western clothes, and had a short, trim moustache. Dr. Cantlie sent the maid to speak with him and find out what he wanted.

Sun laughed and spoke to the party in English. Even then they failed to recognize him and he had to tell them who he was. The Cantlies were extremely interested in his new efforts for the Movement and suggested that he come to England to further spread his doctrine, and that he be their guest while there. He promised to look them up if and when he got to London. At present, however, he explained, his interest was in California and its large Chinese population.

His ship sailed from Hawaii for San Francisco, in June 1896. Behind him he left an active and well – organized Hawaiian group of his countrymen —— nearly nine – tenths of the Chinese population of the Islands.

San Francisco's Chinatown —— a veritable 'small China' transplanted, was ready and eager to receive him. They were well aware of his work and had heard, from relatives in China and Hawaii, of the abortive first revolutionary attempt at Canton. His quiet, intense speeches did not fall on unresponsive ears. Rich and poor came to hear him and stayed to pledge their support in whatever means they were able. They joined the fast –

growing Uplifting Society, took the oath of allegiance, and money again poured in to finance the Cause.

From San Francisco, Dr. Sun made a short speaking tour of the small outlying California towns where Chinese market gardeners and farmers met to listen to his words. (Here, again, he found instant and loyal support.) Some had little to give but their belief in the Movement, but it was something that at last men were waking to the need for support and unified action. And again there were new members for the Progressives.

On his way across country to New York, his next goal, Dr. Sun continued his speech – making and organization of new branches to his society —— stopping over in the major cities. Everywhere he found enthusiasm amongst the younger men and at least a frank interest on the part of the elders. It was naturally harder for the older people to believe that anything could actually come of this young revolution.

Revolutions in China were an old story and quite common even in ancient times —— but they followed a certain pattern, more talk than action, and while a few were bloody and many were of long duration, they all ended in the same way by accomplishing little. Sun Yat Sen's idea of a free and democratic China, doing away with all of the old traditions, was something almost beyond belief. Terrible and wonderful in the extreme. If he could bring it about it would be magnificent —— if he failed, the people would reap the chaos of an inate (innate?) Manchu government.

To a man, the followers of Sun Yat Sen realized the extreme danger of their position. Not only to themselves, but to each member and branch of their family in China and abroad. At the first inkling of guilt, the Manchus would distribute death and seize property without mercy. Still, loyalty to the Cause, and to the new leader did not falter. Many gave all their property and life's savings, and dedicated their lives to the Revolution. It was amazing how swiftly the society grew.

In New York, Dr. Sun stayed with a friend, Tong Phong, one of his Iolani schoolmates, who now ran a curio shop. He intended to sail shortly for England. Unknown to him, word of his arrival in New York had reached the representatives of the Manchu government there, and when they learned of his journey to England, they wired the London Manchu Legation to seize him. Dr. Sun, of course, knew nothing of this when he sailed.

Usually he was very cautious in his travels. Knowing the danger of ever – present Manchu spies, he booked passage under assumed names, but for some reason, he felt quite safe in England. Word had reached him by now, of course, that the Chinese minister in Washington had done his best to have him taken captive and returned to China. But the plans had failed and Dr. Sun, not aware of the wire to the London Legation, considered himself quite safe.

In London, he went to the home of the Cantlies where he was warmly received, and where he stayed as an honored guest during his visit.

Dr. Sun had two objectives in visiting England at this time. One was to organize the local Chinese in his movement, the other to interest and enlist the financial aid, if possible, of some sympathetic Englishmen. He did not have marked success along either line at the time. There were few Chinese in England, and as to the English loan for munitions which he had hoped to arrange, they were kindly and sympathetic enough, but unwilling to involve themselves in so new and unproven a cause. They did not refuse him outright however, but suggested that they would watch and wait awhile, and he could then come to them again.

The blow fell on a quiet Sunday in October. While on his way to church, Dr. Sun was hailed by another Chinese who asked him if he were Japanese or Chinese. Since Dr. Sun had cut his queue and adopted western clothes, he was often taken for a Japanese. He explained to his countryman that he was Cantonese, and the other man saying he was also Cantonese, they spoke in Punti as they strolled along. Presently they were joined by another Chinese and the two urged Dr. Sun to come to their rooms for a talk. Dr. Sun explained that he was to meet Dr. Cantlie at church. Still a third Chinese joined them and the first one left. In passing a house with an open door, Dr. Sun was forced by the remaining two, to enter. He still suspected nothing until they slammed and bolted the door. He realized with a shock that he was inside the Chinese legation!

Ever since the Washington legation had wired them, of course, they had been on the lookout for him. They at once made it clear to him that he was a prisoner. A search of his person proved very disappointing since he carried no papers on him. But they knew that he must have left papers at Dr. Cantlie's where he was living, and promptly sent a representative to get them. Fortunately Dr. Cantlie refused to give them up in Sun's absence.

Dr. Sun said that Sir Halliday McCartney was his chief inquisitor at this time and he told the revolutionist that he was to be sent back to China by ship and would remain a prisoner until the ship sailed. The legation was much chagrined at failing to get hold of Dr. Sun's papers, for if they had managed this, they would have known the names and addresses of all these active in the Revolution and there would have been tremendous and dire repercussions in China.

For twelve days Dr. Sun was held captive in an upstairs room of the legation. He learned that he was to be shipped to China under the fiction of being a lunatic, and he knew that unless he managed to escape before he was put aboard ship, he would certainly be killed upon arrival in China. He made up his mind to try and get word to Dr. Cantlie. It was impossible to bribe the legation people but they had left him his money and the contents of his pockets.

Since his room was high above the street overlooking an areaway, Dr. Sun decided to write a message to Cantlie, wrapping it about a coin, and try to get it onto the sidewalk or street where some passerby might discover it. His first attempts ended in complete failure.

Either the paper came off the coins or they failed to reach beyond the roof, and at last when one did succeed in getting to the street, it was picked up by a legation member and a closer guard than ever was put on him. Almost in despair, Dr. Sun commanded himself to God and stood ready to accept his fate. He said afterwards that it was the only moment of utter defeat he had ever known.

With hope all but abandoned, since they had made it impossible for him to throw any more messages from the windows, Dr. Sun was sitting alone one day when a servant entered to replenish the coal fire. On the spur of the moment, he explained his position to the man and asked him if he could get a message to Dr. Cantlie's house. The servant was cautious but he at least listened to the story and finally accepted the scrap of paper Dr. Sun had written on, and the last of his money. The next hours of waiting and suspense were the longest of Dr. Sun's life.

His duties completed, the servant left the legation and from his high window Dr. Sun watched his departure knowing full well that it is his last chance of escape. He had wrapped 150 pounds about the note to Cantlie, telling the servant, " I am in grave danger here. They are going to ship me back to China and kill me. Here is a note to the only friend who may help me. He lives on this street. If you will deliver the note to him, there are 150 pounds for you. "

The servant did not go directly to Dr. Cantlie, however. He took the note and the money home to discuss it with his wife. Fortunately, she was a shrewd and astute woman, and says of course they must help the poor man. Scribbling a note to Dr. Cantlie herself, she took Sun's card and putting on her shawl, went to the Cantlie house to deliver it in person, even though it was eleven – thirty at night. She was afraid that she might get her husband in trouble at the Legation if his name was connected with the affair, so she has signed the message merely 'a Friend' and after slipping it under the front door, rang the bell and disappeared.

Dr. Cantlie coming downstairs in his pajamas found both notes. He wasted no time but dressed at once and set out for Scotland Yard. At the Embankment, the chief commissioner told him bluntly that it was nothing to do with the Yard and that they would not act. Dr. Cantlie, realizing the gravity of Sun's situation and the pressing time element, went in desperation to the Foreign Office where he had a personal friend. Here at last he got some cooperation. The friend carried the tale at once to Lord Salisbury, who without further waste of time, phoned Scotland Yard and told them to surround the Legation and rescue Dr. Sun.

This was barely twenty hours before Sun was to be spirited away to his doom. Burly plainclothesmen from the Yard formed a cordon about the Embassy where Sun was held captive, and an inspector with a derby hat and a no‑nonsense air about him, put a heavy thumb on the Legation doorbell.

At the sight of actual force, the Manchu ambassador was frightened nearly out of his wits. He played sick and sent his secretary to the door to deal with the barbarians. If one may judge, the conversation went something like this:

" I'm Inspector So‑and‑so from Scotland Yard. Is the ambassador in?"

" His Excellency is ill. I am his personal secretary. May I assist you?"

" Yes. We understand you have a certain Dr. Sun here, who is being held prisoner. We want to see him. "

" Oh, but there has been some mistake, Inspector. We have no such person here. "

" No? Then you won't object if we search the house —— we must follow up these rumors. "

" But —— you have no right. "

" I have a proper warrant. Either you produce Dr. Sun at once, or we search the house from garret to cellar. "

" This is an outrage against the Chinese Empire!"

" Maybe. But what you've got to understand is that you're not in China now —— you're in England! And the quicker you produce what we want, the easier it will be for you—— and your Empire!"

A few moments later, a pale but smiling Sun was reunited with his friend, Dr. Cantlie.

This was to be his narrowest escape, and also the most widely publicized, for the British newspapers made a field day of the event, getting Dr. Sun to write an account of his adventure for the London Times. In a twinkling the name of Dr. Sun Yat Sen of China spread abroad and became a worldwide topic.

The publicity pleased Dr. Sun, not for himself, but because at last his Cause was made clear to the world as well as his own people, and he hoped the soliciting of aid would be made much easier.

ı   He remained for a short time with the Cantlies, always studying and working for a better way to carry on his well beloved Cause. Dr. Cantlie later remarked upon the fact that Sun never let a moment go to waste.

He read constantly, military works, constitutional history, political science, in preparation for the great job ahead once China was ready to raise her place as a Republic. He knew that someone must teach them the fundamentals of the new form of government he advocated. But through all the hardships and seemingly insurmountable obstacles, he never lost faith in the dream he had for a free China.

V
Europe, the Straits and China again

When he left London, Dr. Sun made a brief tour of the other large European cities —— Brussels, Paris and Berlin. But there were few Chinese to be contacted and his real business lay in the Straits Settlements, especially Singapore with its large Oriental population and its numerous wealthy merchants.

The banking houses of Europe had given him only coy replies and vague promises. How, they countered, could they lend money to a new government that had yet to be formed? Their sympathy, however, was a latchstring for future use.

In the Straits Settlements it was quite a different matter. Here again, Dr. Sun found loyalty amongst his own people and concrete proof of their interest. Going about his work of conversion diligently and patiently, amongst rich and poor alike, he raised some $60,000 in funds. The Singapore people realized that it would be a long time before the blow for freedom could be struck with any hope of success. It takes time to lay the groundwork for a revolution. But they were patient and willing to wait. Singapore became and remained, one of the staunchest strongholds of the Revolutionary party —— always ready to give Dr. Sun protection or aid. And many times he took advantage of this, while on the run from the Manchus.

It was a constant source of amazement to those who knew him, how Dr. Sun managed to keep in close personal touch with all of his scattered branch societies, especially as he was always on the go. But he managed not only to keep track of the activities of each group, but also to get word to them of his own progress. Much of the correspondence came through Hawaii, where it was handled by the local society, which in turn routed news to Dr. Sun abroad, and also kept him supplied with funds for personal use, taken from the treasury.

Dr. Sun did not care about money as far as he himself was concerned. In later years I used to tax him about traveling with practically nothing in his pockets, telling him it did not look well for a leader of his position to have to ask for money as he went along. He would always laugh and say, " I dont need money. I get what I want wherever I go. " It was quite true.

When organization of the Movement was once established, he could travel from one end of the world to the other merely on his name. There was always transportation available, a house and food ready to his hand, funds when he asked for them —— though he seldom did for anything but a business transaction, and even motorcars and boats were obtainable if needed.

When Dr. Sun came to Hawaii after the failure of his first revolt, during which time my uncle, Luke Ho Tung, was killed by the Manchus, I told Dr. Sun that I would like to be a doctor myself and study medicine. Sun said: " Why do you want to do that? I am a doctor already and I have given it up. There is much greater work ahead. If you want to really learn something, study under K´ang – yu – wei, and learn politics and government. "

K´ang – yu – wei was a great Chinese scholar and liberal. He had been called to the court of the Manchus to advise the young Emperor, Kuang Hsu, on a more modern government.

But I told Dr. Sun that I was too old to go to school again. " Then, if you want to help me," said Sun, " go into politics here, organize the societies in Hawaii. " I told him that I would do that. I remained in charge of our society for many long years and often sent Dr. Sun sums of money upon request, from our treasury.

The job was made more difficult for me due to the fact that my father had been seized by the Manchu government on the rumor that he had some revolutionary connections, and for his sake I had to work quietly and under cover. I also had to wear my queue, though living in Hawaii, for ten years longer for his sake, since to cut it would have been a revolutionary act and might have caused his death.

The poor old man had long been retired, living in our native village, and of course had no connection with the movement. After the establishment of the Republic he became one of the elders of the district. He had gone outside one day to stroll about the rice patch when he was seized and imprisoned in Canton.

Luckily, he was a scholar and could write, and they made him something of a secretary. But for six long years he was to remain in prison, while I tried every way I could think of to bring about his release. In the end I brought it about through Wu Ting Feng, the Chinese ambassador to Washington, who effected his release, but in the interim I had spent $10,000 through the Chinese courts to no avail.

Dr. Sun wished to set up a permanent headquarters in Japan, first because it was close to China, and secondly, because of the large Chinese population at Yokohama and Tokyo. There were quite a large number of Chinese students then in Tokyo, and Sun thought that if he could gain their sympathy and interest, they in turn would be ideally suited to spreading his doctrine inside China. It was becoming increasingly difficult for him to enter and leave China, as the Manchu dragnet for him widened. Many of the Japanese were friendly towards his movement and gave him money for the Cause, and every aid available.

Although there was a large price on his head now, Dr. Sun managed to make many trips to China. Usually, he traveled in disguise and incognito, still it is a miracle that he escaped detection. He dressed as beggar, coolie, fisherman —— even as a woman on occasions, but his luck always held. He knew the importance of preaching his doctrine personally —— for almost the whole Movement was built upon his own compelling and magnetic personality. But even though he was always able to make even his 'mixed' audiences understand him, he knew that he could not possibly travel everywhere. So he hit upon the plan of writing out his teachings, and having them printed in small undercover revolutionary printing shops and later distributed to the various tea – houses throughout the land. Here they were read aloud to all.

This may strike you as a clumsy, slow way of spreading news, but it was in fact the only way, considering the complexities of the Chinese language.

The Chinese for the most part, speaking of the 400, 000, 000, learn and understand only the dialect of their particular province and class. There is no such thing as a 'universal' language in China, even today. It will be slow in coming. So that even a man who makes a speech to the multitude is translated again into each of the many dialects. Mandarin has always been the official and court language of course, but at that time only a few could be scholars or afford the time and leisure required to study it.

But though few could read, there was always at least one man available in every village who both read and wrote. He then would translate the paper to his local people. And the beauty of the written word was that though the spoken dialects differed to the point of foreignness to each other, the written word was always the same! Hence the same paper could be translated into each of the dialects by its local reader with universal ease. It was the solution to the problem of reaching all the people. So at last the people of China began to rally to the banner of the new leader and waken to the Revolutionary Cause. It was a slow process, this waking up of the Dragon that had slept long under the yoke of the Manchus, but the coils here and there were beginning, to tremble with life and the great jaws to flex themselves. Internal China was stirring again after two hundred and sixty years of lethargy!

The defeat of China in the war with Japan in 1894 – 95 clearly showed the world, and especially China, that a change of some sort was vital, else China would be conquered and divided. Even the Imperial Throne was aroused, and young Kuang Hsu, under the guidance of the scholar, K'ang – yu – wei, began a series of 'reforms'. In September 1898, he issued edits abolishing the use of Chinese classics exclusively in public examinations for office; encouraging Western education and travel; establishing colleges and modernizing the army.

All of these were sweeping changes, too sweeping as a matter of fact. Many felt that they should have come more slowly, not all at once. but the little group of reformers inside the Palace had a reason for haste. They knew that the wily old Dowager Empress would stop them if she could, and they meant to rid themselves of this danger. Young Kuang Hsu ordered his General, Yuan Shih Kai, to surround her palace and hold her prisoner while the reform was carried out. It was a bold move and would have worked, had the plot succeeded. But Yuan Shih Kai, a double – dealing, unprincipled man who had bought his way into power and did not intend to lose it, saw his chance of playing one side against the other to his own advantage, and went to the Empress quietly, with his own story. He told her Kuang Hsu had ordered him to put her to death. This was high treason of course, and the Dowager Empress now had all the 'proof' she needed to seize the throne herself. This she promptly did, with Yuan Shih Kai at her heels. The young Emperor was taken prisoner, held captive, and a huge price was put on the heads of K'ang – yu – wei and his brother with five other reformers who were beheaded. K'ang – yu – wei had escaped in a British boat. He took refuge in Japan as Dr. Sun had done, and the Empress swiftly declared all of the new edicts void.

Dr. Sun continued his written teachings which now found an even more eager audience inside China. For the most part, he used the classics and simple Chinese history to illustrate his meaning. He explained that the people needed better food, education and more freedom, in order to progress, and that China must progress to exist. In the past, he took pains to point out, corrupt governments had been overthrown, and therefore the people must have faith and now move without fear.

Also, the sporadic revolts continued under Dr. Sun. All told he was to try nine times before final success. Most of the early revolts failed due to poor or hasty planning, lack of coordination, or the untimely discovery by the enemy.

Once a barrel of arms broke open on the dock, giving the plot away. A second time two parties failed to unite their strength at the crucial moment. Again, gunpowder exploded by accident in a central warehouse. Even those most faithful to the Cause lost heart as failure after failure piled up. In Europe the Movement became something of a joke —— a zealot trying to move a mountain with his bare hands!

But Dr. Sun did not waver. If anything, his zeal burned brighter with each failure. He went doggedly ahead adding new tentacles to his octopus, welding them on with the fire and strength of his own determination.

China, however, was becoming an unsafe base from which to work and once more new horizons beckoned.

VI

The Organization of American and Europe

Although the Empress Dowager ruled the Dragon Throne once more as absolute monarch, since the fiasco of Kuang Hsu's reform attempt, it was recognized by the world powers and China herself, that the old way of government would not do for long.

China, through her enforced concessions to other nations, her loss of Formosa and Korea, had displayed to the world the extent of her inner weakness. In 1897 China had lost Kiao Chow to Germany. In 1899 Kwang Chow Bay was lost to France.

Even the Empress, with her hatred of western methods, was aroused to the need for China to protect herself.

She had two enemies now working directly against the Throne —— Dr. Sun and K´ang – yu – wei, who was preaching a constitutional monarchy from his haven in Japan. And her hatred of the barbarians whose outlandish mode of government had inspired these men, knew no bounds. She was ripe therefore for any suggestion from the opportunists and shrewd plotters of her court, provided they could help her get rid of the accursed foreign devils, whom she blamed for the whole thing.

While this turmoil brewed and bubbled in the Forbidden City, Dr. Sun went faithfully ahead with his own plans for a change of government. With unrest in the Imperial Court, anything was liable to happen, and he meant to waste no opportunity that presented itself.

From Japan he again started his circuit of Hawaii, the United States and Europe. His second world tour was even more of a success than the first —— mainly because the world was at last cognizant of the name, Sun Yat

Sen, and his work for China.

When he reached San Francisco, he found not only avid interest amongst the Chinese, but also amongst certain Americans. After his speech one night, Dr. Sun was approached by a young American hunchback, a student at Stanford University.

" I admire what you are trying to do for China," he told Dr. Sun, " I would like to throw in my lot with you. "

There was instant liking and respect between the two serious young men.

The American had been introduced to Dr. Sun, as Homer Lea, by the two young Chinese students who brought him to the meeting. They explained to Dr. Sun, that Lea was something of a military genius, and shortly afterwards Dr. Sun made the young American his military advisor. He also arranged for Homer Lea to go to China in the company of two young Chinese who were to sail soon from New York.

Dr. Sun again traveled his old route to New York —— stopping over in the larger cities to speak to his followers. Everywhere, the movement had grown and the society membership swollen to a remarkable extent. The local treasuries continued to gather funds for the Cause and even Dr. Sun was amazed at the speed with which his organization had spread.

In Europe, as in America, there was a more cordial welcome ready for him, but the banking firms still resisted any definite promise of financial aid. They did agree, however, to watch and wait.

At many times the Movement, for all its outward success, seemed futile to those who were close to it. Failure after failure began to daunt even the stauncher followers, and many advised Dr. Sun to give it up. But he remained firm in his determination to proceed, and I am convinced that it was his own intrepid spirit and iron resolve that finally brought about the success of the revolution.

Many people are inclined to regard the Chinese Revolution as merely a phase in the political history of the land. But when you seriously consider the stupendous obstacles involved, in all their ramifications, it is impossible not to realize that it was the greatest, most far – reaching change in the entire history of the nation.

Consider the background from which it had sprung. The active mind of a young Cantonese village boy, whose thoughts had become imbued with the teachings of the West. Behind him rose the always small but eager group of other young Chinese, who have come under the Western or European influence. This handful of intrepid spirits faced the traditions of two thousand years. Picture if you can, this vast land with its 400, 000, 000 population, the majority of whom were illiterate. A land where no common language existed, where there was little development of resources or travel and communication —— a land steeped in the ancient lore of its ancestors, sleeping away its centuries behind the great walls erected to insure its isolation. A civilization that had endured for thousands of years was being threatened by the ideals of one man. Not only did this man wish to change the government of his people, but every phase of life as well! It is little wonder that people both in China and abroad questioned even the remote possibility of success. The greater wonder, is that in spite of the odds so many all over the world, in all walks of life, were willing to cast their lot with the dauntless young leader, Sun Yet Sen.

Since the Korean defeat, the Manchus had been forced to admit the need for learning the ways of more progressive nations. This was bitter pill for the Dowager Empress, whose deep hatred for the so – called barbarians´ had reached new heights since the attempted reform of Emperor Kuang Hsu and K´ang – yu – wei. She was ripe therefore for the suggestion by Prince Tuan, one of her courtiers, that an attempt be made to drive all the foreign devils´from the land.

So came the Boxer Rebellion of 1900, starting in the north and continuing in a reign of blood and carnage against the whites and all Christian Chinese, until the American, French, British and other allied troops put down the revolt and marched triumphantly into Peking.

The royal family had been forced to flee north to Si Ann. But even in defeat, the Empress was still the tenacious, wily old spider, ruling her domain by sheer cunning. She held Emperor Kuang Hsu a prisoner, and continued to place a huge price on Dr. Sun's head as well as that of the reformist, K'ang – yu – wei. And since Homer Lea, Dr. Sun's young American military advisor, had taken part in the Boxer trouble, she added a third reward of ten thousand dollars for his head.

Dr. Sun had been abroad during the early part of the Boxer outbreak, but he returned to his base in Japan. All three rebels, Sun, Homer Lea and K'ang – yu – wei had by now taken refuge there to lay plans for their coming activities.

Dr. Sun approached K'ang – yu – wei to see if they could not consolidate their two movements, but K'ang – yu – wei declined, with the explanation that, while Dr. Sun advocated a clean break from old ways, and a real Republic, he did not agree that China was yet ready for such a drastic change, and preferred instead a constitutional monarchy, putting Emperor Kuang Hsu back on the throne. Homer Lea, now General Lea, saw the whole matter from a military point of view. He tried to explain that unity at this time was more important than their personal aims for China. Before they could attempt any new form of government, the Mauchus must be overthrown!

When it was clear to him that this cooperation was not to be had, he told Dr. Sun that he would return to America, where he could be of more use training Chinese cadets for the revolution, and raising funds. These volunteer troops, he suggested, could later be secretly introduced into China to honeycomb the Manchu army and help bring about its disintegration, once the Revolution was begun. In the meantime Dr. Sun was to continue his work for the Republic, and K'tang – yu – wei, with his newly formed Po Wong Wui, or 'Save the Young Emperor Society' (designed to free Kuang Hsu) was to preach his doctrine of reform. There would be time enough to iron our personal differences, once the overthrow of the Manchus was accomplished.

Before he left Japan, Dr. Sun introduced Homer Lea to the man who was to be his second in command, General Huang Hsing, a husky fighting man devoted to Dr. Sun and his Cause.

Huang was a great swordsman. He had learned swordsmanship from the Japanese, practicing with the heavy – bladed Samurai sword, which developed tremendous shoulders and arm muscles. He was at all times a calm, capable, loyal soldier into whose hands Dr. Sun thrust the active part of the fighting. It was also decided that the troops raised in China and abroad, would serve directly under General Huang, with General Homer Lea mapping out the campaigns and returning at the final hour to execute them.

While General Homer Lea returned to the United States and began in secret to organize and drill bands of Chinese cadets for the Cause, Dr. Sun continued his sporadic revolts, doomed to failure, but serving to keep alive the interest in China and her Movement. He had planned a revolt for the fall of 1900, and a group under foreign trained officers and men made up partly of Japanese and Caucasian sympathizers, was readied for the attack. Although a small force was to be sent, it was thought that after their first success they would be joined by eager Chinese troops of the district. The revolutionists, who were to await the arrival of Sun Yat Sen, took cover near Macao.

Dr. Sun sailed from Yokohama, but upon arrival at Hongkong, he was refused a landing since the Manchu government had warned the British that a revolt had been planned. The Manchu spies were both diligent and effective. Dr. Sun could no doubt have slipped ashore, but he discovered that the society treasurer, who carried funds necessary to the revolt, had also been refused entry at Hongkong and had been forced to go on to Singapore. Sun followed him, only to discover that the man had been arrested there and the money was being held by the authorities. Since time was of paramount importance, Dr. Sun did some of his best explaining to get the money returned to him, telling these in charge that he needed it to carry on his business —— but carefully failing to mention the nature of that business! He was finally successful, but still more precious time had been wasted and he was forced to rush back to Hongkong by the next boat. He landed with little trouble, but the British kept such a careful check of his activities that he was unable to go directly to his men. He sent word changing the meeting place to another area, but the unforeseen delays had caused him to wait too long. Surprise was now out of the question, and the revolutionists had counted on this element as their chief weapon of attack. Manchu spies informed headquarters at Canton that a body of armed soldiers were nearby, and Canton sent troops at once to intercept them. Four thousand royal troops soon put to flight the hardy little band of six hundred revolutionists.

Dr. Sun, and those who escaped with him, were forced to take refuge again in Japan and Singapore. The increasing pressure from the Imperial Palace upon the ports of entry, made it almost impossible for Dr. Sun to land or embark. Even the treaty and concession ports in China were now closed to him, and at long last even Japan refused him landing. But he managed after some difficulty to return to his Yokohama headquarters where he began at once to lay the groundwork for his next revolt.

In 1901 the Dowager Empress was forced to sign a treaty with the eight powers, with payment of 45, 000, 000 taels or about $62, 500, 000 in indemnity. This was a further blot on the escutcheon of Imperial Rule, and a very thoughtful China began more and more to consider the worth of reform activities. Throughout the unsuccessful revolts of 1903, 1904, and 1907, Homer Lea in America, K'ang – yu – wei in Japan and General Huang in China, worked diligently to raise funds, train troops and keep alive the fire of revolution.

In 1904 Dr. Sun went to Hawaii and the United States, attempting to raise the $2, 500, 000 he knew he needed to carry out his plans. Everywhere he received an enthusiastic reception. He was surprised and pleased at the progress General Lea had made in training his volunteer troops, recruited from the Chinese settlements in the States. There was even a troop formed in Manila and of course one in Hawaii. None of these men had had any previous military training, yet they turned into crack troops, even though for the most part they had started training with broomsticks.

In the spring of 1905, Dr. Sun journeyed to Europe, where he tried once more to solicit aid from the banking firms there. He had little success, but again they were not adamant in their refusals, and indeed seemed to admire his tenacity. Through his European tour, Dr. Sun preached his " San Min Chu Yi" or five – power constitution, modeled after the American theme —— of, by and for the people. He also formed the first society group at Antwerp, with thirty sworn members, in Berlin. Still a third was formed in Paris with ten members. At last, the Movement could claim a truly universal membership.

By constant practice, Dr. Sun had become an excellent and powerful orator. Besides a convincing, magnetic approach, he had added the valuable trick of raising his audience to an emotional pitch, and swaying them by the power of suggestion. His name had become a household word throughout China and the Chinese settlements abroad, and there was a strong sympathy for him amongst the other races in Europe and America.

He was popular in some cases because he was a Christian; because he had an English education; because he was a progressive, striving to enlighten China—— all of these things counted in various quarters. But the wise leaders realized a still more important item, from a selfish point of view. Dr. Sun stood to become the titular head of China, should be succeed in his revolution, and one must always be prepared to back the winner.

Every nation with trade treaties or agreements in the treaty ports, had a stake in the final outcome. They realized, that even a weak, shaken, ill – ruled China, was still a rich and powerful country from the economic point of view, and one to be reckoned with eventually in the balance of world power. They began to realize that Dr. Sun could without doubt head China, should he carry out his plans. Interest amongst the banking houses began at last to take definite shape, and it looked as if the entire financial burden would not have to be faced by the faithful Chinese at home and abroad.

VII
The Family

I wish to devote at least a short chapter to the family of Sun Yat Sen, since it has been my privilege to know them intimately.

The Chinese family is a very closely – knit group, even today, and forms an integral part of the character of each member. Since each one has a definite niche in the family group and never steps out of it, I will start with the head of the house, the father.

Dr. Sun's father, Sun Tat Sung, was a poor but honest farmer, and an elder of our village. I remember him as an old man who always carried a small fan with, which he used to slap his thigh gently as he walked. He shared his rice crop, in the Chinese manner, with the owner of his land——some three and a half acres.

Though most of the houses in the village were brick with tiled roof, all were without trees or lawns. On either side of Sun Tat Sung's house, however, three wealthy merchants from Hongkong had built three large mansions with surrounding grounds. I recall we used to go to these places as to a park.

Besides his wife and children, Sun Tat Sung had taken into his home the wives of his two brothers. These 'aunts' were more or less left to the care of their brother – in – law since their husbands had journeyed forth to seek their fortune and had never returned. One had gone to the gold rush in California and no doubt died there; the other went to Ning Po and failed to return. Communication was extremely slow and undependable in those days and so the ladies remained in ignorance of the fate of their spouses to the end. Their loss, however, had left a lasting fear and bitterness towards the outside world, a thing which the children of the family had to fight when they wanted to leave home.

The second head of the house, Sun Yat Sen's mother, who had come from a neighboring village, was a good – sized woman, with clear features, a dark Punti complexion and the traditional tiny, bound feet. In later years her face was lined, and she lived to reach her eighties, but died unfortunately before her son became president of China.

Ah Mi or Sun Mi, was their eldest child, a second son died, very young, and a girl came next before Sun Yat Sen. He also had a younger sister later. Sun Mi, being the eldest went abroad first, selecting Hawaii as so many of his countrymen were doing in those days. He was an industrious young farmer, settling on a plot outside Honolulu. He prospered from the first, and returned shortly to the village to recruit more Chinese labor for the plantations in Hawaii. Going back to Honolulu, he first set up shop as a merchant on Maui, and when this venture prospered, bought a ranch near Kula and began to raise cattle. He was one of the first cattlemen on the island of Maui, and an extremely successful one.

I remember about this time Sun Mi arranged passage for his mother to come and visit him. He had also married a girl from near our village and had a son and two daughters. His mother was much impressed with all she saw on Maui, little guessing that because of her other son, it would become her place of exile.

When she returned to the village, we all gathered to hear her tell of her visit. The thing that made the most lasting impression —— and which scarcely any of us believed, was her tale of the 'portable'houses in Hawaii. Their houses, she explained, were not substantial like ours, but were frame – houses and moved from one side of the island to the other!

When Sun Mi sent for his younger brother to come to him in Hawaii in order that he might secure an education, he did not know of course the results that would ensue. He thought that young Sun Yat Sen would join him eventually in carrying on his business, and even went so far in his generosity as to legally deed his young brother one – half the store. Then, of course, followed the dreadful repercussions of the desire on Sun Yat Sen's part to become a Christian, and secondly his disfigurement of the village idol, Buck Dai. When word of this outrage reached Sun Mi he ordered his brother to come to him in Hawaii, where he upbraided him for his actions and demanded that he return his half of the deeded property as a punishment. This, Sun Yat Sen did willingly, signing the document in the presence of a lawyer. He explained to Sun Mi that money and property meant nothing to him. He never changed his mind on this score. To Sun Mi, the hard – working merchant and rancher, this seemed the height of youthful folly. Sun Yat Sen, in turn, tried to convince his brother that a change from the old order was essential to China. This news of course, fell on deaf ears. Sun Mi would listen to none of it. He was shocked and disgraced by his brother's actions and flatly told him so.

Sun Yat Sen returned to his medical studies in Canton, but shortly after his visit to Peking and the failure of his petition to the government concerning reformation of the educational and agricultural laws ——— when he saw that force and action alone could work the changes necessary, he made one more visit to Sun Mi in Hawaii. He had become something of an orator by this time, though he was new to the tricks of the trade, and he was able to convince Sun Mi, against his will, that he was in the right. From that moment, when Sun Mi threw in with him – the first substantial merchant to become a convert to the Cause ——— he gave his young brother aid in every way possible, using his considerable fortune to further the Cause, and working with untiring loyalty for the Revolution.

While Sun Yat Sen was still studying medicine his father died. He was in his late seventies. His wife then became head of the household, and she wrote to Sun Yat Sen telling him that she had selected a bride for him.

This selection of a wife for the son of a house may seem strange to the Occidental mind, but in reality many Western nations have and still do make use of it; i. e. the marriages 'arranged' in France, Spain, Portugal, Italy, etc. In many ways it is a success, since it usually unites two families of the same social standing, the same tastes and creed.

The girl selected by Sun's mother was from a neighboring village ——— a country girl of Punti origin, even darker complexioned than Sun's mother.

The procedure for a wedding was rather a lengthy and serious business. At first Sun's mother sent for a 'go – between' to ask the girl's mother for a report of the year, month, day and hour of the girl's birth. This was written on a piece of red paper and submitted to the boy's family for a month.

During this time the boy's mother consulted a fortune teller to look up the girl's horoscope as compared to the boy's. If there was no bad luck indicated, she called the bearer of the birth paper to ask the girl's mother how much money, cakes, pork and jewelry she would ask for the betrothal. In return the bride's mother would send a suit of clothing to the groom. If both sides agreed, the groom sent a flower – decked sedan chair to the bride's home with his own birth paper and presents.

The bride, veiled with a red handkerchief, was carried then to the groom's house. When the chair arrived it was greeted by firecrackers. The groom opened the door of the chair, and an old woman carried the bride into the house, passed a small bonfire, straight to her room. At last the groom was invited to meet his bride.

The male guests and brothers escorted the groom to the bedroom of the bride. He lifted the red veil from her face with his fan. This is the first glimpse he has had of his bride's face. But he leaves at once with the escorts. Dinner for the bridal pair is served to them alone later, the bridegroom is supposed to first pick up a piece of chicken for good luck. The woman who has come from the bride's family makes the remark that the two will live harmoniously as husband and wife, and after her statement all of the guests leave except the immediate family and the guests from afar.

The bride and groom have retired to their bedroom. But in the early morning there is another ritual for the bride. Custom demands that she serve her new mother – in – law hot water to wash her face, followed by a cup of tea with sweetmeats. Later the bride and groom, dressed in their best, 'kow – tow' to the father and mother and senior members of the family to show their obedience and respect.

In three days they go to the bride's home to pay their respects, and a last feast attended by close relatives will be given the new couple.

The Chinese marriage, based as it is upon family ties and economic stability, is far from being the whirlwind love – match of the western world, but due perhaps to its solemnity and tradition it is usually a contented and lasting union out of which grows deep affection. I am certain that Sun Yat Sen appreciated the many good qualities of his bride and had he not been so absorbed first in his studies and then in his revolutionary work, I believe they would have come to understand each other much better. As it was, Sun left his bride almost as soon as he was married, and returned alone to finish his medical studies in Hongkong. Lu Szu remained in the Sun home at Tsuei Heng, and in time bore her husband three children, a boy, Sun Fo, and two girls. Their father was seldom home, however, and it was natural that his wife and mother both complained about his continual absence. I have never known anyone kinder or more considerate than Sun, and I know if it had been anything but his work for China, he would no doubt have given it up and come home to please the family. But his eyes were on the future of China, and nothing could swerve him from his purpose.

When the first revolt was in readiness, Dr. Sun realized the danger to his family should anything go amiss. He had them leave Tsuei Heng therefore and move to a boarding house in Hongkong where he hoped they would be safe in the British concession.

Old Mrs. Sun complained bitterly at having to leave her village at this time due to the actions of her young son. Their boarding house in Hongkong must not have been as secret as Sun hoped, for after the failure of the first revolt, Manchu spies came to the house asking permission to make a search. Fortunately the owner of the place was an Englishman, and he refused to allow a search unless they first produced a legal warrant, also adding that he would sue them for any disturbance or upset should they fail to find what they were seeking. After discussing it between themselves, they went away.

It was because Sun felt that even the concessions would no longer be safe for them that he asked me to take them to Sun Mi in Hawaii.

Again, of course, there was much bitterness and unhappiness on the part of both women, when told they must go to live outside China. Their complaints did not lessen with the years, either. Often when I visited them at Sun Miś on Maui, the old mother would tell me of her disappointment and grief at her son's actions. And poor Lu Szu would weep at the mere mention of the Revolution. Neither of the women knew or cared to know much of the work Sun Yet Sen was doing. In China, women did not often mix in politics, their sphere was the home mud the family. But in this, Lu Szu felt that she had been cheated. And of course hers was not an ordinary life by our standards. She had her children, of course, and a comfortable existence in Sun Miś home with her mother – in – law and Sun Miś wife and son and daughter. But of her husband she saw next to nothing. And she was aware constantly of his personal trials and dangers, without being able to help in any way. It was a hard position to fill, difficult for any woman, but doubly so for a simple village girl who was bewildered by the swift changes of her life since marriage.

Sun Yet Sen was always very fond of his children and especially of Sun Fo, his only son. He was a bright and active boy. His father sent him to St. Louis School, a Catholic school in Honolulu, and later he attended Columbia and University of California. At present, he is Vice – President of China.

Of the two little girls, one died quite young, the other is the wife of Tai En Sui, who was an Ambassador to Mexico.

Most of Dr. Suns family returned to China after the revolution and still reside there. Sun Mi settled in Macao, and his mother lived nearby, though she died just before her son was inaugurated president. Lu Szu is still living in Macao, and of course, Sun Fo and his family live there. For them the exile ended in 1911 —— as it did for so many other revolutionary sympathizers.

There has been much discussion and some criticism, too, of Dr. Suns marriage to Soong Chingling, in 1914 in Japan. I met Chingling's elder sister Eling, later Madame Kung, when she was Dr. Suns secretary. I did not meet Chingling. But it is quite understandable that she was well fitted not only to help him with his tremendous work for China, but to envision it as well. Dr. Sun had known her family for years, since her father, Charles Soong, was one of his close friends. Of course, in the eyes of the Chinese it was not proper to discard a first wife who had at all times remained a loyal and faithful spouse, but as the younger generation explained, China was no longer living in or by the past. She was stepping forward and shedding the old ways as she went. I do not condone either school of thought——there must be good in both, and certainly Sun Yat Sen never did a selfish or unworthy deed in his life, knowingly. To the exclusion of all else, he gave his entire existence to China. And I know that China is grateful.

VIII
Preparations for 1910

The Revolutionists, under Dr. Sun, had at last reached the stage were it looked as if real success might be in sight. Their organization inside China and abroad, was strong and vigorous. They had enlisted the sympathy and aid of many Americans and influential Europeans who saw that the Imperial Throne was growing more unstable daily, while Dr. Sun and his followers gained in strength and numbers. All who saw Sun at this time found him to be high – minded, sincere and devoted to his Cause. His integrity was beyond question, and his sense of honor bound his friends to him as nothing else could have.

Then in 1908 one more advantage fell to the rising young leader and his party. The Empress Dowager died. First with the aid of her unscrupulous court doctors and a eunuch, Li Liang Ying, She had poisoned young Emperor Kuang Hsu in 1908. She now left another child on the throne Pu Yi, a small boy of around three. But she tried to protect the Ching dynasty in ordering a meeting of the Assembly which was called however by a restricted electorate —— a fictitious parliament, which ended in nothing as Dr. Sun had expected.

China was no longer as passive to these false promises of the Manchus, thanks to Dr. Sun's written works, speeches and the newspapers that had begun to appear all over the land. Dr. Sun's first paper started in 1899, the China Daily News for which he sent Chen Siu Pak to Hongkong as Editor.

It was still a difficult time for him to travel, as even Japan would not knowingly harbor the arch revolutionist, but he moved about in his usual quiet way, going incognito as much as possible and personally checking all of the last minute details.

Homer Lea told him that the American cadets were ready and invited him to inspect them. General Huang´s forces in China were ready and waiting. Káng – yu – wei was in America on a trip of inspection of his own Po Wong Wui society, but since the death of the Emperor Kuang Hsu, was ready, Lea thought, to join forces with Dr. Sun. Dr. Sun did not need K´ang – yu – wei —— he had his own following, far larger and stronger, and certainly Káng – yu – wei could not aid him in anyway. Still Dr. Sun saw the advantages of a united strength once China declared her freedom to the world.

Káng – yu – wei, unlike the modest, unassuming Dr. Sun, went to America in full panoply as scholar and Court advisor, and his name was awe – inspiring to the humble Cantonese of the Coast cities. Banquets, receptions, suites at the Waldorf Astoria in New York were his. The Chinese in the States soon found that this leader did not come quietly, or in simple dress, as did Dr. Sun, to deliver a stirring message of faith and hope, and having done so, silently stealed away in the night.

And though Káng – yu – wei was a man of distinguished background, he did not make the lasting and endearing impression of Sun Yat Sen. While among the Chinese troops of General Lea, there was unrest due to the fact that they had seen Káng – yu – wei to be little of a military man. Since most of the troops realized the danger of having a non – military leader, they were not pleased, and already those who had joined the Po Wong Wui, were ready to join Dr. Sun´s party.

General Homer Lea played up to Káng – yu – wei´s flamboyant role, however, as good politics to swerve public attention from the quietly working Dr. Sun, who was busy putting the finishing touches on the coming revolution. An interview with President Theodore Roosevelt was arranged for Káng – yu – wei. This gave General Lea a legitimate excuse to travel to New York with the reformist, and covered a real purpose of his trip which was to meet Dr. Sun.

Sun Yat Sen, with the stage now fully set for what he hoped would be the last revolt to free China, stopped over in Los Angeles long enough to address the Chinese there who had given so loyally to the Cause. He had often addressed them before, but always incognito, just as a speaker for the Cause. Now, before the large Chinese gathering with a sprinkling of interested Americans who had come at General Homer Lea's invitation, his real identity was made known to them.

Those who heard his speech said that it was moving, poignant and beautiful. His audience, hearing his quietly sincere pledge for a free and democratic China, realized that here was the one man fit to lead them, not only into revolution —— but if successful, to lead China herself !

At the New York meeting shortly afterwards, between Dr. Sun, K'ang – yu – wei and Homer Lea, the old argument began on the score of a Republic for China or a Constitutional Monarchy. But, as General Lea explained to the scholar K'ang – yu – wei, he no longer had much of a following, since most of his group had already turned to Dr. Sun. And since the death of the Emperor Kuang Hsu, it seemed he had no valid excuse even for a " Save the Young Emperor Society. " Between the blunt, forceful arguments of General Lea on one side and the quiet persuasive logic of Dr. Sun on the other, K'ang – yu – wei at last conceded the field to Dr. Sun, agreeing to aid the Republic in anyway that he could.

With no longer any division of leadership, Dr. Sun set the actual date for the beginning of hostilities for January 1912. Both Dr. Sun and General Lea were confident this time of success. They had labored long and painstakingly to lay a sound groundwork for the conflict. Former mistakes had taught them the pitfalls to be avoided. China was honeycombed with Lea's trained officers and General Huang's eager troops. There were spies and revolutionary sympathizers inside Peking and even in the Manchu army, awaiting call. The people were ready. The Chinese all over the world were poised to follow Dr. Sun in his move to free China. As far as Dr. Sun was concerned, there only remained the final arrangement of loans and trade agreements to insure his new government recognition once it was established.

For this purpose, Lea was to go to Europe to see the Rothschild interests, while Dr. Sun finished his campaigning in the States. General Lea could travel abroad openly, as he had been invited by Kaiser Wilhelm of Germany to review the Royal troops. His astute books the 'Valor of Ignorance', an amazing scientific analysis of modern warfare, published in 1908, had given him an instant worldwide reknown.

Fate, however, as so often happens had decreed that these plans should go awry.

On October tenth, 1911, while Dr. Sun was in Denver, he received a cablegram from General Huang. Since the code book to decipher the message was locked up in his luggage, and he thought it merely a routine matter or appeal for funds, he decided to wait until morning. He came down to the dining room for breakfast with the undeciphered cable still in his pocket, when his eye lit on a headline in the morning newspaper. " Wuchang in hands of Revolutionists. " He bought a paper at once and read the news telling of the realization of his lifelong dreams —— ten thousand miles from the place in which it was happening. Deciphering General Huang's cables he found it a verification of the news.

On April 27th, 1911, General Huang and his men stormed the Governor's Yamen at Canton. They fought brilliantly and well —— so well that although General Huang lost two fingers and seventy – two of his brave dare – to – dies, later buried on Yellow Flower Mount, it displayed to the nervous Ching Dynasty the vigor and skill of the new Revolutionary forces. No longer were they facing rank amateurs, but well – trained seasoned troops, fired with a personal determination and daring.

General Huang's dispersed troops, who had only fallen back under overwhelming odds, begged to try again. But the General held them in check, until on October 9th, an untimely explosion of a bomb stored in the Russian concession set off the Revolution with a literal bang!

Immediately the Revolutionary headquarters were raided and thirty members taken with the membership ledger. It was imperative that something be done at once. The remaining members used Sun Yat Sen's name to open the real Revolution and all the provinces were notified to each command their own soldiers. In a matter of weeks, fifteen provinces were taken by the revolutionists. Everywhere they met with success. The Imperial army, finding itself weakened and betrayed by the revolutionary spies and sympathizers within its own ranks was forced to realize defeat.

Dr. Sun's first thought was to return to China as swiftly as possible, but on consideration he realized in his unselfish way, that he could better serve China now by going to Europe and helping General Lea complete the financial and trade business.

It was a great day for China —— at long last they had something substantial to present to the World Powers collateral for their recognition as a free and equal nation.

IX
Success of the Revolution
——Sun Made First President

As quickly as possible, Dr. Sun sailed for England, and in London went at once to the home of his friends, the Cantlies.

For several days telegrams had been arriving at the house for Sun. Prior to his arrival, one was missent to the Manchu Legation addressed to Sun Wen (Dr. Sun's official name) and since Mrs. Cantlie who received it, could not prove that Sun was there yet, the messenger was about to return it. Mrs. Cantlie painstakingly copied the Chinese characters on another piece of paper however, before releasing it. When Dr. Sun arrived sometime later, she presented it to him. It was not until the next morning however that her curiosity as to the message was satisfied, when Dr. Sun modestly admitted that it was an invitation to become first president of China.

The Cantlies were delighted with this news, but Dr. Sun assured them that he would only accept, temporarily, and only if no better man could be found for the job.

General Lea joined Dr. Sun in London, and they concentrated on a last try for the loan so badly needed now by a raw, new government. The banking houses told them that first they must have proof that it was a full – fledged government with a permanent and not 'provisional' president and assembly. To bring this about, of course, Sun would have to first return to China. So the money he had hoped to present to China for her new Republic was not forthcoming. But one boon was granted him – the bankers agreed to stop the Manchu loans at once.

Sailing from France, through Suez, with General Lea accompanying him, the return to China was something of a triumphant procession for Dr. Sun. When the ship stopped at Singapore, children threw flowers at his feet, and everywhere the joyous smiling faces of his people greeted him as the conquering hero. Through all the acclaim, however, Dr. Sun was quietly pleased, but reserved and modest. He did not choose the limelight for himself, and he saw, unlike the multitude who thought the struggle was over, that China faced an even harder battle to maintain what she had won.

He landed openly for the first time in many long hard years, at Shanghai on December 24th —— under his official name, Sun Wen. At once he vas received with enthusiasm as the natural leader of the new Republic.

When asked if he had come with the funds so badly needed by the infant government, he replied sadly that he brought only himself. But he pointed out that money would be forthcoming from the World Powers, once the new Chinese government was established on a permanent basis and formally recognized.

Only five days after landing, Sun Yat Sen was elected first president of China by the assembly of seventeen provinces which met at Nanking, chosen the new capital of the land.

It was the greatest day in China's history. After a nearly bloodless revolution, so carefully had it been planned and executed, China was at last a free nation! And after years of toil, effort and personal sacrifice, Sun Yat Sen, the village boy with but an ideal and a dream to steer by, had guided his people from the darkness into the light, and what he hoped would be a safe harbor as a free Republic.

As he watched the celebrating and reviews before the old Ming Tombs, during his inauguration January 1st, 1912, he was aware that his work had only just begun. There was so much still to do for China, and he was so anxious for his newlyborn Republic to have its chance for life! In a sense, perhaps, he was too afraid for its immediate rather than its future life.

I received a vacation about this time from my firm in Honolulu, and sailed for China January 16, 1912, with twenty other overseas members of the Tung Ming Hui Society, taking with me young Sun Fo, now a young man of twenty.

We went to Nanking upon arrival, and found President Sun already swamped with outside advice.

Dr. Sun had some preliminary laws for his people that were the changes we had all looked forward to —— adoption of the universal calendar, cutting off of the queue, and the forbidding of bound feet. This satisfied all, but the president's advisors were of two factions.

The young progressives from overseas, who had followed loyally and given freely to the Cause, who demanded a sweeping change and complete new form of government. And the older scholars of China, who wished him to adopt what was good in the old system and incorporate it into the new government, thus giving China a chance to accustom herself to the change.

The latter sounded like good advice to Dr. Sun, who for the first time in his life had grown cautious, through his fear of making a mistake that would endanger his infant Republic. These older men, he argued, had long been in government and politics, and there were even some of the younger men among them, including Sun's own secretary, the writer, Wang Ching Wei, who favored the old ways.

The third and minor group of advisors, including the militarists and General Lea and Huang, pointed out the urgent necessity of marching to the north at once and finishing the job of ousting the Manchus at Peking and thus taking and uniting all of China. They pleaded with Sun that if this was not done immediately, the whole Cause would be lost —— if not now, eventually —— and it would all have to be done over again.

On the other hand, the civil advisors explained to the president that such a move would cost money which they did not have at present, and they pointed out that they could very well stand on their laurels since they now controlled China in any case. It was much more important that they secured China recognition at once as a world power, than that they conquered a few frightened Manchus and Northern provinces that could be taken any time.

What sorry advice for new China! This little group to the north that was to form the rift in all future Chinese unity. Had the one step been taken to consolidate China at that time there would have been no question of disunity down through the years —— and politically China would have been far ahead.

Sun and many others believed this advice, however, and the die was cast. The China uplifting Society, which had now grown into the present day Kuomingtang, cancelled all further military advancement. Shortly afterwards, General Lea suffered a stroke and returned to America to die. Before going, however, he cautioned Sun again not to abandon the move to the north.

I know that General Huang felt the same, for I overheard his telephone conversation to the president's office, when he spoke to Secretary Wang. The president's secretary told him bluntly that the president had ordered him to cease hostilities. To a question from General Huang, Wang replied: " It is the president's order, what can you do about it?" and hung up.

The next day General Huang suffered a hemorrhage, caused many said, by the intensity of his feelings over the matter.

Always completely loyal to Dr. Sun, both as a personal friend and a military leader, General Huang followed instructions in this case as usual, but quite against his will.

A man quick to take advantage of this end to hostilities was Yuan Shih Kai, who was in command of the Manchu army, a man of strength and cunning always able to turn the tables to his own advantage. He recognized the security of the new republic and speedily joined their ranks.

It is necessary here, I think, to give a brief summary of the background of this man who proved himself not only an opportunist, but the archenemy of China. Certainly no one could have presented more of a contrast to Dr. Sun than Yuan Shih Kai.

He was from the north, Ho Nan, where his family had belonged to the lesser officialdom and one grandfather had held the rank of mandarin. As a young man he was a licentious, debauched rake who spent money like water —— a fault he was never to overcome —— and who gambled his wife 's jewels away in an evening's play. It was unfortunate that his wife, whose father was also a mandarin, was going next day to his birthday celebration. As he was very wealthy, it was the custom for his children and guests to deck themselves in their best. Due to the absence of the jewels, Yuan's wife was forced to appear in very simple dress compared to the others. One of her father's serving maids asked her why she had come in such a simple costume, and the humiliation was too much for Yuan's wife. She left her father's house without presenting herself to him and returned home in anger and tears. She knew of course what had happened, and strangely she was the one person Yuan feared.

When he finally returned, he found his wife weeping bitterly and she upbraided him to such an extent that he felt forced to make the boasting reply that given the chance, he could also go to Peking and secure a title. His wife amazed him by taking him at his word. Taking 500 from her savings, she offered it to him with the taunt that he would never succeed.

Stung by her accusations, Yuan Shih Kai started at once for Peking. Of course $300 of the money was spent on gambling and liquor before he reached his destination. But all through his life ran a streak of devil's luck. In Peking he sought the advice of one of his Ho Nan associates who had attained the rank of mandarin. This man advised Yuan to go to Military school, since Yuan's uncle was a ranking officer and might aid him. But this sounded too slow and dull to Yuan. Instead he went to consult the old scholar Hse Shih Chang, later Kuang Hsu's tutor, and the scholar told him that if he hoped to pass any of the official examinations he must study the various classics used as subject matter. Again Yuan balked at the toil envolved and asked the scholar to give him one of the books used as examination material. He said he could copy it when the time came and thus pass the examination.

Hse Shih Chang told him that was all very well, provided they based his examination upon that particular book —— a chance in a thousand. Yuan's luck held however, his examination was based on the identical book he held, and after copying it out, he passed, attaining his title. He now entered the military as an officer, and under his uncle's influence went to Korea in charge of the Chinese garrison there.

Here he behaved in his usual manner, insulting the Japanese ambassador, and through his negligence eventually losing Korea. He fled to Shanghai, but was emboldened soon after to buy his way into the Imperial court through the unscrupulous eunuch, Li Liang Ying. The eunuch, who had the ear of the Empress Dowager, and knew that his own reward would be forthcoming, succeeded in having Yuan appointed Inspector General of the Imperial army to head the military school for cadets, Pei Yang.

I have already told how he betrayed the young Emperor Kuang Hsu, by distorting his story to the Empress Dowager, and how in her new entourage he became even more powerful in Court circles. At last, when the Dowager died, Yuan Shih Kai saw his opportunity to become even Emperor, if he played his cards right.

The Dowager left the boy, Pu Yi, on the throne, with his father to rule as regent until Pu Yi could rule. But Pu Yi's father knew of Yuan's designs on the throne and his fear and mistrust went so far that he took to carrying a gun and even attempted to kill Yuan. Failing this, the royal family presented Yuan with a length of silk, or Hong Lo, with which to strangle himself in the time honored manner. But Yuan Shih Kai had no such sense of honor, instead he retreated to his home in Ho Nan, where he remained until the revolution.

As soon as the revolution broke, a member of the frightened royal family, Prince Ching, journeyed in person to Yuan's house to beg him to return and head the Imperial army.

Yuan was now in a position to drive a hard bargain. If he returned, he said, he must have complete control not only of the armed forces, but of the royal household as well. When this was grudgingly promised him, he returned. But his eye was on the main chance, and when he saw beyond doubt which way victory lay, he made haste to dicker with the Revolutionists. He was an experienced man in government, and Dr. Sun believed him when he said he was truly a Republican at heart and was sorry for his past misdeeds.

The only possible excuse for Sun's belief in such a man, is, that he had such a high integrity and sense of honor himself that he trusted all others. Yuan Shih Kai had no such scruples. He was crafty and cunning and knew, from his court training, how to pull strings. Dr. Sun's secretary, Wang, owed Yuan Shih Kai a personal debt —— the General had saved his life in getting him released from prison, and it was easy to persuade Wang that he must sway Sun into turning over the Presidency of China to Yuan.

There were others, too, who sincerely trusted Yuan, as Sun did. But the young Chinese, especially those from overseas and those in the troops who could not have the wool pulled over their eyes. They knew Yuan Shih Kai was interested solely in personal power, that he wanted not a free Republic, but armies to control the land so that he might cut his way to the Dragon Throne and rule as the Manchus had.

At the peace conference of the north and south at Shanghai he instructed his representative to advocate a constitutional monarchy. But the Nanking representative, Wu Ting Feng, demanded recognition of the Republic first, before a discussion of any other form of government. Yuan's representative was forced to grant this which so angered Yuan Shih Kai, that he recalled the man and carried on the rest of the conference by telegraph.

The first rift between Sun Yat Sen and his old followers came at this moment. I went with others of his boyhood friends and overseas members to beseech him to abandon the idea of turning over the hard won presidency to such a man as Yuan Shih Kai.

We held a conference after hours in his office, and from 7: 00 to 11: 00 P. M. , argued with the president to reconsider his decision.

Sun said, in effect, " You overseas Chinese know nothing of conditions in China. Yuan Shih Kai is a capable and experienced man, moreover he is in a position to bring about the abdication of the Emperor, which is necessary if we are to show the world that we have a true Republic and not just a provisional one. "

Backed up by Wang, and others, it was difficult to sway Sun from this point of view. We then asked if he would not at least send troops to the north to finish the job of conquering China.

Sun told us that finances would not permit a northern expedition. We explained that since we had raised money before, we could do it again. But once more the president's secretary, Wang Ching Wei, advised against such a waste of time, money and energy, and Sun listened to him. Wang later proved himself the weak creature he was, when in the last war he became the puppet ruler of the Chinese Government in Shanghai for the Japanese. It was unfortunate that Sun Yat Sen had to be surrounded by such men at the time of the first critical period in the history of the Republic.

Many of the overseas Chinese who had come to China to aid Sun, saw the futility of remaining and left for abroad. Since I was on vacation for a while longer, I remained. But Sun Yat Sen's plan to get Yuan Shih Kai accepted by the people was not an instant success. The man was not popular, and the newspapers ran long stories disclosing his true character. To overcome this, Sun ordered his secretary to print opposing stories, telling of Yuan's experience as an official, and generally building him up as a presidential candidate. Sun's name, naturally, held great weight with his people and at last they accepted the word of their leader on the surface, if not underneath.

The peace terms demanded by the royal household became another thorn in the side of the young revolutionists. The demands included keeping the Forbidden City for the royal family, maintaining of the Palace Guard, a substantial revenue for the Emperor's personal needs, and the right of the Emperor to receive obeisance from those who called upon him. Many of us did not see where the Manchus had a right to 'demand' anything in the future. And we were opposed to even a slight continuation of the old ways. But Sun Yat Sen again trusted Yuan Shih Kai, saying that it was of first importance to secure an immediate abdication. So the articles were signed over the protests of a few and the grumbling of many —— Sun thinking as always that what he did was best for China. It was of course his gravest and only mistake. Had any other substitute been chosen it might have worked, but Yuan Shih Kai was completely untrustworthy.

Sadly, Sun's true friends began to drift away, and he was left surrounded by the wily Yuan and his supporters, and the elders who for one reason or another sought to have him turn his infant Republic over to Yuan Shih Kai.

On February 12, 1912, the Manchu Emperor abdicated. Three days later, Sun Yat Sen resigned as President. Cables came to him from all over the world begging him to at least serve out his term of office, but he stood firm in his decision to thus get rid of the Manchus without further fighting.

He returned to Canton and I went with him. While working in his office there I met Soong Eling, elder sister of Chingling later Madame Sun.

Dr. Sun was offered the post of Commissioner of Railroads, which he accepted, but the funds ran out in three short months and that was an end to it.

Dr. Sun asked me to remain in China, but I told him that since I could not do any material good there, I would return to Hawaii. It was a sad parting and a lasting farewell, since I never saw him again.

X

Chaos of First Administration
——Treachery

In spite of his trust in Yuan Shih Kai, Dr. Sun had taken the precaution of posting his ever – faithful General Huang in Nanking, to keep an eye on the new President. Yuan Shih Kai was a past master at deceit, however, and expanded and armed his troops behind General Huang's back.

Yuan shih Kai was a man in his fifties when he became president. He was a well set up man of military bearing ——but the leopard had not changed his spots. He still drank, smoked and gambled to excess, and had added the vice of opium. In one year as president he spent $4, 000, 000 mostly on personal luxuries and to buy the protection he felt he needed from his spies, troops and other followers.

He felt safer in the north, and steadily refused to come down to Nanking, the chosen capital. He ruled instead from Peking. In later years various Revolutionists attempted to kill or poison him, but his spies were so astute and well paid that they always failed. On another occasion when his sedan chair was attacked, only one of his bearers was slain. Again his luck held out.

In 1913, the Nanking Assembly had elected Yuan President, and Li Yuan Hung, vice – president. The latter was a mandarin and Lieutenant General of two provinces. They were a fit pair, although Li was the weaker and therefore less dangerous of the two. And both had no scruples about killing off any who stood in their way.

One thing Sun Yat Sen had not reckoned with, was that his resignation would effect (affect?) the loans promised on the strength of his presidency. In most cases the loans were cancelled, and China was left with a green new

Republic and no monies with which to develop it properly. Funds at this time were essential, for under the Manchus China had grown steadily more backward as compared to her sister nations, and the tremendous jobs of refinancing, reconversion, and industrial development, had to be started at once.

President Yuan, soon proved true to his former reputation. Having secured some money on loan, 25, 000, 000 pounds, from European sources, contracted without the consent of the assembly, he began to rule with the iron hand of despotism learned from his Manchu teachers. He was treacherous, cruel and without any sense of honor.

Early in May 1913, Dr. Sun learned that Yuan was planning to kill him. Dr. Sun, having discovered that Yuan was using his loan to better equip his army, had written the foreign nations to stop granting loans to the president. This enraged Yuan to such an extent that he had his troops surround the house of Sun's friend, Dr. Lee, where he was visiting, and demanded Sun be turned over for trial and decapitation at Peking. Dr. Sun, while amazed at such an act on Yuan's part, made his escape through Dr. Lee's back door while his friend engaged the troops in front. Reaching his home, he was told that it had also been visited and watched.

Remaining incognito, Dr. Sun attempted for three weeks to reach his old faithful General Huang, but was unable to do so. At last he traveled to Hongkong, from there to Canton, and at last reached General Huang's headquarters at Hoochow, where he requested him to help get his family to Japan. The two friends agreed to separate and meet later in Japan. They traveled disguised as river men, which enabled them to frequent the waterfronts. Sun sailed from Macao in a fishing boat that landed at Moji, Japan, after twelve days. He learned on arrival that the loyal General Huang had already been in Nagasaki five days, having successfully accomplished Dr. Sun's mission.

Once more an exile, Dr. Sun wrote Yuan Shih Kai a stinging letter of rebuke in which he accused him of being a traitor to his country and his people. Sun added that he would rise against Yuan just as he rose against the Manchus, for at last he realized what lay underneath the mask of false promises Yuan had given him.

Although, for his own sake, Dr. Sun was once more advised by friends and followers to take the line of least resistance and conform to the present governmental policy, Sun still believed firmly in the people of China was determined to see that they got a fair deal.

Most of Dr. Sun´s followers had joined him in Japan, including the Soong family. He had taken Eling´s younger sister, Chingling, just back from college in America, as his secretary when Eling became Madame Kung. Shortly after, in 1914, Chingling and Dr. Sun were married.

In 1913, Yuan Shih Kai had succeeded, by getting rid of those of the assembly who opposed his wishes, in securing a five – year term. In 1914 he increased this term of office to ten years, with the provise that he choose his successor. All of this, of course, was merely the preliminary to his declaring himself Emperor —— the first and last of his desires. By devious means, bribes and threats, he ´received´ requests from his people asking for a constitutional monarchy. But in 1916 he went the necessary step farther and proclaimed himself Emperor.

Yuan Shih Kai had at last gone too far. His loans were used up, he had stripped his land of anything of value as collateral, including the salt tax, and he found that without the ready money he had always poured forth upon his followers like water, he could not be sure of their loyalty. I think for the first time he was frightened, for only abject fear or madness could have accounted for his act of brutality in slaying his favorite concubine and her newly born child one night with his sword.

After a brief term as Emperor he was forced to reinstate the Republic, and he died three months later, his death no doubt partially due to his failure. He was, I think, the most ruthless, selfish man in the history of China.

XI

Trials of Come – back
——Partial Success

In 1915, during World War I, Japan had forced her twenty one demands upon China, and Yuan Shih Kai, who was then working towards his monarchy, signed the documents.

Dr. Sun ordered his adherents in Kwang Tung, Hu Nan and other strongholds to rebel. General Lung Chi Kuang serving Yuan, killed about ten thousand of these rebels. But the revolts continued. Dr. Sun ordered his other military leaders to various places to stage revolts —— Li Lieh Jiun was sent to Yunnan, Jiu, to Shantung, Chiu and Chen to Kwang Tang, and General Huang to Hu Nan, and all of the southern provinces joined in.

Li Yuan Hung, succeeded Yuan Shih Kai as president, maintaining the Republic at least in form. But Dr. Sun realized that he must begin all over again to free his people. Force was necessary this time, and he intended to waste no words where they would accomplish nothing. He worked diligently and carefully for his new revolution. Funds had again been sent from his faithful followers abroad, thus enabling him to carry on.

At last, in 1917, he was able to return to China to organize the military government. In May, the northern generals rebelled, and General Chang Shiun compelled Li Yuan Hung to dissolve parliament, and put the disposed Emperor, Pu Yi, back on the throne. It seemed as if China was doomed to return to her old vices.

Then in 1917 the southern provinces revolted successfully, and Dr. Sun once more returned to Canton to take his place in the local government administration. In August, former parliamentary members gathered at Canton to reorganize a local parliament. It was decided to resume a military government for the time being in order to carry out the fight against the Peking forces. Sun Yat Sen was elected Generalissimo of the Army and Commander of the Navy. Sun had advised the southern delegates that they must make a new and separate government in the south which could in time take over the north. As the head of this new government, Sun was for a time absolute dictator.

It was clear to him at last, that a tremendous job faced China if she was to consolidate the old ways and the new, in any degree of permanence. Always a man of peace and not of force, Sun found it difficult to abandon his old way of using words instead of bullets. But it was a necessary evil before China could emerge as a unified nation. These were days of trial and disillusionment for many. But Sun Yat Sen, firm in his resolve for a new Republic, of, by and for the people, knew no discouragement. He continued to use his military influence to send armies to the north.

He was quite aware now that there were those about him whom he could not trust. The various warlords in particular, were like Yuan Shih Kai, ready to play both sides against each other to feather their own nests. They could not be depended upon, and yet Sun was forced to make use of them. There were others in his group who wanted, as had been the case before, to adopt many of the old ways and wait before making any radical changes in government. And there were those among the younger men who could not wait, who chafed at any delay. Sun Yat Sen was the buffer between them, and the anchor to which they clung. A less determined and deliberate man might well have been swayed by public opinion —— or lost his head altogether, but Sun knew when to wait and when to act and his calm reserve never stood him in better stead.

The Peking government had by now gone through yet another change, ousted Pu Yi, and resumed their own Republic with the Royalists, electing as President, Feng Kuo Chang. He was at once pressed by the Germans to ally himself to them in World War I.

Sun Yat Sen had opposed such a move as early as 1915, claiming that China, as an infant Republic, was in no position to take care of herself, let alone aid an outside power. She could not afford to carry on her internal wars let alone tackle one of major importance.

The see – saw between the north and the south continued, but without material effect. And Dr. Sun abandoned Canton for Shanghai in 1918, where he began work on a report called " The International Development of China" ⸺ outlining the immediate needs of his country for the other world powers. It was clear to him that aid must come from outside China if she was to be saved. In his outline, Sun, pointed out that in helping China to expand, the Powers would benefit themselves. It was a simple plan to have capitalism create socialism in China.

Once more, he found his chief support in the wealthy overseas Chinese, many of whom responded with their entire fortunes. Dr. Sun continued to make his pen do the work of a sword, and wrote many articles of wide – spread interest for the Reconstruction Magazine, also advocating his 'hard to know, easy to act', policy to his people. A statement that it was simple to do things, but difficult to know what was the correct thing to do.

Besides his writing, Dr. Sun was busily engaged in arranging another military move to regain control of Canton for his Republic. The funds from overseas aided him, and he even mortgaged his house in the French concession at Shanghai, a gift of overseas members. This mortgage was in turn paid off by them, only to be mortgaged again as the need arose. Throughout his life, Dr. Sun never thought of himself or his family but only of the Cause to which he had dedicated himself.

In 1920 he journeyed to Nagasaki on a tour of inspection of the more modern Japanese shipping methods. A council of his followers was held there to see if anything could be done about the development of China's resources and internal communications, but all were of the opinion that first there must be peace and unity in the land.

After careful plotting with General Chen, the liberation of Canton was once more affected, and Dr. Sun was invited to return.

On April 27, 1921 the Canton parliament elected Dr. Sun President of the Republic, and inaugurated him May 5th. It was a personal triumph and at last a step forward. But again intrigue and jealousy surrounded him, and General Chen and others failed to give him their true support.

Regardless, Sun began plans at once for a northern campaign through Kwangsi.

Russia, due partly to her own revolution, had maintained an active interest in Dr. Sun's work for sometime. They now sent a representative, from Canton to Kwangsi to see him. Many foreigners felt that, since peace seemed far from a possibility in China, they should divide into a northern and southern province which would be able to demand equal recognition. Dr. Sun, on the other hand, would not hear of this. It must be a union of all the people, he argued.

He was, however, willing to hold a peace conference with General Wu Pei Fu, of the north when the latter suggested it in 1921. But as usual the plan was abandoned by the north before it ever materialized.

Dr. Sun meanwhile had ordered General Chen Chiung Ming to move on the North, not realizing that the general was not a true supporter. General Chen countered that the army was not ready. The president demanded action, and Chen sullenly advanced making only a pretense of fighting and bringing about a dismal failure. When Sun accused him of insubordination Chen retaliated by blaming the president for lack of aid. In April, Sun sent soldiers to Kwangsi to dismiss Chen but the wily General returned to Canton with his forces and surrounded the Presidential offices, peppering it with machine gun fire. Both Sun and his wife had narrow escapes from the city before joining each other on a gunboat which landed them at Shanghai.

Sun remained there from 1922 to 1923, carrying on negotiations for a peace settlement between the North and South. He had been approached once more by the government at Peking to help solve the problem. It was clear that neither side was getting anywhere with their constant warfare. Dr. Sun worked tirelessly and earnestly to bring about a meeting of the old members of the original Parliament, and succeeded at last in getting them to return to Peking for a conference. All were bitterly disappointed when they found that the North maintained their same old ideas and prejudices. Since nothing could be accomplished the whole matter was abandoned. It had looked like success at first, for after General Chen's uprising against Sun, the local soldiers of Ho Pei and Feng Tien had begun fighting among themselves. Ho Pei proved victorious, and drove the President Feng Kuo Chang away, putting in his place Li Yuan Hung, and recalling their parliament.

China's internal strife which would surely strangle her hopes of becoming a world power, seemed insurmountable to all but her faithful champion —— Sun Yat Sen. With the patience of a father with a difficult child he again prepared to take her hand and lead her into the light.

XII
The Russian Influence

Casting about for aid of any sort in January 1923, since funds were low and support dwindling with the repeated failures, Dr. Sun met a sympathetic Soviet representative, Adolf Joffe. The Russian did not come empty handed, but offered Dr. Sun financial as well as military aid. Realizing sadly his past mistakes in refusing well meant advice from outside friends, Sun was now eager to accept help where he found it. This was to mark the beginning of the great Soviet influence in South China.

Dr. Sun's power in Canton was restored to him in February 1923 and the soldiersunanimously elected him their leader. He found also that the attitude in Hongkong had changed to a more friendly and cooperative one.

On his return to Canton, however, Sun found chaos through out the whole south, due mainly to lack of funds. The troops who had not been paid, began a mutiny which ended in general looting of the countryside and general disaster. While Dr. Sun was attempting to deal with this new disorder, another Russian, Michael Borodin, arrived from the Soviet with an appointment to act as advisor to the South.

At first his salary was paid from Moscow, but later was assumed by the Southern Chinese Government. Sun believed firmly in Borodin who became virtual prime minister of the South. It was all too clear to the Republic that outside help and advice were of vital importance to their success.

At this time of internal strife Sun Yat Sen still dared to dream of a true Republic for all China, world recognition, and a place as an equal world power —— but he saw the trouble ahead, the possibility of failure, and all of this was doubled by the fact that his health was failing. It would be little wonder if he had taken the easiest way out —— the way of surrender. But Sun Yat Sen was not born to give up his ideals. He did not spare himself. Revolt after revolt, failure after failure, personal tribulation, humiliation and criticism, all of these things he could bear. But to abandon his hopes and dreams for a free China was not possible.

The last days of his rule in Canton grew to be his hardest. The troops terrorized the countryside, raiding and looting at will, while a veritable civil war raged between bandit troops and city merchants. Despairing of bringing order out of this chaos alone, Sun realized that the Russians offered his only actual aid, and he turned more and more in their direction.

In an address given in Canton in 1923, Sun said: " We no longer look to the western powers. Our faces are turned towards Russia. " Yet he had only accepted aid from Russia when his other sources of aid failed. The Russians did help him materially. Under Borodin he founded the Whampoa Military School where young cadets were trained under Russian officers in the latest modern methods. And he ordered a northern expedition which was successful in dismissing Chow Kuan as President, and putting in Tuan Chi Juei as temporary president. He in turn requested Sun to visit Peking for a final conference to see what agreements could be reached for a lasting and consolidated peace.

Although at long last the end of hostilities seemed in sight and was partially due to the help of the Russians, I do not believe that Sun Yat Sen ever thought of China as a follower of the Marx doctrine. It is true that the two revolution – freed countries had certain problems and aims in common, but China was not morally or spiritually adaptable to communism. Dr. Sun's dream for China was that she become a free Republic. It had been his dream since boyhood and it was certainly his dream to the last.

There has been a great deal of discussion about Dr. Sun 's attitude towards Russia and, whether he meant to adopt the communistic teachings and point of view. It has in fact been taken up by the North and is the present hue and cry that splits the country. I believe that Dr. Sun's feelings in this instance have been misconstrued.

That he was grateful to Russia for her aid and support in a trying moment I have no doubt, but that he ever seriously contemplated incorporating her creed into his own for China I seriously question. If one thing is clear from Dr. Sun's own writings, it is that he had a single desire for China —— and that one desire was freedom, in the form of a Republic, of, by and for, the people.

XIII
Illness—Death—Will to People

Sun agreed to go to the peace meeting in Peking, and he had made arrangements for representatives from the World Powers to attend as well as the Chinese delegates.

Although he was in ill health, suffering a hemorrhage before he even left Canton, he did not spare himself to personally lay the groundwork for what he hoped would be the lasting peace he had worked so long to secure. He insisted upon carrying out every detail himself, and made long arduous journeys to Japan, Shanghai and Tientsin, making long speeches in person to unite his people.

At Tientsin he suffered an attack diagnosed as liver disease, and upon reaching Peking he was forced to enter the hospital in the Peking Union Medical College. An exploratory operation disclosed that he had cancer of the liver and that nothing could be done. He was taken to the home of his friend, Wellington Koo, where he remained until his death at 9: 30 A. M., March 12, 1925. With him at his death were his wife, Chingling, his son, Sun Fo, and his daughter. He insisted on dying with his hand outside the cover —— as a Christian. And his wife saw that he was buried with Christian rites as she knew he would have requested.

On April 5th, the day of the funeral, the body was carried in state to the assembly hall of the Peking Union Medical College and arranged with floral wreaths and a huge picture of Sun Yat Sen as a background.

The large picture was later carried in front of the hearse and large crowds gathered to pay homage to their late leader.

Dr. Sun had requested a small funeral and no monument, but he reckoned without the reverence and love of his people who began at once to raise funds for a great tomb. A temporary resting place was chosen at Pi Yun, an old monastery near the Summer Palace.

All over the world Chinese held memorial services of their own and mourned the passing of their great leader, the true father of the Republic of China.

But if he had gone, he had not done so without leaving full instructions behind for his people. In sum total these instructions told the faithful followers of his aim to secure liberty and equality in China, and his realization that only a solid and lasting unity could bring this about. He pointed out that the Republic as such, was not a true success and he prayed that they would follow his published works for National Reconstruction, General Principles of Reconstruction, Fundamentals of Democracy and the Manifesto of the First National Convention of Representatives, until completely achieved.

He ordered them to carry out at once, the People's Conference, which he had been in Peking to attend.

To his family he left his blessings and wish that they continue his work. He left his house, books and clothes to his wife, Chingling, saying that his son and daughters now grown, could stand on their own feet. He had little else than his personal belongings to leave, for he had never been acquisitive for himself or his family.

When the Kuomingtang, or Nationalists, set up Nanking as the Capital, a site was picked out for the tomb of Sun Yat Sen to be erected with funds gathered from his followers. The architecture was to be Chinese, with an altar before it. Since it was to be built on a hillside, Purple Hill, surrounded by the trees Sun loved, a long flight of steps were to lead up to it.

The great monument was erected not far from the Ming Tombs, as a signal that the village boy had at last conquered the oppressors of China. The great leader came more at death into the hearts of all his people than he ever did in life, and a sorrowing country buried him with full honors.

The granite and marble tomb was ready in 1929, and in June of that year the Father of the Chinese Republic was given his final burial on the side of Purple Mountain outside Nanking. Present were his family, Madame Sun, Sun Fo (then Minister of Railways at Nanking, carrying out his father 's dream for adequate transportation in China), close relatives and friends, and General Chiang Kai – shek, now President of China, who had long been one of Sun Yat Sen's disciples.

Starting from the Kuomingtang headquarters the procession, flanked by an enormous throng, travelled slowly along the recently built memorial highway to the tomb. At the exact stroke of twelves all China —— and all Chinese gathered throughout the world, held a respectful silence in memory of their leader.

In the four years since his death, the fame of Sun Yat Sen had travelled far and wide. Already he had become something of a saint and a legend and his name was a symbol of freedom throughout China.

On his deathbed he had said: " Let us strive peacefully to free China. " And many adopted this as their slogan. The schools paid him daily tribute in a salutation to the Father of the Republic.

Sun Yat Sen may have known in his last hours, that his dream for China was not yet complete. But as always his hopes for her and his trust in the people of China sprang bright and fresh from his teachings, as the waters from Golden Betel Spring in his old village of Tsuei Heng.

And there is no question now in the minds of those at home or abroad, that Sun Yat Sen, the brave, unselfish idealist, is to remain as the greatest liberator to rise from China.

It is true that a great man needs no other monument than his work —— but Sun Yat Sen has, besides the magnificent tomb at Nanking, a separate shrine in the hearts of 450, 000, 000 Chinese who revere him as the flame and foundation of their Republic of China.

XIV
China Today

Today the eyes of the world are more on China than ever before in her history. She has fought a long and arduous war under the most difficult circumstances. Certainly the stamina and character of her people has been tested and proven worthy beyond a doubt.

This is no longer the China of Sun Yat Sen's boyhood or mine. It is no longer the somnolent dragon dreaming of past glories under the yoke of the Manchus, which put the rank of scholar first and that of soldier last. Instead, China today is a wide – awake land, progressive in spirit and completely cognizant of her position in world affairs. How this position is to be taken advantage of is another matter.

General Homer Lea made a statement which seems very apt at the moment: " A strong China means our protection in the Orient. " For, as has been proven in his military outline " The Valor of Ignorance" , he foresaw the aggressive policy of Japan in the Far East. But the lesson has not come too late, and I think that today as never before the Western world in particular, realizes the value of China as a balance of power in the Eastern hemisphere. Strategically, materially and fundamentally, she is in a position to enact the role of peaceful guardian of the East. It is vital however that she be fitted and equipped to take on or fulfill this responsible role.

Few liberators have taken the trouble to leave their people such complete instructions for carrying on their new government as did Sun Yat Sen. In his Fundamentals of National Reconstruction, ´his Constitution, ´ and General Principles, ´ he laid down in the greatest detail the rules for executing his governmental policy. Those rules, despite dissension at various times, are still the backbone of the Chinese Republic.

It has long been the cry that China must set her own house in order before she can be reckoned a serious contender for world power. So far this has not been accomplished. China has not yet been truly unified——though she came closest to being so during the war with Japan. And if the last twenty some years since Dr. Sun's death have seemed slow years of progress to the outside world, they have been years of definite accomplishment within China.

As always, China is an unwieldy and slow – moving country. This is due in part to her national characteristics, and partially to the old faults which Dr. Sun was fighting and which have never been fully overcome. Namely, the slow spread of mass education, the absence of a common language, the lack of full development of resources, and the difficulties of wholesale transportation. It must also be realized that ten years of war destroyed and maimed what little advance had been made along these lines. Therefore the period of reconstruction and reconversion for China must of necessity be a longer one than in most other countries. She needs aid at present, as do most war – weary lands, to begin the work ahead. But China, unlike the others in many cases, has assets of her own. She has rich undeveloped resources. And she has unlimited man – power. These two things alone can save her in time.

But time has become the one commodity of which the world is shortest. America barely had time to arm for this last war, neither did Great Britain. Vigilance and readiness have been proven the only guarantee of safety. Therefore, China cannot make use of her time honored recipe —— nor can the world afford to let her. From a purely selfish point of view, it is necessary to help China grow and maintain her strength in order that she may in turn help her benefactors.

Many have felt that because of her constant internal warfare, China is not capable of regenerating her state. To the other powers, China seems disorderly and politically weak. The same was true, argue outsiders, when Sun Yat Sen was alive, and China beyond declaring herself a Republic has done little to form herself into one. These same critics, however, forget the stupendous obstacles involved in executing that simple order.

At the time of Sun Yat Sen's death, only a handful of men knew even the rudimentary principles of a free government ——and of these not all could be trusted. It had been the fashion in Court circles to play the winner against all odds and to look after yourself first. It took time for the very different doctrine of personal sacrifice, and unselfish devotion to the Cause, the teachings of Sun Yat Sen, to sink in, let alone be adopted for use.

Yet in spite of the old obstacles and the new, China has made progress nationally and politically since Dr. Sun's death. In the thirties her imports had risen to a new high, she had pretty well stamped out the opium market, her manufacture especially in cotton and silk and flour had advanced greatly and her transportation system was at least a reality and in definite operation. Compared to Japan she may have seemed slow to modernize, but considering her size as compared to Japan the two countries appear like an elephant and a mouse.

And in the war with Japan, China's very remoteness and size were her salvation. China has never really needed to fear aggression. Time after time she has seen enemies on her doorsteps only to retreat into the vastness where they either give up in despair or conquer temporarily, only to be assimilated by China as time goes by. She has swallowed up many of her conquerors like the great slow – moving dragon she is.

Unity of China however, must and will be accomplished in time. It will be an enormous job and a slow one. Uniting China is much like uniting Europe —— only a much larger and more disorganized Europe. The people are slow to take to a new idea —— but once they have done so they have proven themselves tenacious and loyal in the extreme. The pity has been that due to lack of education and communication they are able to be swayed by bad leaders as well as good. This is not the fault of the people but of the unscrupulous few who always prey on the many. China's first job therefore is to give all of her people a true and clear picture of events. When this is accomplished —— be it now or a hundred years from now, China will stand solidly shoulder to shoulder behind the right leader, and the other things will follow as a matter of course. The world will then have no criticism to make of China as a responsible world power —— and Sun Yat Sen's dream for a free and equal China will be complete.

The outside world must have faith in the meantime, and patience and trust, as in the beginning of China's revolutionary struggle. For although war has slowed up the process the battle is more than half won, and China stands on her own merits today as never before.

I myself am going back to China shortly, to revisit the land of my birth, to wander in the little village where Sun Yat Sen made his first bid for the freedom of his people. I know that I shall see outward signs of chaos and confusion throughout the land and that my heart shall be saddened at the sufferings and upheaval of war. But if, through my travels, the spirit of my old friend, Sun Yat Sen, walks with me, as I know it shall, my faith in China will not diminish.

The days of that first revolution seem far away now to many, but to me they are still very clear. I recall the anxieties, the sacrifices, the high burning zeal and courage of the first dare – to – dies, and I am thankful that I was able to play even a minor part in the great drama of the life of Sun Yat Sen. He would probably say, in his quiet, unassuming manner, that I have spoken too much about the unimportant things and too little of the important ones. But I think that there is a place for the unimportant details of a great man's life, for I believe the man is truly as important as his work. As those of us who knew Sun Yat Sen from childhood, pass on, the man himself will become lost in legend and history. And I take the liberty of believing that some at least, will want to know the full story of his background in order to appreciate more fully his accomplishments. If I have done this even in part, supplying some of the gaps in the story, I am grateful.

China's road to complete fulfillment of her Republic may be a long one. But as long as Sun Yat Sen's memory lives enshrined in the hearts of his people, China cannot fail ——for there was no failure in the life history of the man who gave his entire life to liberate his people.

封面设计：张希广

责任印制：张道奇

责任编辑：贾东营

图书在版编目（CIP）数据

我所认识的孙逸仙：童年朋友陆灿的回忆／陆灿，
（美）泰勒（Taylor，B. T.）著：黄健敏译．－北京：文
物出版社，2008.10

ISBN 978-7-5010-2575-6

Ⅰ．我… Ⅱ．①陆…②泰…③黄… Ⅲ．孙中山（1866～
1925）－生平事迹 Ⅳ．K827＝6

中国版本图书馆 CIP 数据核字（2008）第 159675 号

我所认识的孙逸仙

——童年朋友陆灿的回忆

陆灿、Betty Tebbetts Taylor 著

黄健敏 译 欧冬红 校

*

文 物 出 版 社 出 版 发 行

（北京东直门内北小街2号楼）

http://www.wenwu.com

E－mail：web@wenwu.com

北京美通印刷有限公司印刷

新 华 书 店 经 销

787×1092 1/16 印张：15.5

2008 年 10 月第 1 版 2008 年 10 月第 1 次印刷

ISBN 978－7－5010－2575－6 定价：29.80 元